Macmillan/McGraw-Hill • Glencoe

Diagnostic and Placement Tests

$2+a^5=$

Macmillan/McGraw-Hill
Glencoe

The **McGraw·Hill** *Companies*

Mc Graw Hill **Macmillan/McGraw-Hill**
Glencoe

Send all inquiries to:
Glencoe/McGraw-Hill
8787 Orion Place
Columbus, OH 43240-4027

ISBN: 978-0-07-888709-3
MHID: 0-07-888709-7

Diagnostic and Placement Tests

Printed in the United States of America.

3 4 5 6 7 8 9 10   045   16 15 14 13 12 11 10 09 08

Table of Contents

This booklet is designed to be used in two ways.

- The twelve tests in this booklet provide tools to assist teachers in making placement decisions with the Macmillan and Glencoe Mathematics series for Kindergarten through Algebra 2:

  Math Connects, Grade K

  Math Connects, Grade 1

  Math Connects, Grade 2

  Math Connects, Grade 3

  Math Connects, Grade 4

  Math Connects, Grade 5

  Math Connects, Course 1

  Math Connects, Course 2

  Math Connects, Course 3

  Math Triumphs, Grades K–8

  Glencoe Pre-Algebra

  Glencoe Algebra 1

  Glencoe Geometry

  Glencoe Algebra 2

- These tests provide valuable diagnostic information teachers may find helpful throughout the school year. See Learning Objectives before each test in this booklet for further information on using these tests as diagnostic tools.

- These tests are also available in Spanish at glencoe.com.

Placement Options

Placement Decisions

In making placement decisions for a student, consider a variety of evidence, such as the student's mathematics grades, classroom observations, teacher recommendations, portfolios of student work, standardized test scores, and placement test scores. Use the results of these placement tests in conjunction with other assessments to determine which mathematics course best fits a student's abilities and needs.

These tests can help determine whether or not students need intervention as well as the level of intervention required. Through strategic intervention, teachers can work with students using on-level content, but strategically choose which content strand(s) need further development. Sometimes, a student may struggle with a particular strand, but overall the student is able to perform on-level.

Intensive intervention is used with students who are struggling with most or all strands of math content and are unable to work on grade-level. These students will need alternative intervention materials to help meet their needs. These materials, such as the *Math Triumphs* programs, offer alternatives that will accelerate achievement in mathematics.

Test Content

These placement tests measure ability, but they are not achievement tests. They cover prerequisite concepts, not every concept found in a Glencoe mathematics textbook or in your state standards.

Mathematics concepts are introduced, developed, and reinforced in consecutive courses. These placement tests measure student mastery of concepts and skills that have been introduced or developed in the student's current mathematics course, that are further developed in the next course, but that are not developed in the following course.

In most situations, these placement tests are given near the end of the current course, in order to help determine student placement for the following year. You can also use these tests in special situations, such as a student transferring into your school mid-year or entering middle school with advanced mathematics ability.

Placement Tests Format

Placement Tests for Kindergarten through Grade 2 use a similar format. All of the tests are oral tests and address the content strands: Number, Operations, and Quantitative Reasoning; Patterns, Relationships, and Algebraic Reasoning; Geometry and Spatial Reasoning; Measurement; Probability and Statistics; and Mathematical Processes and Tools. The Kindergarten, Grade 1, and Grade 2 tests each contain 15 questions. The Kindergarten and Grade 1 tests require students to follow simple directions in order to answer each question, while the Grade 2 test is multiple-choice.

Placement Tests for Grades 3 through Algebra 1, use the same format. Each contains 30 multiple-choice questions and addresses the content strands: Number, Operations, and Quantitative Reasoning; Patterns, Relationships, and Algebraic Reasoning; Geometry and Spatial Reasoning; Measurement; Probability and Statistics; and Mathematical Processes and Tools.

The placement tests for Geometry and Algebra 2 also contain 30 multiple-choice questions. However, the Geometry test covers content strands for Algebra 1 including: Functional Relationships, Properties and Attributes of Functions, Linear Functions, Linear Equations, and Inequalities, and Quadratic and Other Nonlinear Functions.

The Algebra 2 test focuses on content strands for Geometry as well as prerequisite skills found in the Algebra 1 strands. The content strands covered in the Algebra 2 placement test include: Foundations of Functions, Linear Functions, Quadratic and Other Nonlinear Functions, Geometric Structure, Geometric Patterns, Dimensionality and the Geometry of Location, Congruence and the Geometry of Size, and Similarity and the Geometry of Shape.

When interpreting scores on the placement tests, consider the student's score on each part, as well as the total score. Scoring Guide Masters before each test can be reproduced and used to record each student's score. A sample of a completed Scoring Guide for Grade 5 is shown below; a sample for Algebra 1 is provided on the next page.

The shaded boxes show the range of scores that corresponds to each placement option. If a student's scores on each part of the test fall in the same shaded range, then that course is probably the best placement decision. If a student's scores fall in different ranges or near range boundaries, then analyze the results for each part and use additional assessment results to help determine placement.

Sample Score and Placement Analysis

On the Grade 5 test, this student scored 8 out of 10 questions correct in Number, Operation, and Quantitative Reasoning, 6 in Patterns, Relationships, and Algebraic Thinking, 2 in Geometry and Spatial Reasoning, 3 in Measurement, 2 in Probability and Statistics. The total number correct was 21 out of 30. **Note:** There is not a direct correlation between the score for each strand and the total test score. Use the total score for class placement decisions, and the scores by strand when working on particular objectives.

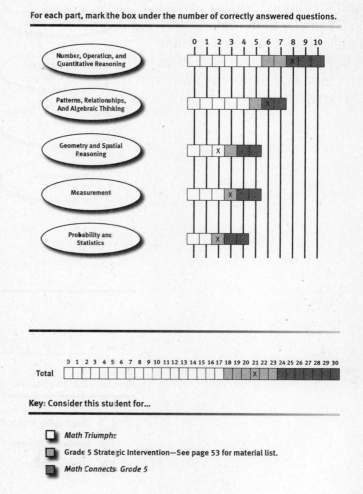

For each part, mark the box under the number of correctly answered questions.

Key: Consider this student for...

☐ Math Triumphs

▨ Grade 5 Strategic Intervention—See page 53 for material list.

▦ Math Connects Grade 5

Sample Analysis

This student scored well in the first two parts of the test, but lower in the remaining sections. If these results are similar to other assessments, this student is likely to need intervention materials for Grade 5, but will likely find Grade 5 too challenging without any intervention materials. The teacher should also note that the student scored particularly low in the Geometry and Spatial Reasoning. This student may require intensive intervention when these skills are taught.

Scoring Placement Test for Algebra 1

Students who score in the Algebra 1 range for each of the four parts are ready for Algebra 1. Students who score in the Pre-Algebra range or below in each of the four parts, are best served by Pre-Algebra.

To place students who score in the Algebra 1 range on only two or three parts, use other factors, such as previous mathematics grades and teacher recommendations.

Sample Score and Placement Analysis

On the Algebra 1 test, this student scored 7 out of 8 questions correct in Number, Operation, and Quantitative Reasoning, 4 in Patterns, Relationships, and Algebraic Thinking, 4 in Geometry and Spatial Reasoning, 3 in Measurement, 5 in Probability and Statistics. The total number correct was 23 out of 30.

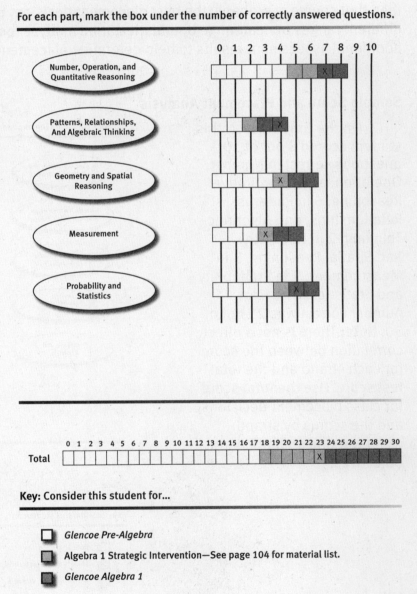

For each part, mark the box under the number of correctly answered questions.

Key: Consider this student for…

☐ *Glencoe Pre-Algebra*

▨ Algebra 1 Strategic Intervention—See page 104 for material list.

▦ *Glencoe Algebra 1*

Sample Analysis

This student could be placed in either algebra course. This student will likely do well in *Pre-Algebra*, but many find *Algebra 1* challenging. This student may need additional help to succeed in *Algebra 1* since some sections show relatively low scores. Check which questions were missed and consider other factors, such as English language or reading difficulties.

These placement tests also provide valuable diagnostic information for classroom teachers. Reproducible learning objective charts list the learning objective for each test question and can be found before each test. By marking each question the student answered incorrectly, you can see which objectives the student has not mastered.

Glencoe's wide variety of supplementary materials, such as the Skills Practice worksheets, Practice worksheets, and Problem Solving Practice worksheets available in the *Chapter Resource Masters*, and the ExamView® *Assessment Suite* CD-ROM, can provide intervention and remedial help. Diagnostic charts for each test, found with the learning objectives pages, describe the intervention that students may require and include a list of Glencoe print and technology materials.

If these tests are given near the end of the student's current course, it is recommended that the diagnostic information be shared with the teacher of that student's next course, in order to provide appropriate intervention during the next year.

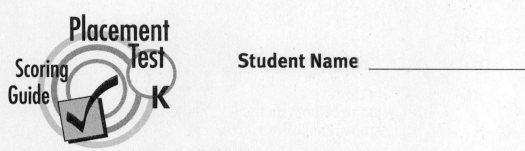

Placement Test K
Scoring Guide

Student Name _____

For each part, mark the box under the number of correctly answered questions.

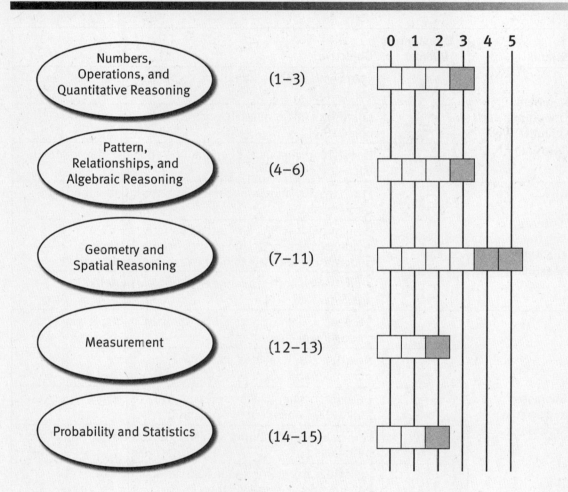

	0	1	2	3	4	5
Numbers, Operations, and Quantitative Reasoning (1–3)				▨		
Pattern, Relationships, and Algebraic Reasoning (4–6)				▨		
Geometry and Spatial Reasoning (7–11)					▨	▨
Measurement (12–13)			▨			
Probability and Statistics (14–15)			▨			

Mark the total number correct below.

	0	1	2	3	4	5	6	7	8	9	10	11	12	13	14	15
Total											▨	▨	▨	▨	▨	▨

Key: Consider this student for...

☐   Strategic Intervention—See page 4 for materials list.

▨   Kindergarten

Placement Test
Learning Objectives
K

Student Name _____

In the column on the left, mark the questions that the student answered *incorrectly*.

Strand	Question Number	Objective
Numbers, Operations and Quantitative Reasoning	☐ 1	Count with understanding and recognize how many in sets of objects.
	☐ 2	Count with understanding and recognize how many in sets of objects.
	☐ 3	Understand meanings of operations and how they relate to each other.
Patterns, Relationships and Algebraic Reasoning	☐ 4	Sort, classify, and order objects by size, number, and other properties.
	☐ 5	Recognize, describe, and extend patterns such as sequences of sounds and shapes or simple numeric patterns and translate form one representation to another.
	☐ 6	Analyze how both repeating and growing patterns are generated.
Geometry and Spatial Reasoning	☐ 7	Recognize, name, build, draw, compare, and sort two- and three-dimensional shapes.
	☐ 8	Describe attributes and parts of two-and three-dimensional shapes.
	☐ 9	Describe, name, and interpret relative positions in space and apply ideas about relative position.
	☐ 10	Find and name locations with simple relationships such as near to and in.
	☐ 11	Recognize geometric shapes and structures in the environment and specify their location such as, above, below, next to.
Measurement	☐ 12	Recognize the attributes of length, volume, weight, and area.
	☐ 13	Compare and order objects according to the attributes of length, volume, weight, and area.
Probability and Statistics	☐ 14	Sort and classify objects according to their attributes and organize data about the objects.
	☐ 15	Sort and classify objects according to their attributes and organize data about the objects.

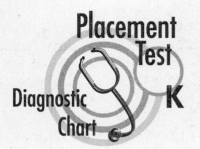

Placement Test
Diagnostic Chart
K

Student Performance Level	Number of Questions Correct	Suggestions for Intervention and Remediation
Intensive Intervention	0–5	Use *Math Triumphs* to accelerate the achievement of students who are significantly below grade level. Students should follow a personalized remediation plan. A variety of materials and instructional methods are recommended. For example, instruction and practice should be provided in print, technology, and hands-on lessons.
Strategic Intervention	6–11	Use additional Intervention and Remediation materials listed on the next page. This list of materials can provide helpful resources for students who struggle in the traditional mathematics program. Strategic intervention allows students to continue to remain in the *Math Connects* program, while receiving the differentiated instruction that they need. Teaching Tips and other resources may also be listed in the Teacher Edition.
Kindergarten	12 or more	Use *Math Connects*. This student does not require overall intervention. However, based on the student's performance on the different sections, intervention may be required. For example, a student who missed 2 or more questions in the Geometry and Spatial Reasoning section may require extra assistance as you cover these skills throughout the year.

A Special Note About Intervention

When using diagnostic tests, teachers should always question the reason behind the students' scores. Students can struggle with mathematics concepts for a variety of reasons. Personalized instruction is recommended for English language learners, students with specific learning disabilities, students with certain medical conditions, or for those who struggle with traditional instructional practice. Teachers should always consider the needs of the individual student when determining the best approach for instruction and program placement.

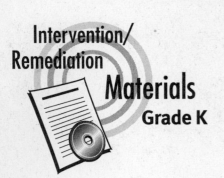

Intervention/
Remediation Materials
Grade K

Print Materials	
Reteach Masters	A brief explanation, along with examples and exercises, for every lesson in the Student Edition. These masters are included in the Chapter Resource Masters.
Skills Practice Masters	Additional practice in computational and application exercises for each lesson in the Student Edition. These masters are included in the Chapter Resource Masters.
Homework Practice Masters	Additional practice in computational and spiral review exercises for each lesson in the Student Edition. These masters are included in the Chapter Resource Masters.
Reteach and Skills Practice Workbook	A consumable version of the Reteach and Skills Masters for each lesson.
Homework Practice Workbook	A consumable version of the Homework Practice Masters for each lesson.

Technology Products	
ExamView® Assessment Suite	Software includes a Worksheet Builder to make worksheets and tests, a Student Module to take tests on-screen, and a Management System to keep student records.
Math Adventures with Dot and Ray	Provides entertaining activities and math games that use a problem-solving format.
Math Songs	Collections of songs, raps, and chants.
Math Tool Chest	Contains inquiry-based concept building software with interactive representations of manipulatives.

**Diagnostic and
Placement
Grade K**

Name _____

Date _____

This test contains 15 questions. Work each problem in the space on this page. Select the best answer. Write the answer as directed.

1 Count the apples. Write the number. _____

2 Put an X on the set of four cherries.

3 Circle the problem that fits the story.

$$\begin{array}{r} 2 \\ -1 \\ \hline 1 \end{array} \qquad \begin{array}{r} 2 \\ +1 \\ \hline 3 \end{array}$$

4 Look at the first square. Circle the squares that are the same size.

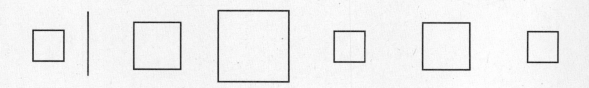

Diagnostic and Placement Tests

5 Circle the shape that comes next.

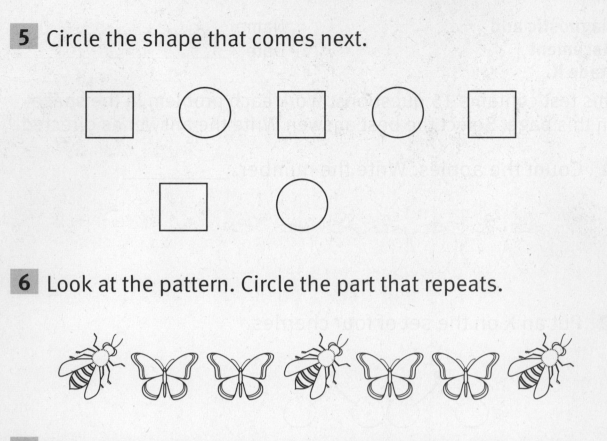

6 Look at the pattern. Circle the part that repeats.

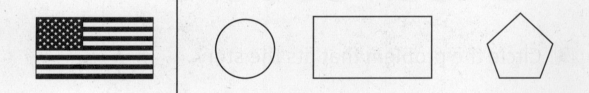

7 Look at the object. Color in the figure that matches the shape of the object.

8 Put an X on the objects that can stack.

9 Put an X on the sailboat that is in the middle.

10 Put an X on the crayon that is under the table.

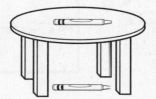

11 Put an X on the object that is next to the tree.

12 Circle the shorter object.

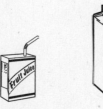

13 Circle the object that holds more.

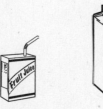

14 Sort the crayons by color. Use tally marks to show how many crayons are in each group.

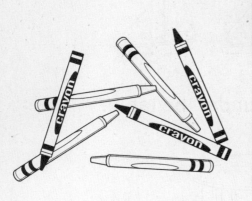

Number of Crayons	
Crayons	Tally

15 Look at the group. Write how many of each pet.

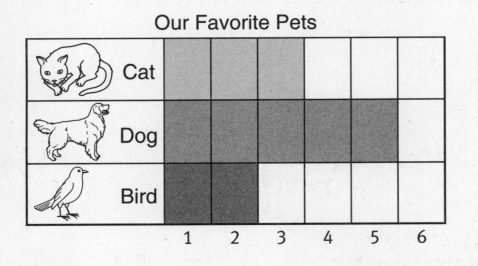

Our Favorite Pets

		1	2	3	4	5	6
Cat							
Dog							
Bird							

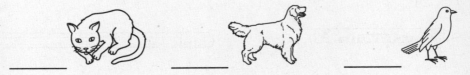

_____   _____   _____

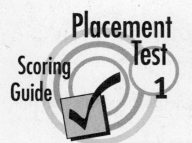

Placement Test 1
Scoring Guide

For each part, mark the box under the number of correctly answered questions.

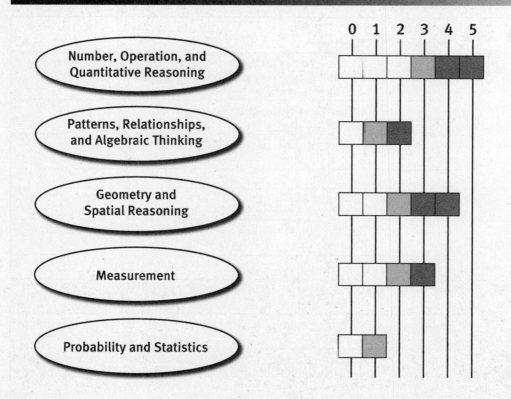

Number, Operation, and Quantitative Reasoning

Patterns, Relationships, and Algebraic Thinking

Geometry and Spatial Reasoning

Measurement

Probability and Statistics

Mark the total number correct below.

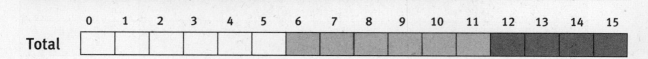

Total	0	1	2	3	4	5	6	7	8	9	10	11	12	13	14	15

Key: Consider this student for...

 Math Triumphs

☐ Grade 1 Strategic Intervention—See page 12 for materials list.

☐ *Math Connects, Grade 1*

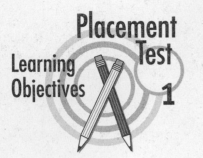

Placement Test 1

Learning Objectives

Student Name _____

In the column on the left, mark the questions that the student answered *incorrectly*.

Strand	Question Number	Objective
Number, Operation, and Quantitative Reasoning	☐ 1	Use one-to-one correspondence and language such as more than, same number as, or two less than to describe relative sizes of sets of concrete objects.
	☐ 2	Use numbers to describe how many objects are in a set (through 20) using verbal and symbolic descriptions.
	☐ 3	Name the ordinal positions in a sequence such as first, second, third, etc.
	☐ 4	Share a whole by separating it into two equal parts.
	☐ 5	Model and create addition and subtraction problems in real situations with concrete objects.
Patterns, Relationships, and Algebraic Reasoning	☐ 6	Identify, extend, and create patterns of sounds, physical movement, and concrete objects.
	☐ 7	Count by ones to 100.
Geometry and Spatial Reasoning	☐ 8	Describe one object in relation to another using informal language such as over, under, above, and below.
	☐ 9	Describe and identify an object by its attributes using informal language.
	☐ 10	Sort a variety of objects including two- and three-dimensional geometric figures according to their attributes and describe how the objects are sorted.
	☐ 11	Describe identify, and compare circles, triangles, rectangles, and squares (a special type of rectangle).
Measurement	☐ 12	Compare and order two or three concrete objects according to length (longer/shorter than, or the same).
	☐ 13	Compare the areas of two flat surfaces of two-dimensional figures (covers more, covers less, or covers the same).
	☐ 14	Compare two objects according to weight/mass (heavier than, lighter than, or equal to).
Probability and Statistics	☐ 15	Use information from a graph of real objects or pictures in order to answer questions.

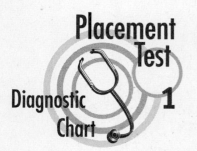

Placement Test 1
Diagnostic Chart

Student Performance Level	Number of Questions Correct	Suggestions for Intervention and Remediation
Intensive Intervention	0–5	Use *Math Triumphs* to accelerate the achievement of students who are two or more years below grade level. Students should follow a personalized remediation plan. A variety of materials and instructional methods are recommended. For example, instruction and practice should be provided in print, technology, and hands-on lessons.
Strategic Intervention	6–11	Use the additional Intervention and Remediation materials listed on the next page. This list of materials can provide helpful resources for students who struggle in the traditional mathematics program. Strategic intervention allows students to continue to remain in the *Math Connects* program, while receiving the differentiated instruction they need. Teaching Tips and other resources are also listed in the Teacher Edition.
Grade 1	12 or more	Use *Math Connects*. This student does not require overall intervention. However, based on the student's performance on the different sections, intervention may be required. For example, a student who missed 2 or more questions in the Measurement section may require extra assistance as you cover these skills throughout the year.

A Special Note About Intervention

When using diagnostic tests, teachers should always question the reason behind the students' scores. Students can struggle with mathematics concepts for a variety of reasons. Personalized instruction is recommended for English language learners, students with specific learning disabilities, students with certain medical conditions, or for those who struggle with traditional instructional practice. Teachers should always consider the needs of the individual student when determining the best approach for instruction and program placement.

Intervention/ Remediation Materials
Grade 1

Print Materials	
Reteach Masters	A brief explanation, along with examples and exercises, for every lesson in the Student Edition. These masters are included in the Chapter Resource Masters.
Skills Practice Masters	Additional practice in computational and application exercises for each lesson in the Student Edition. These masters are included in the Chapter Resource Masters.
Homework Practice Masters	Additional practice in computational and spiral review exercises for each lesson in the Student Edition. These masters are included in the Chapter Resource Masters.
Reteach and Skills Practice Workbook	A consumable version of the Reteach and Skills Masters for each lesson.
Homework Practice Workbook	A consumable version of the Homework Practice Masters for each lesson.
Problem Solving Workbook	A consumable version of the Problem Solving Masters for each lesson.

Technology Products	
ExamView® Assessment Suite	Networkable software includes a Worksheet Builder to make worksheets and tests, a Student Module to take tests on-screen, and a Management System to keep student records.
Math Adventures with Dot and Ray	Provides entertaining activities and math games that use a problem-solving format.
Math Songs	Collections of songs, raps, and chants.
Math Tool Chest	Contains inquiry-based concept building software with interactive representations of manipulatives.

This test contains 15 questions. Work each problem in the space on this page. Select the best answer. Circle the correct answer.

1 The number of hearts is _____ the number of triangles.

more than
less than
equal to

2 How many diamonds?

◇ ◇ ◇ ◇ ◇
◇ ◇ ◇ ◇ ◇ ◇
◇ ◇ ◇ ◇ ◇

16   17   18   19

3 Circle the third fruit in the row.

4 Which picture shows a cookie split into 2 equal parts?

5 Write a number sentence that shows how many hats Maria bought in all.

_____

6 Draw the next shape in the pattern.

◯ ◯ ▢ ◯ ◯ ▢ ◯ ◯ ____

7 What number comes after 39?

37   38   40   41

8 Put an X on the crayon that is under the table.

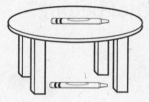

9 Which set of words best describe the shape?

triangle, 3 sides
square, 4 equal sides
rectangle, 4 sides
circle, 0 sides

10 Draw a line to show in which group the baseball belongs.

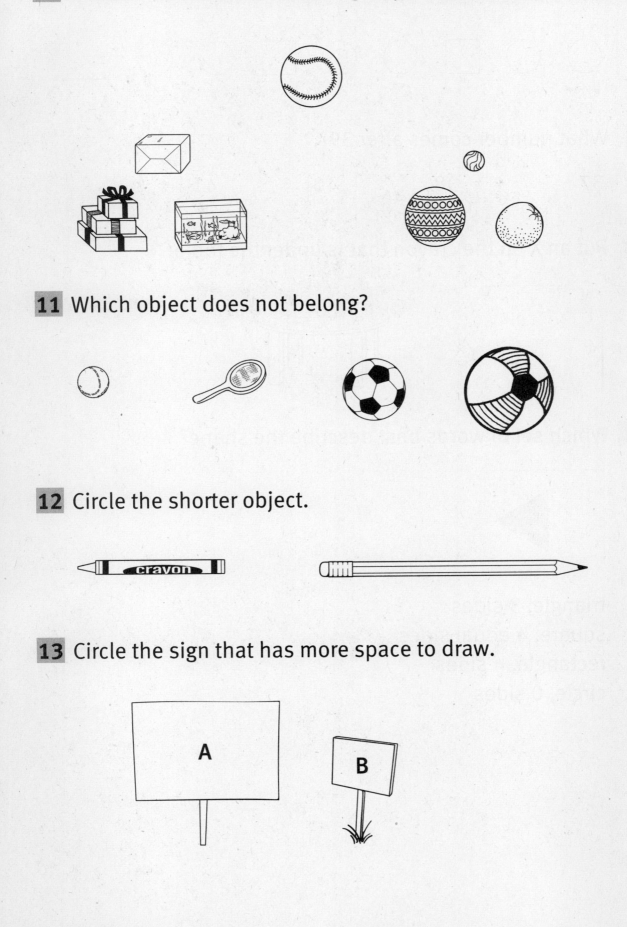

11 Which object does not belong?

12 Circle the shorter object.

crayon

13 Circle the sign that has more space to draw.

A

B

14 Which is the heaviest?

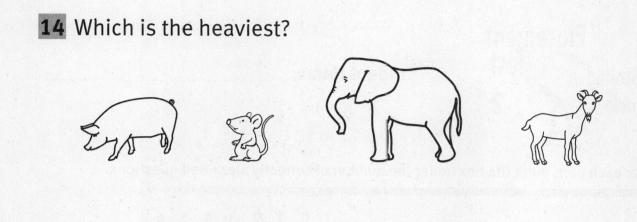

15 Look at the group. Write how many of each pet.

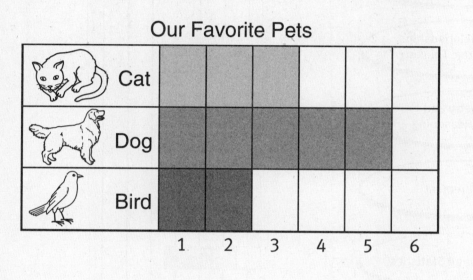

Our Favorite Pets

_____   _____   _____

Placement Test 2

Scoring Guide

Student Name _____

For each part, mark the box under the number of correctly answered questions.

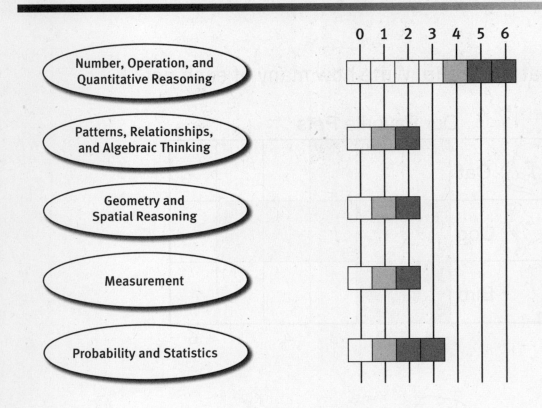

Mark the total number correct below.

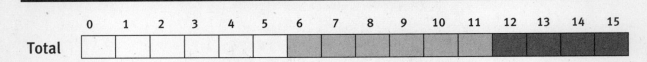

Key: Consider this student for...

☐ *Math Triumphs*

◻ Grade 2 Strategic Intervention—See page 21 for materials list.

◼ *Math Connects, Grade 2*

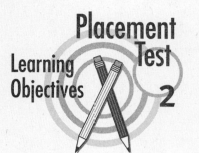

Placement Test 2

Learning Objectives

In the column on the left, mark the questions that the student answered *incorrectly*.

Strand	Question Number	Objective
Number, Operation, and Quantitative Reasoning	☐ 1	Compare and order whole numbers up to 99 (less than, greater than, or equal to) using sets of concrete objects and pictorial models.
	☐ 2	Identify individual coins by name and value and describe relationships among them.
	☐ 3	Model whole numbers in groups of tens and ones.
	☐ 4	Use appropriate language to describe part of a set such as three out of the eight crayons are red.
	☐ 5	Model and create addition and subtraction problems with concrete objects and write corresponding number sentences.
	☐ 6	Use concrete and pictorial models to apply basic addition and subtraction facts (up to $9 + 9 = 18$ and $18 - 9 = 9$).
Patterns, Relationships, and Algebraic Reasoning	☐ 7	Identify, describe, and extend concrete and pictorial patterns in order to make predictions and solve problems.
	☐ 8	Identify patterns in related addition and subtraction sentences (fact families for sums to 18).
Geometry and Spatial Reasoning	☐ 9	Describe and identify two-dimensional geometric figures, including circles, triangles, rectangles, and squares (a special type of rectangle).
	☐ 10	Describe and identify two- and three-dimensional geometric figures according to a given attributes using informal and formal language.
Measurement	☐ 11	Compare and order two or three concrete objects according to length (from longest to shortest).
	☐ 12	Combine and decompose plane and solid figures (e.g., by putting two congruent isosceles triangles together to make a rhombus), thus building an understanding of part-whole relationships as well as the properties of the original and composite shapes.
Probability and Statistics	☐ 13	Use organized data to construct real-object graphs, picture graphs, and bar-type graphs.
	☐ 14	Draw conclusions and answer questions using information organized in real-object graphs, picture graphs, and bar-type graphs.
	☐ 15	Draw conclusions and answer questions using information organized in real-object graphs, picture graphs, and bar-type graphs.

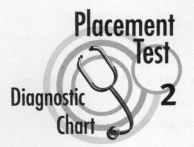

Placement Test 2
Diagnostic Chart

Student Performance Level	Number of Questions Correct	Suggestions for Intervention and Remediation
Intensive Intervention	0–15	Use *Math Triumphs* to accelerate the achievement of students who are two or more years below grade level. Students should follow a personalized remediation plan. A variety of materials and instructional methods are recommended. For example, instruction and practice should be provided in print, technology, and hands-on lessons.
Strategic Intervention	6–11	Use the additional Intervention and Remediation materials listed on the next page. This list of materials can provide helpful resources for students who struggle in the traditional mathematics program. Strategic intervention allows students to continue to remain in the *Math Connects* program, while receiving the differentiated instruction they need. Teaching Tips and other resources are also listed in the Teacher Edition.
Grade 2	12 or more	Use *Math Connects*. This student does not require overall intervention. However, based on the student's performance on the different sections, intervention may be required. For example, a student who missed 1 or more questions in the Measurement section may require extra assistance as you cover these skills throughout the year.

A Special Note About Intervention

When using diagnostic tests, teachers should always question the reason behind the students' scores. Students can struggle with mathematics concepts for a variety of reasons. Personalized instruction is recommended for English language learners, students with specific learning disabilities, students with certain medical conditions, or for those who struggle with traditional instructional practice. Teachers should always consider the needs of the individual student when determining the best approach for instruction and program placement.

Print Materials

Reteach Masters	A brief explanation, along with examples and exercises, for every lesson in the Student Edition. These masters are included in the Chapter Resource Masters.
Skills Practice Masters	Additional practice in computational and application exercises for each lesson in the Student Edition. These masters are included in the Chapter Resource Masters.
Homework Practice Masters	Additional practice in computational and spiral review exercises for each lesson in the Student Edition. These masters are included in the Chapter Resource Masters.
Reteach and Skills Practice Workbook	A consumable version of the Reteach and Skills Masters for each lesson.
Homework Practice Workbook	A consumable version of the Homework Practice Masters for each lesson.
Problem Solving Workbook	A consumable version of the Problem Solving Masters for each lesson.

Technology Products

ExamView® Assessment Suite	Networkable software includes a Worksheet Builder to make worksheets and tests, a Student Module to take tests on-screen, and a Management System to keep student records.
Math Adventures with Dot and Ray	Provides entertaining activities and math games that use a problem-solving format.
Math Songs	Collections of songs, raps, and chants.
Math Tool Chest	Contains inquiry-based concept building software with interactive representations of manipulatives.

This test contains 15 questions. Work each problem in the space on this page. Circle the best answer.

1 Which sign makes the number sentence 43 ◯ 34 true?

= + > <

2 If a pencil costs 15¢, what coins could Markel use to buy the pencil?

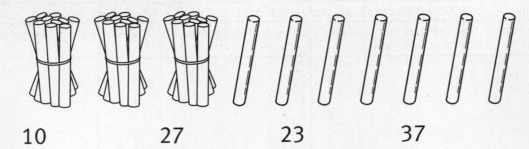

3 What number is modeled below?

10   27   23   37

4 Which sentence describes the set of objects?

There are 9 shaded circles.
Four out of 9 circles are shaded.
Half of the circles are unshaded.
Five out of 9 circles are shaded.

5 Which number sentence tells how many more triangles than squares?

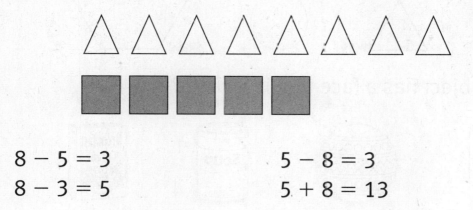

$8 - 5 = 3$ $5 - 8 = 3$

$8 - 3 = 5$ $5 + 8 = 13$

6 Which number sentence tells how many in all?

○○○○○○○○ ○○○○○

$8 + 6 = 14$ $8 - 6 = 2$

$4 + 3 = 7$ $4 - 3 = 1$

7 Which object comes next in the pattern?

8 What number makes the number sentence true?

$3 + 6 = \boxed{} + 3$

3   4   5   6

9 Which shape is a triangle?

10 Which object has a face that is a circle?

11 List the items from longest to shortest.

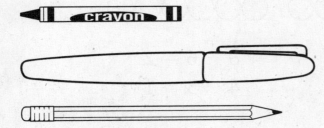

crayon, pencil, marker

pencil, marker, crayon

marker, pencil, crayon

crayon, marker, pencil

12 The triangles below can be combined to form which shape?

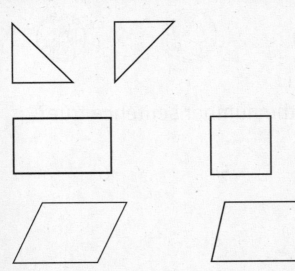

13 Which set of shapes matches the picture graph?

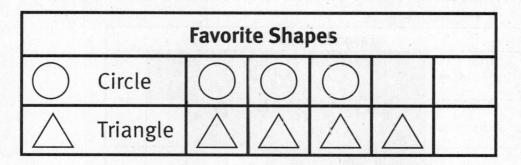

14 Tanya and Marcell asked their friends which pet is their favorite. The results are shown below.

Our Favorite Pets

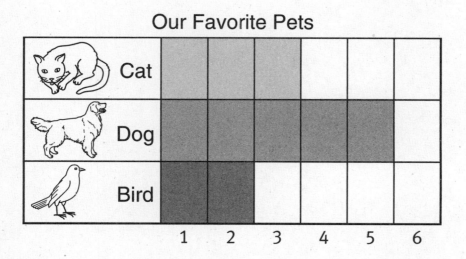

How many more chose dogs than cats?

1   2   3   4

15 The class voted on their favorite fruits. The results are shown below. Which sentence describes the results?

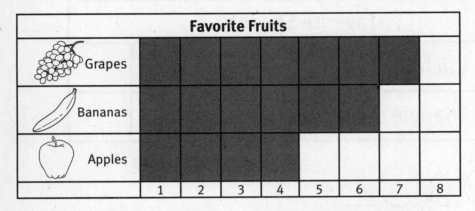

No one chose apples as their favorite fruit.

Bananas are the favorite fruit.

More students like apples than grapes.

Fewer students like bananas than grapes.

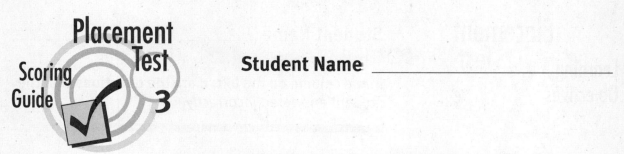

Placement Test 3
Scoring Guide

Student Name _____

For each part, mark the box under the number of correctly answered questions.

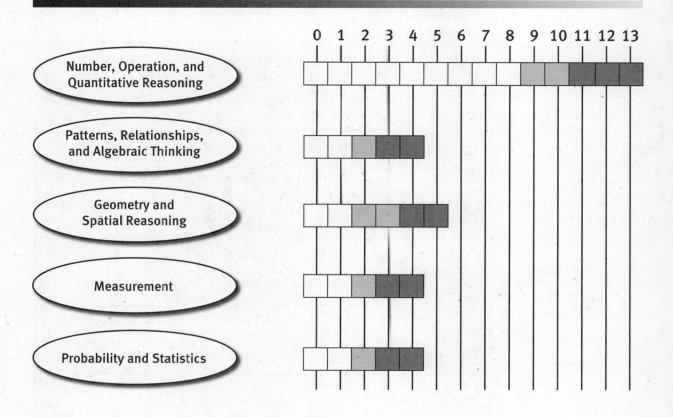

	0	1	2	3	4	5	6	7	8	9	10	11	12	13
Number, Operation, and Quantitative Reasoning														
Patterns, Relationships, and Algebraic Thinking														
Geometry and Spatial Reasoning														
Measurement														
Probability and Statistics														

Mark the total number correct below.

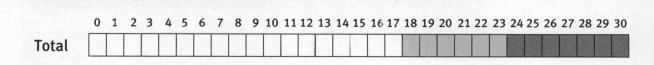

Total 0 1 2 3 4 5 6 7 8 9 10 11 12 13 14 15 16 17 18 19 20 21 22 23 24 25 26 27 28 29 30

Key: Consider this student for...

☐ *Math Triumphs*

▨ Grade 3 Strategic Intervention—See page 31 for materials list.

▪ *Math Connects, Grade 3*

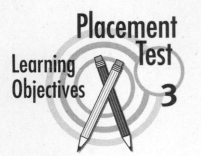

Placement Test 3
Learning Objectives

Student Name _____

In the column on the left, mark the questions that the student answered *incorrectly*.

Strand	Question Number	Objective
Number, Operation, and Quantitative Reasoning	☐ 1	Use concrete models of hundreds, tens, and ones to represent a given whole number (up to 999) in various ways.
	☐ 2	Use place value to read, write, and describe the value of whole numbers to 999.
	☐ 3	Use place value to compare and order whole numbers to 999 and record the comparisons using numbers and symbols $(<, =, >)$
	☐ 4	Use concrete models to represent and name fractional parts of a set of objects (with denominators of 12 or less).
	☐ 5	Use concrete models to determine if a fractional part of a whole is closer to 0, $\frac{1}{2}$, or 1.
	☐ 6	Recall and apply basic addition and subtraction facts (to 18).
	☐ 7	Model addition and subtraction of two-digit numbers with objects, pictures, words, and numbers.
	☐ 8	Model addition and subtraction of two-digit numbers with objects, pictures, words, and numbers.
	☐ 9	Determine the value of a collection of coins up to one dollar.
	☐ 10	Model, create, and describe multiplication situations in which equivalent sets of concrete objects are joined.
	☐ 11	Select and apply appropriate methods to estimate sums and differences or calculate them mentally, depending on the context of the numbers involved.
	☐ 12	Model, create, and describe division situations in which a set of concrete objects is separated into equivalent sets.
	☐ 13	Select addition or subtraction to solve problems using two-digit numbers, whether or not regrouping is necessary.
Patterns, Relationships, and Algebraic Reasoning	☐ 14	Use patterns in place value to compare and order whole numbers through 999.
	☐ 15	Use patterns and relationships to develop strategies to remember basic addition and subtraction facts. Determine patterns in related addition and subtraction number sentences (including fact families) such as $8 + 9 = 17$, $9 + 8 = 17$, $17 - 8 = 9$, and $17 - 9 = 8$.
	☐ 16	Generate a list of paired numbers based on a real-life situation such as a number of tricycles related to number of wheels.
	☐ 17	Identify, describe, and extend repeating and additive patterns to make predictions and solve problems.

Strand	Question Number	Objective
Geometry and Spatial Reasoning	☐ 18	Describe attributes (the number of vertices, faces, edges, sides) of two- and three-dimensional geometric figures such as circles, polygons, spheres, cones, cylinders, prisms, and pyramids, etc.
Geometry and Spatial Reasoning	☐ 19	Describe attributes (the number of vertices, faces, edges, sides) of two- and three-dimensional geometric figures such as circles, polygons, spheres, cones, cylinders, prisms, and pyramids, etc.
	☐ 20	Use attributes to describe how 2 two-dimensional figures or 2 three-dimensional geometric figures are alike or different.
	☐ 21	Cut two-dimensional geometric figures apart and identify the new geometric figures formed.
	☐ 22	Use whole numbers to locate and name points on a number line.
Measurement	☐ 23	Read and write times shown on analog and digital clocks using five-minute increments.
	☐ 24	Identify concrete models that approximate standard units of length and use them to measure length.
	☐ 25	Select a non-standard unit of measure such as a bathroom cup or a jar to determine the capacity of a given container.
	☐ 26	Select a non-standard unit of measure such as square tiles to determine the area of a two-dimensional surface.
Probability and Statistics	☐ 27	Draw conclusions and answer questions based on picture graphs and bar-type graphs.
	☐ 28	Use data to describe events as more likely or less likely such as drawing a certain color crayon from a bag of seven red crayons and three green crayons.
	☐ 29	Use data to describe events as more likely or less likely such as drawing a certain color crayon from a bag of seven red crayons and three green crayons.
	☐ 30	Draw conclusions and answer questions based on picture graphs and bar-type graphs.

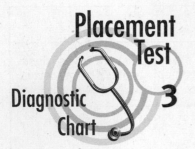

Student Performance Level	Number of Questions Correct	Suggestions for Intervention and Remediation
Intensive Intervention	0–17	Use *Math Triumphs* to accelerate the achievement of students who are two or more years below grade level. Students should follow a personalized remediation plan. A variety of materials and instructional methods are recommended. For example, instruction and practice should be provided in print, technology, and hands-on lessons.
Strategic Intervention	18–23	Use the additional Intervention and Remediation materials listed on the next page. This list of materials can provide helpful resources for students who struggle in the traditional mathematics program. Strategic intervention allows students to continue to remain in the *Math Connects* program, while receiving the differentiated instruction they need. Teaching Tips and other resources are also listed in the Teacher Edition.
Grade 3	24 or more	Use *Math Connects*. This student does not require overall intervention. However, based on the student's performance on the different sections, intervention may be required. For example, a student who missed 2 or more questions in the Measurement section may require extra assistance as you cover these skills throughout the year.

A Special Note About Intervention

When using diagnostic tests, teachers should always question the reason behind the students' scores. Students can struggle with mathematics concepts for a variety of reasons. Personalized instruction is recommended for English language learners, students with specific learning disabilities, students with certain medical conditions, or for those who struggle with traditional instructional practice. Teachers should always consider the needs of the individual student when determining the best approach for instruction and program placement.

Intervention/ Remediation Materials
Grade 3

Print Materials

Reteach Masters	A brief explanation, along with examples and exercises, for every lesson in the Student Edition. (Two pages for Problem-Solving Lessons and one page per lesson for all other lessons.) These masters are included in the Chapter Resource Masters.
Skills Practice Masters	Additional practice in computational and application exercises for each lesson in the Student Edition. These masters are included in the Chapter Resource Masters.
Homework Practice Masters	Additional practice in computational and spiral review exercises for each lesson in the Student Edition. These masters are included in the Chapter Resource Masters.
Study Guide and Intervention Workbook	A consumable version of the Study Guide and Intervention Masters for each lesson.
Skills Practice Workbook	A consumable version of the Skills Practice Workbook Masters for each lesson.
Practice Workbook	A consumable version of the Practice Masters for each lesson.
Prerequisite Skills Workbook	Arithmetic study guide and practice pages for each of the prerequisite skills that review basic math concepts.

Technology Products

ExamView® Assessment Suite	Networkable software includes a Worksheet Builder to make worksheets and tests, a Student Module to take tests on-screen, and a Management System to keep student records.
Math Adventures with Dot and Ray	Provides entertaining activities and math games that use a problem-solving format.
Math Songs	Collections of songs, raps, and chants.
Math Tool Chest	Contains inquiry-based concept building software with interactive representations of manipulatives.

Mathematics Chart

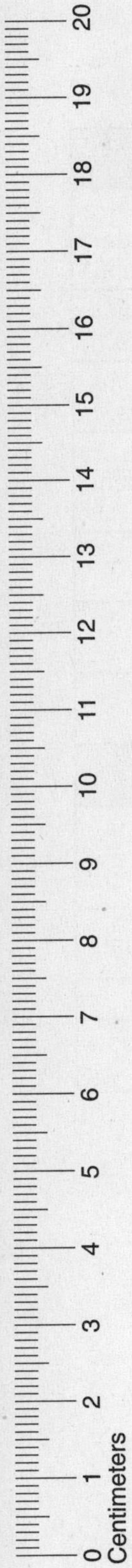

LENGTH	TIME
Metric	1 year = 365 days
1 meter = 100 centimeters	1 year = 12 months
1 centimeter = 10 millimeters	1 year = 52 weeks
	1 week = 7 days
Customary	1 day = 24 hours
1 yard = 3 feet	1 hour = 60 minutes
1 foot = 12 inches	1 minute = 60 seconds

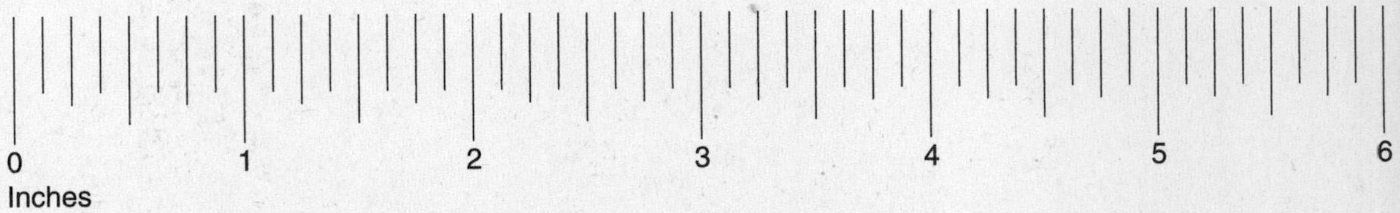

Centimeters

Inches

Diagnostic and Placement Grade 3

Name _____

Date _____

This test contains 30 multiple-choice questions. Work each problem in the space on this page. Select the best answer. Write the letter of the answer on the blank at the right.

1 Which number is shown by the blocks?

1 _____

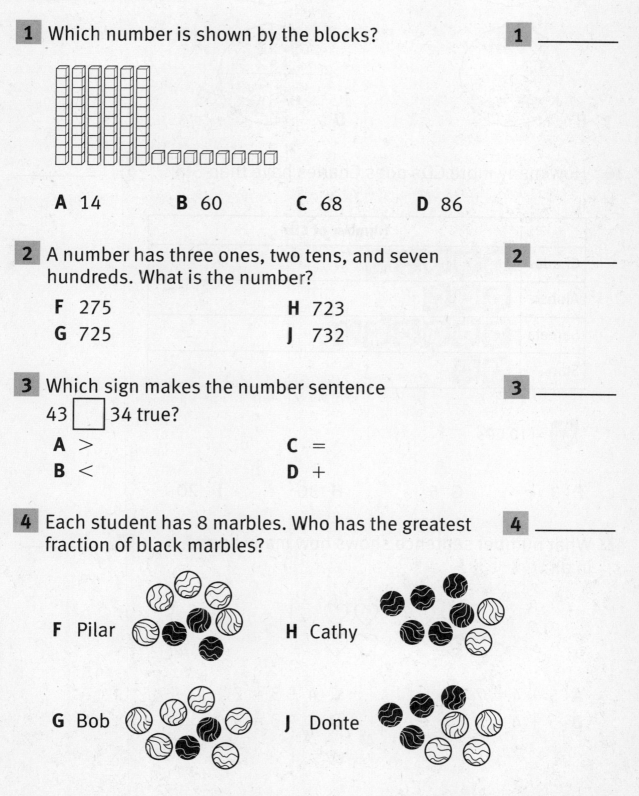

A 14   **B** 60   **C** 68   **D** 86

2 A number has three ones, two tens, and seven hundreds. What is the number?

2 _____

F 275   **H** 723

G 725   **J** 732

3 Which sign makes the number sentence
43 [ ] 34 true?

3 _____

A >   **C** =

B <   **D** +

4 Each student has 8 marbles. Who has the greatest fraction of black marbles?

4 _____

F Pilar

G Bob

H Cathy

J Donte

5 Which pizza is closest to half eaten?

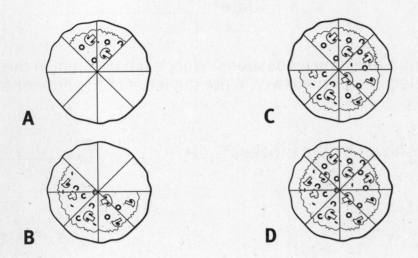

A

C

B

D

6 How many more CDs does Charles have than Stan?

6 _____

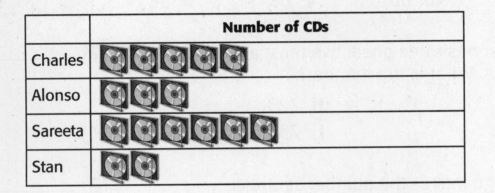

	Number of CDs
Charles	
Alonso	
Sareeta	
Stan	

 = 10 CDs

F 3   **G** 5   **H** 30   **J** 20

7 What number sentence shows how many hearts in all?

7 _____

♡ ♡ ♡   ♡ ♡
♡ ♡   ♡ ♡

A 5 + 4 = 7   **C** 4 + 3 = 7
B 5 + 4 = 9   **D** 4 + 3 = 9

8 Molly has 6 stickers. She gives 3 stickers to her friend. Identify how many stickers Molly has now and the operation that you use to calculate it.

    F 9; addition

    G 3; subtraction

    H 2; division

    J 18; multiplication

8 _____

9 Mykia has 2 dimes, 3 nickels and 4 pennies. How much money does she have?

    A $0.39   **B** $0.34   **C** $0.29   **D** $0.24

9 _____

10 Sam, Liana, Frank and Terrell went fishing. Each person caught four fish. How many fish were caught all together?

    F 8   **G** 4   **H** 12   **J** 16

10 _____

11 Sanden purchased 4 packs of gum for $0.95 each. Estimate to find the total amount Sanden spent.

    A $1.00   **B** $2.00   **C** $3.00   **D** $4.00

11 _____

12 A teacher had 20 pieces of chalk. He wanted to give each of his 5 students the same number of pieces. How many pieces of chalk should he give each student?

    F 5   **G** 6   **H** 4   **J** 2

12 _____

13 Fumiko has 34 soccer cards. He gives 20 to his sister. Which number sentence shows how many soccer cards Fumiko has left?

    A $34 + 20 = 64$ **C** $54 - 20 = 34$

    B $34 - 20 = 14$ **D** $20 + 14 = 34$

13 _____

Diagnostic and Placement Tests

14 What is the missing number?
30, 32, 34, __, 38, 40, 42

  F 33   **G** 35   **H** 36   **J** 37

15 Which of these can be used to check the answer to the problem below?

$$5 + 7 = 12$$

  A $7 + 12 = 9$ **C** $4 + 8 = 12$
  B $17 - 5 = 12$ **D** $12 - 7 = 5$

16 Onatah noticed wagons have 4 wheels. Which table could she use to determine the number of wheels on four of these wagons?

F

Wagons	1	2	3	4
Wheels	4	6	8	10

G

Wagons	1	2	3	4
Wheels	4	8	12	16

H

Wagons	1	2	3	4
Wheels	4	8	16	20

J

Wagons	1	2	3	4
Wheels	4	8	16	32

17 Look at the pattern in the table.

Starfish	1	2	3	4
Points	5	10	15	?

How many points do 4 starfish have?

  A 16   **B** 20   **C** 25   **D** 30

18 As part of an experiment, Consuela releases four objects down a ramp to see if they roll down the ramp or slide down the ramp. Which object is most likely to slide down Consuela's ramp?

18 _____

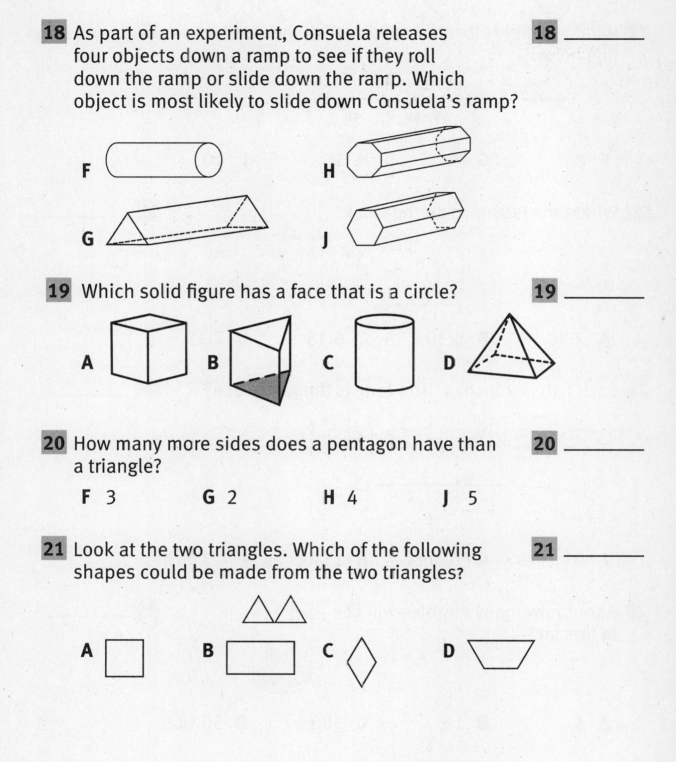

19 Which solid figure has a face that is a circle?

19 _____

20 How many more sides does a pentagon have than a triangle?

20 _____

F 3   **G** 2   **H** 4   **J** 5

21 Look at the two triangles. Which of the following shapes could be made from the two triangles?

21 _____

Diagnostic and Placement Tests

22 What number is located at Point *A* on the number line below?

22 _____

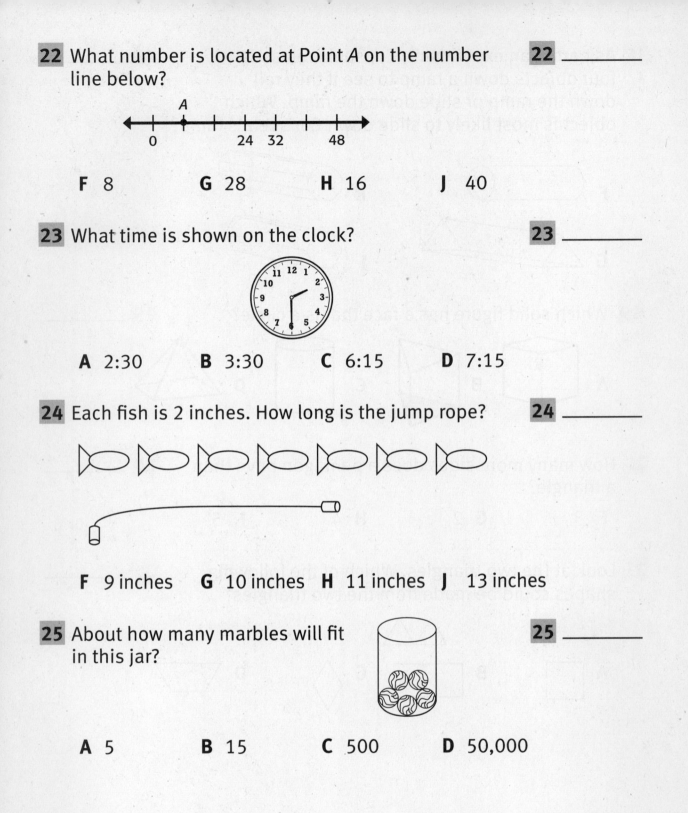

F 8   **G** 28   **H** 16   **J** 40

23 What time is shown on the clock?

23 _____

A 2:30   **B** 3:30   **C** 6:15   **D** 7:15

24 Each fish is 2 inches. How long is the jump rope?

24 _____

F 9 inches   **G** 10 inches   **H** 11 inches   **J** 13 inches

25 About how many marbles will fit in this jar?

25 _____

A 5   **B** 15   **C** 500   **D** 50,000

26 What is the area of this house?

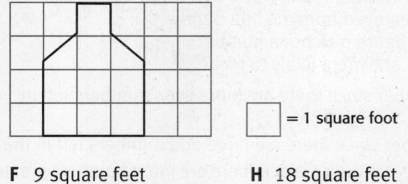

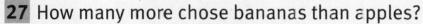

☐ = 1 square foot

F 9 square feet **H** 18 square feet

G 8 square feet **J** 10 square feet

27 How many more chose bananas than apples?

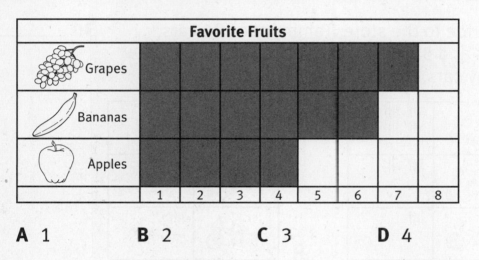

A 1 **B** 2 **C** 3 **D** 4

28 Julia places 3 yellow, 4 red, 6 green, and 2 purple candies in a bag. She then chooses a candy at random and records its color. Which color is she more likely to choose?

F yellow **G** purple **H** red **J** green

26 _____

27 _____

28 _____

29 There are 10 pieces of paper in a hat each
numbered 1–10. Two numbers, 7 and 8,
are picked and removed from the hat. Sandy
reaches into the hat to pick out a number.
Which number is she more likely to pick?

29 _____

   A An even number since there are more even numbers left in
     the hat

   B An odd number since there are more odd numbers left in the hat

   C A number greater than 5 since there are more numbers greater
     than 5 left in the hat

   D A number less than 6 since there are more numbers less than 6
     left in the hat

30 During a ride to the store, Tommy sees 36 cars,
18 trucks and 5 bikes. Which tally table shows
how many cars, trucks and bikes he sees?

30 _____

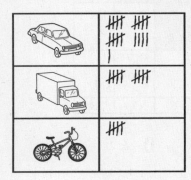

F

G

H

J

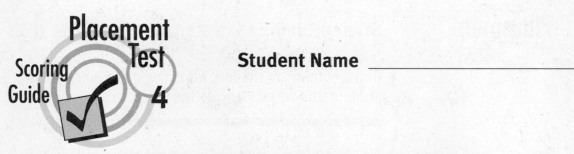

Placement Test 4
Scoring Guide

Student Name _____

For each part, mark the box under the number of correctly answered questions.

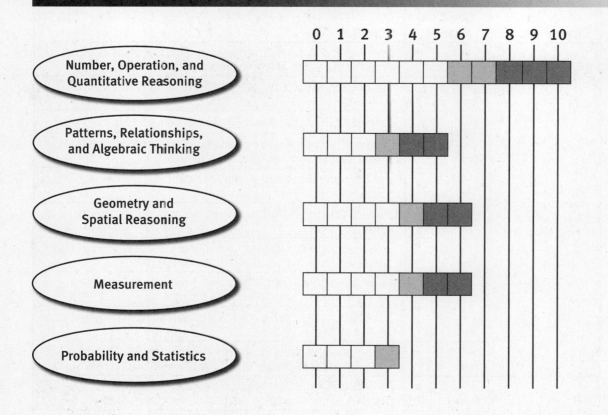

Mark the total number correct below.

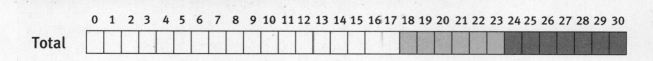

Key: Consider this student for...

 Math Triumphs

Grade 4 Strategic Intervention—See page 45 for materials list.

Math Connects, Grade 4

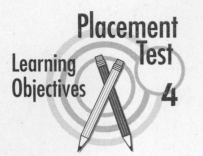

Placement Test 4
Learning Objectives

In the column on the left, mark the questions that the student answered *incorrectly*.

Strand	Question Number	Objective
Number, Operation, and Quantitative Reasoning	☐ 1	Use place value to read, write (in symbols and words), and describe the value of whole numbers to 999,999.
	☐ 2	Use place value to compare and order whole numbers to 9,999
	☐ 3	Determine the value of a collection of coins and bills.
	☐ 4	Compare fractional parts of whole objects or sets of objects in a problem situation using concrete models.
	☐ 5	Use fraction names and symbols to describe fractional parts of whole objects or sets of objects.
	☐ 6	Model addition and subtraction using pictures, words, and numbers.
	☐ 7	Select addition or subtraction and use the operation to solve problems involving whole numbers through 999.
	☐ 8	Learn and apply multiplication facts through 12 by 12 using concrete models and objects.
	☐ 9	Solve and record multiplication problems (up to two digits times one digit).
	☐ 10	Round whole numbers to the nearest ten or hundred to approximate reasonable results in problem situations.
Patterns, Relationships, and Algebraic Reasoning	☐ 11	Identify and extend whole-number and geometric patterns to make predictions and solve problems.
	☐ 12	Identify patterns in multiplication facts using concrete objects, pictorial models, or technology.
	☐ 13	Identify patterns in related multiplication and division sentences (fact families) such as $2 \times 3 = 6$, $3 \times 2 = 6$, $6 \div 2 = 3$, $6 \div 3 = 2$.
	☐ 14	Generate a table of paired numbers based on real-life situations such as insects and legs.
	☐ 15	Identify, describe patterns in a table of related number pairs based on a meaningful problem and extend the table.

Strand	Question Number	Objective
Geometry and Spatial Reasoning	☐ 16	Identify, classify, and describe two- and three-dimensional geometric figures by their attributes. Compare two-dimensional figures, three-dimensional figures, or both by their attributes using formal geometric vocabulary.
	☐ 17	Identify, classify, and describe two- and three-dimensional geometric figures by their attributes. Compare two-dimensional figures, three-dimensional figures, or both by their attributes using formal geometric vocabulary.
	☐ 18	Identify congruent two-dimensional figures.
Geometry and Spatial Reasoning	☐ 19	Identify lines of symmetry in two-dimensional geometric figures.
	☐ 20	Use models, including number lines, to identify equivalent fractions.
	☐ 21	Locate and name points on a number line using whole numbers and fractions, including halves and fourths.
Measurement	☐ 22	Use linear measurement tools to estimate and measure lengths using standard units.
	☐ 23	Use standard units to find the perimeter of a shape.
	☐ 24	Use concrete and pictorial models of square units to determine the area of two-dimensional surfaces.
	☐ 25	Use concrete models that approximate cubic units to determine the volume of a given container or other three-dimensional geometric figure.
	☐ 26	Use a thermometer to measure temperature.
	☐ 27	Tell and write time shown on analog and digital clocks.
Probability and Statistics	☐ 28	Collect, organize, record, and display data in pictographs and bar graphs where each picture or cell might represent more than one piece of data.
	☐ 29	Interpret information from pictographs and bar graphs.
	☐ 30	Use data to describe events as more likely than, less likely than, or equal likely as.

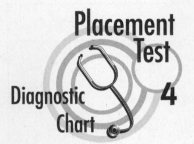

Student Performance Level	Number of Questions Correct	Suggestions for Intervention and Remediation
Intensive Intervention	0–17	Use *Math Triumphs* to accelerate the achievement of students who are two or more years below grade level. Students should follow a personalized remediation plan. A variety of materials and instructional methods are recommended. For example, instruction and practice should be provided in print, technology, and hands-on lessons.
Strategic Intervention	18–23	Use the additional Intervention and Remediation materials listed on the next page. This list of materials can provide helpful resources for students who struggle in the traditional mathematics program. Strategic intervention allows students to continue to remain in the *Math Connects* program, while receiving the differentiated instruction they need. Teaching Tips and other resources are also listed in the Teacher Edition.
Grade 4	24 or more	Use *Math Connects*. This student does not require overall intervention. However, based on the student's performance on the different sections, intervention may be required. For example, a student who missed 2 or more questions in the Measurement section may require extra assistance as you cover these skills throughout the year.

A Special Note About Intervention

When using diagnostic tests, teachers should always question the reason behind the students' scores. Students can struggle with mathematics concepts for a variety of reasons. Personalized instruction is recommended for English language learners, students with specific learning disabilities, students with certain medical conditions, or for those who struggle with traditional instructional practice. Teachers should always consider the needs of the individual student when determining the best approach for instruction and program placement.

Intervention/Remediation Materials
Grade 4

Print Materials

Reteach Masters	A brief explanation, along with examples and exercises, for every lesson in the Student Edition. (Two pages for Problem-Solving Lessons and one page per lesson for all other lessons.) These masters are included in the Chapter Resource Masters.
Skills Practice Masters	Additional practice in computational and application exercises for each lesson in the Student Edition. These masters are included in the Chapter Resource Masters.
Homework Practice Masters	Additional practice in computational and spiral review exercises for each lesson in the Student Edition. These masters are included in the Chapter Resource Masters.
Study Guide and Intervention Workbook	A consumable version of the Study Guide and Intervention Masters for each lesson.
Skills Practice Workbook	A consumable version of the Skills Practice Workbook Masters for each lesson.
Practice Workbook	A consumable version of the Practice Masters for each lesson.
Prerequisite Skills Workbook	Arithmetic study guide and practice pages for each of the prerequisite skills that review basic math concepts.

Technology Products

ExamView® Assessment Suite	Networkable software includes a Worksheet Builder to make worksheets and tests, a Student Module to take tests on-screen, and a Management System to keep student records.
Math Adventures with Dot and Ray	Provides entertaining activities and math games that use a problem-solving format.
Math Songs	Collections of songs, raps, and chants.
Math Tool Chest	Contains inquiry-based concept building software with interactive representations of manipulatives.

Mathematics Chart

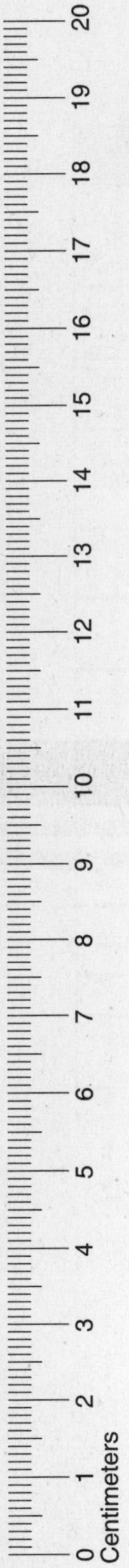

LENGTH	TIME
Metric	1 year = 365 days
1 meter = 100 centimeters	1 year = 12 months
1 centimeter = 10 millimeters	1 year = 52 weeks
	1 week = 7 days
Customary	1 day = 24 hours
1 yard = 3 feet	1 hour = 60 minutes
1 foot = 12 inches	1 minute = 60 seconds

Centimeters

Inches

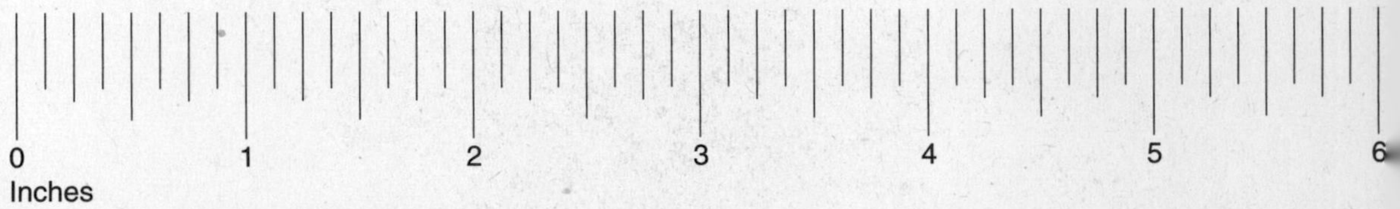

Diagnostic and Placement Grade 4

Name _____

Date _____

This test contains 30 multiple-choice questions. Work each problem in the space on this page. Select the best answer. Write the letter of the answer on the blank at the right.

1 Which number has a 3 in the tens place and a 9 in the thousands place?

1 _____

   A 2935   **B** 3592   **C** 9235   **D** 9253

2 Which set of numbers is in order from least to greatest?

2 _____

   F 4324, 4432, 4243, 4234   **H** 4243, 4234, 4324, 4432
   G 4432, 4324, 4243, 4234   **J** 4234, 4243, 4324, 4432

3 Kiyoshi has three quarters, five dimes, and one nickel in her piggy bank. Identify Kiyoshi's total amount of money and the operation used to calculate it.

3 _____

   A $1.10, addition   **C** $1.30, addition
   B $1.10, multiplication   **D** $1.30, multiplication

Diagnostic and Placement Tests

4 Marley makes an apple pie and a blueberry pie to serve at Thanksgiving dinner. After dessert, she notices that $\frac{3}{8}$ of the apple pie remains and $\frac{1}{4}$ of the blueberry pie remains. Which statement is TRUE concerning Marley's observation?

4 _____

F More apple pie remained than blueberry pie because $\frac{3}{8} > \frac{1}{4}$.

G More blueberry pie remained than apple pie because $\frac{3}{8} > \frac{1}{4}$.

H More apple pie was eaten than blueberry pie because $\frac{3}{8} < \frac{1}{4}$.

J Both pies had the same amount remaining because $\frac{3}{8} = \frac{1}{4}$.

5 What fraction of the group of animals is cows?

5 _____

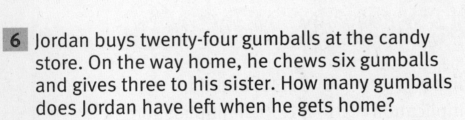

A $\frac{5}{2}$ **B** $\frac{2}{3}$ **C** $\frac{3}{5}$ **D** $\frac{2}{5}$

6 Jordan buys twenty-four gumballs at the candy store. On the way home, he chews six gumballs and gives three to his sister. How many gumballs does Jordan have left when he gets home?

6 _____

F 13   **G** 14   **H** 15   **J** 16

7 Which sign goes in the box to make the number sentence true?

7 _____

$$42 \ \boxed{} \ 7 = 35$$

A +   **B** −   **C** ×   **D** ÷

8 Drew owns 4 sheets of stickers. Each sheet has 12 stickers. Which number sentence shows how to find the total number of stickers Drew owns?

8 _____

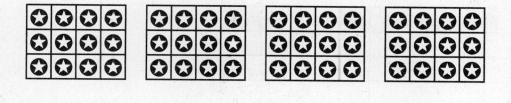

F $12 + 4 = \square$ **H** $12 \times 4 = \square$

G $12 - 4 = \square$ **J** $12 \div 4 = \square$

9 Heather and Matt both collect rocks. Heather says that she has thirty-two rocks in her collection. Matt says that he has three times as many rocks as Heather does. Which number sentence could Heather use to find the number of rocks in Matt's collection?

9 _____

A $32 + 3$ **C** 32×3

B $32 - 3$ **D** $32 \div 3$

10 To enter a dog show, Tehya must weigh her Great Dane and record his weight rounded to the nearest ten pounds. Tehya's Great Dane weighs 123 pounds. Which weight should Tehya record for the dog show?

10 _____

F 100 pounds   **H** 125 pounds

G 120 pounds   **J** 130 pounds

Diagnostic and Placement Tests

11 The table below shows the number of crayons in each box. If every box has the same number of crayons, how many crayons will be in 8 boxes?

11 _____

Number of Boxes	Number of Crayons
1	8
2	16
3	24

A 8   **B** 32   **C** 64   **D** 72

12 A line of ants is moving across Denise's picnic blanket. She counts 6 legs on the first ant, 12 legs on the first two ants, and 18 legs on the first three ants. If Denise continues to count, how many legs will she count on the first 12 ants?

12 _____

F 24 legs   **G** 56 legs   **H** 60 legs   **J** 72 legs

13 Which completes the fact family for the following set of number sentences?

13 _____

$$4 \times 2 = 8, 2 \times 4 = 8, 8 \div 2 = 4$$

A $8 \div 4 = 2$ **C** $4 \div 2 = 2$

B $8 \div 2 = 4$ **D** $4 \div 8 = \frac{1}{2}$

14 Hector saves $5.00 of his allowance every week. After 12 weeks he has $60.00 saved. Which table could he use to show the amount of money he will save after 20 weeks?

14 _____

F

Week	Money Saved
15	$65.00
16	$70.00
17	$75.00
18	$80.00
19	$85.00
20	$90.00

H

Week	Money Saved
15	$75.00
16	$80.00
17	$85.00
18	$90.00
19	$95.00
20	$100.00

G

Week	Money Saved
15	$70.00
16	$75.00
17	$80.00
18	$85.00
19	$90.00
20	$95.00

J

Week	Money Saved
15	$80.00
16	$85.00
17	$90.00
18	$95.00
19	$100.00
20	$105.00

15 Bianca is building a tower with wooden blocks. She counts the number of blocks on each level and records it in the chart below.

15 _____

Level	1	2	3	4	5
Blocks	20	16	12	8	4

Which statement describes the number of blocks on each level of her tower?

A Bianca adds 4 blocks with every level of the tower.

B Bianca adds 6 blocks with every level of the tower.

C Bianca subtracts 6 blocks with every level of the tower.

D Bianca subtracts 4 blocks with every level of the tower.

16 Which best describes this figure?

16 _____

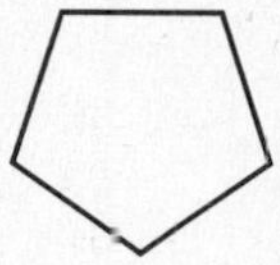

F pentagon   **G** hexagon   **H** triangle   **J** octagon

Diagnostic and Placement Tests

17 Which shape is this can of soup? 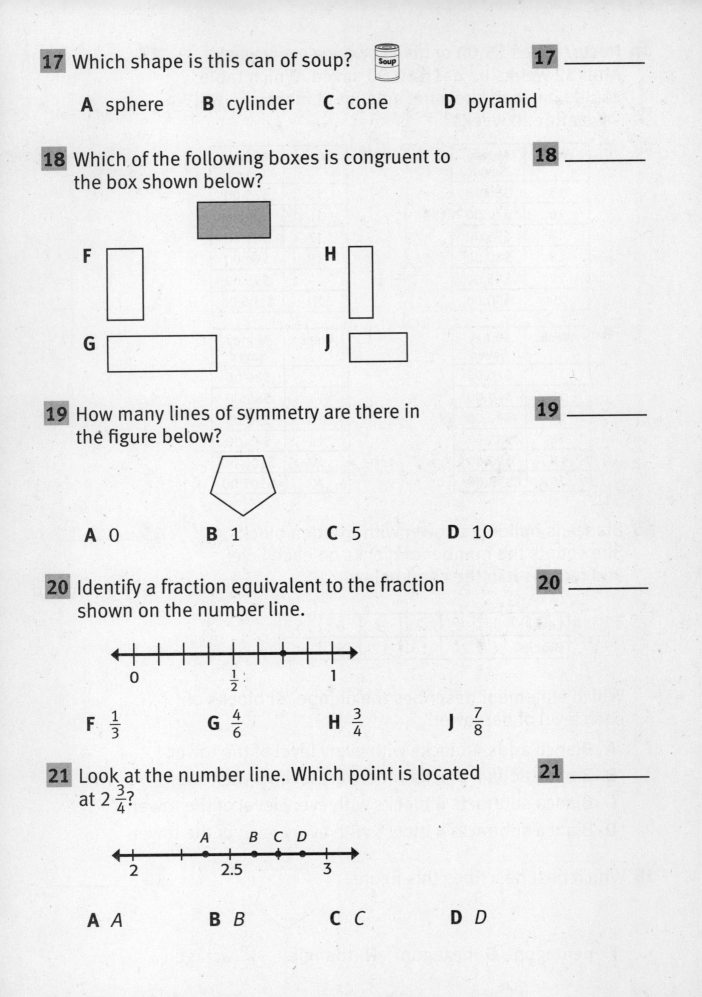 **17** _____

   A sphere   **B** cylinder   **C** cone   **D** pyramid

18 Which of the following boxes is congruent to the box shown below?   **18** _____

F

H

G

J

19 How many lines of symmetry are there in the figure below?   **19** _____

   A 0   **B** 1   **C** 5   **D** 10

20 Identify a fraction equivalent to the fraction shown on the number line.   **20** _____

0    $\frac{1}{2}$ 1

   F $\frac{1}{3}$ **G** $\frac{4}{6}$ **H** $\frac{3}{4}$ **J** $\frac{7}{8}$

21 Look at the number line. Which point is located at $2\frac{3}{4}$?   **21** _____

A   B C D

2   2.5   3

   A A   **B** B   **C** C   **D** D

22 Measure the length of the ribbon in centimeters. About how long is the ribbon?

22 _____

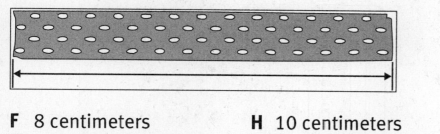

F 8 centimeters   **H** 10 centimeters

G 9 centimeters   **J** 11 centimeters

23 A classroom is shaped like a rectangle with a length of 30 feet and a width of 24 feet.

23 _____

30 ft

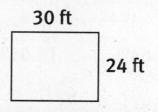

24 ft

What is the perimeter in feet of the classroom?

A 54 feet   **B** 84 feet   **C** 108 feet   **D** 720 feet

24 What is the area of this figure?

24 _____

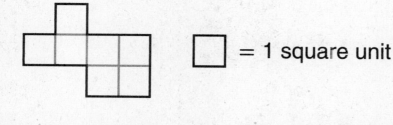

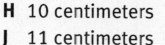 = 1 square unit

F 4 square units   **H** 7 square units

G 6 square units   **J** 8 square units

25 What is the volume of the figure?

25 _____

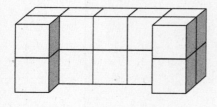

= 1 cubic unit

A 10 cubic units   **C** 14 cubic units

B 12 cubic units   **D** 16 cubic units

Diagnostic and Placement Tests

26 Look at the thermometer. What temperature does it read?

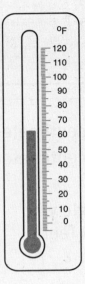

F 62°F   **G** 63°F   **H** 64°F   **J** 65°F

27 Which clock is set to 4:45?

A

B

C

D

28 Kenji spun a spinner 10 times. The results are shown in the tally chart. Which graph shows these results?

Spin Results	
White	|||
Red	~~||||~~
Blue	||

28 _____

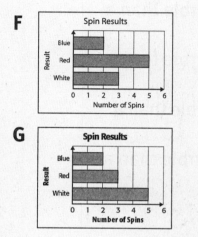

29 _____

29 The bar graph shows the number of students who voted for each color. Which tally chart matches the data in the bar graph?

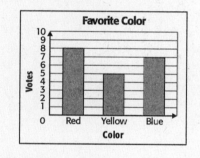

A

Favorite Color	
Red	~~||||~~
Yellow	~~||||~~ |||
Blue	~~||||~~ ||

C

Favorite Color	
Red	~~||||~~ |||
Yellow	~~||||~~
Blue	~~||||~~ ||

B

Favorite Color	
Red	~~||||~~ ||||
Yellow	~~||||~~	
Blue	||||

D

Favorite Color	
Red	~~||||~~ |||
Yellow	||||
Blue	~~||||~~

30 Andrés places 4 red, 4 blue, 3 yellow, and
5 green marbles in a bag. He then chooses
one marble at random and records its color.
Which statement accurately predicts his results?

   F Andrés is more likely to draw a red marble than a
green marble.

   G Andrés is more likely to draw a red marble than a
blue marble.

   H Andrés is less likely to draw a blue marble than a
yellow marble.

   J Andrés is less likely to draw a blue marble than a
green marble.

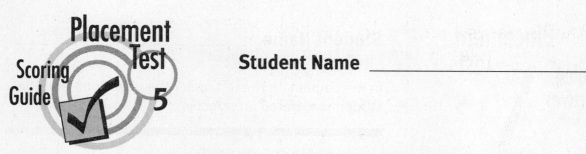

Placement Test 5
Scoring Guide

Student Name _____

For each part, mark the box under the number of correctly answered questions.

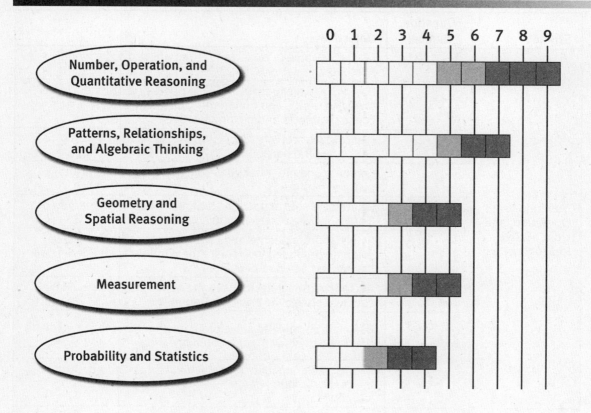

	0	1	2	3	4	5	6	7	8	9
Number, Operation, and Quantitative Reasoning										
Patterns, Relationships, and Algebraic Thinking										
Geometry and Spatial Reasoning										
Measurement										
Probability and Statistics										

Mark the total number correct below.

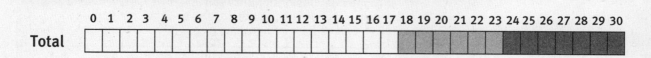

Total	0	1	2	3	4	5	6	7	8	9	10	11	12	13	14	15	16	17	18	19	20	21	22	23	24	25	26	27	28	29	30

Key: Consider this student for...

☐ *Math Triumphs*

◼ Grade 5 Strategic Intervention—See page 60 for materials list.

◼ *Math Connects, Grade 5*

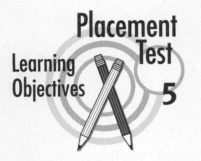

Placement Test 5
Learning Objectives

Student Name _____

In the column on the left, mark the questions that the student answered *incorrectly*.

Strand	Question Number	Objective
Number, Operation, and Quantitative Reasoning	☐ 1	Use place value to read, write, compare and order whole numbers through 999,999,999.
	☐ 2	Use place value to read, write, compare and order decimals involving tenths and hundredths, including money, using concrete objects and pictorial models.
	☐ 3	Use concrete objects and pictorial models to generate equivalent fractions.
	☐ 4	Compare and order fractions using concrete objects and pictorial models.
	☐ 5	Relate decimals to fractions that name tenths and hundredths using concrete objects and pictorial models.
	☐ 6	Select appropriate methods and apply them accurately to estimate products or calculate them mentally, depending on the context and numbers involved.
	☐ 7	Add and subtract decimals to the hundredths place using concrete objects and pictorial models.
	☐ 8	Use multiplication to solve problems (no more than two digits times two digits without technology).
	☐ 9	Round whole numbers to the nearest ten, hundred, or thousand to approximate reasonable results in problem situations.
Patterns, Relationships, and Algebraic Reasoning	☐ 10	Use patterns and relationships to develop strategies to remember basic multiplication and division facts (such as the patterns in related multiplication and division number sentences (fact families) such as $9 \times 9 = 81$ and $81 \div 9 = 9$).
	☐ 11	Use patterns and relationships to develop strategies to remember basic multiplication and division facts (such as the patterns in related multiplication and division number sentences (fact families) such as $9 \times 9 = 81$ and $81 \div 9 = 9$).
	☐ 12	Use patterns to multiply by 10 and 100.
	☐ 13	Use patterns to multiply by 10 and 100.
	☐ 14	Describe the relationship between two sets of related data such as ordered pairs in a table.
	☐ 15	Describe the relationship between two sets of related data such as ordered pairs in a table.
	☐ 16	Describe the relationship between two sets of related data such as ordered pairs in a table.

Strand	Question Number	Objective
Geometry and Spatial Reasoning	☐ 17	Identify and describe right, acute, and obtuse angles.
	☐ 18	Identify and describe parallel and intersecting (including perpendicular) lines using concrete objects and pictorial models.
Geometry and Spatial Reasoning	☐ 19	Use translations, reflections, and rotations using concrete models.
	☐ 20	Use reflections to verify that a shape has symmetry.
	☐ 21	Locate and name points on a number line using whole numbers, fractions, such as halves and fourths, and decimals, such as tenths.
Measurement	☐ 22	Estimate and use measurement tools to determine length (including perimeter), area, capacity and weight/mass using standard units (SI) and customary.
	☐ 23	Perform simple conversions between different units of length, between different units of capacity, and between different units of weight within the customary measurement system.
	☐ 24	Estimate volume in cubic units.
	☐ 25	Use a thermometer to measure temperature and changes in temperature.
	☐ 26	Quantify area by finding the total number of same-sized units of area that cover the shape without gaps or overlaps.
Probability and Statistics	☐ 27	Use concrete objects or pictures to make generalizations about determining all possible combinations of a given set of data or of objects in a problems situation.
	☐ 28	Use concrete objects or pictures to make generalizations about determining all possible combinations of a given set of data or of objects in a problems situation.
	☐ 29	Interpret bar graphs.
	☐ 30	Interpret bar graphs.

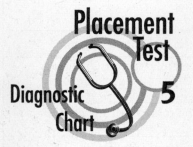

Student Performance Level	Number of Questions Correct	Suggestions for Intervention and Remediation
Intensive Intervention	0–17	Use *Math Triumphs* to accelerate the achievement of students who are two or more years below grade level. Students should follow a personalized remediation plan. A variety of materials and instructional methods are recommended. For example, instruction and practice should be provided in print, technology, and hands-on lessons.
Strategic Intervention	18–23	Use the additional Intervention and Remediation materials listed on the next page. This list of materials can provide helpful resources for students who struggle in the traditional mathematics program. Strategic intervention allows students to continue to remain in the *Math Connects* program, while receiving the differentiated instruction they need. Teaching Tips and other resources are also listed in the Teacher Edition.
Grade 5	24 or more	Use *Math Connects*. This student does not require overall intervention. However, based on the student's performance on the different sections, intervention may be required. For example, a student who missed 2 or more questions in the Measurement section may require extra assistance as you cover these skills throughout the year.

A Special Note About Intervention

When using diagnostic tests, teachers should always question the reason behind the students' scores. Students can struggle with mathematics concepts for a variety of reasons. Personalized instruction is recommended for English language learners, students with specific learning disabilities, students with certain medical conditions, or for those who struggle with traditional instructional practice. Teachers should always consider the needs of the individual student when determining the best approach for instruction and program placement.

Intervention/Remediation Materials
Grade 5

Print Materials	
Reteach Masters	A brief explanation, along with examples and exercises, for every lesson in the Student Edition. (Two pages for Problem-Solving Lessons and one page per lesson for all other lessons.) These masters are included in the Chapter Resource Masters.
Skills Practice Masters	Additional practice in computational and application exercises for each lesson in the Student Edition. These masters are included in the Chapter Resource Masters.
Homework Practice Masters	Additional practice in computational and spiral review exercises for each lesson in the Student Edition. These masters are included in the Chapter Resource Masters.
Study Guide and Intervention Workbook	A consumable version of the Study Guide and Intervention Masters for each lesson.
Skills Practice Workbook	A consumable version of the Skills Practice Workbook Masters for each lesson.
Practice Workbook	A consumable version of the Practice Masters for each lesson.
Prerequisite Skills Workbook	Arithmetic study guide and practice pages for each of the prerequisite skills that review basic math concepts.
Technology Products	
ExamView® Assessment Suite	Networkable software includes a Worksheet Builder to make worksheets and tests, a Student Module to take tests on-screen, and a Management System to keep student records.
Math Adventures with Dot and Ray	Provides entertaining activities and math games that use a problem-solving format.
Math Songs	Collections of songs, raps, and chants.
Math Tool Chest	Contains inquiry-based concept building software with interactive representations of manipulatives.

Mathematics Chart

LENGTH	CAPACITY AND VOLUME
Metric	**Metric**
1 kilometer = 1000 meters	1 liter = 1000 milliliters
1 meter = 100 centimeters	**Customary**
1 centimeter = 10 millimeters	1 gallon = 4 quarts
Customary	1 gallon = 128 ounces
1 mile = 1760 yards	1 quart = 2 pints
1 mile = 5280 feet	1 pint = 2 cups
1 yard = 3 feet	1 cup = 8 ounces
1 foot = 12 inches	

MASS AND WEIGHT	TIME
Metric	1 year = 365 days
1 kilogram = 1000 grams	1 year = 12 months
1 gram = 1000 milligrams	1 year = 52 weeks
	1 week = 7 days
Customary	1 day = 24 hours
1 ton = 2000 pounds	1 hour = 60 minutes
1 pound = 16 ounces	1 minute = 60 seconds

Perimeter		Area	
square	$P = 4s$	rectangle	$A = \ell w$ or $A = bh$
rectangle	$P = 2\ell + 2w$ or $P = 2(\ell + w)$		

Centimeters

Inches

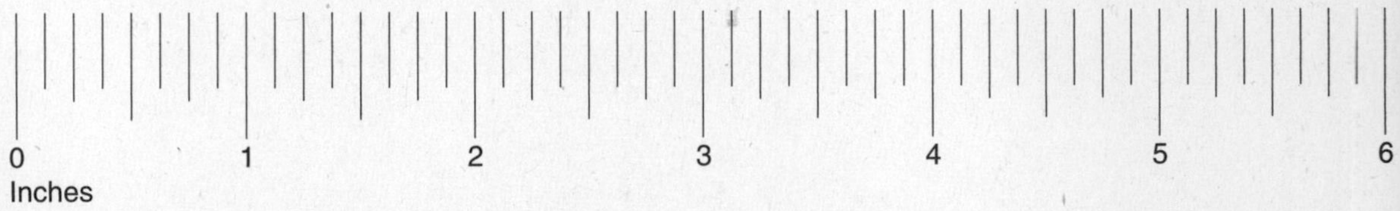

Diagnostic and Placement Grade 5

Name _____

Date _____

This test contains 30 multiple-choice questions. Work each problem in the space on this page. Select the best answer. Write the letter of the answer on the blank at the right.

1 The number 9,020,730 is read as which of the following: **1** _____

   A nine billion, twenty million, seventy-three

   B nine million, two thousand, seven hundred thirty

   C nine million, twenty thousand, seven hundred thirty

   D nine hundred two thousand, seventy-three

2 Which of the following numbers is the greatest?   **2** _____

   F 11.6   **G** 2.09   **H** 4.63   **J** 1.17

3 Inali and his friends ate $\frac{1}{2}$ of a pizza.   **3** _____

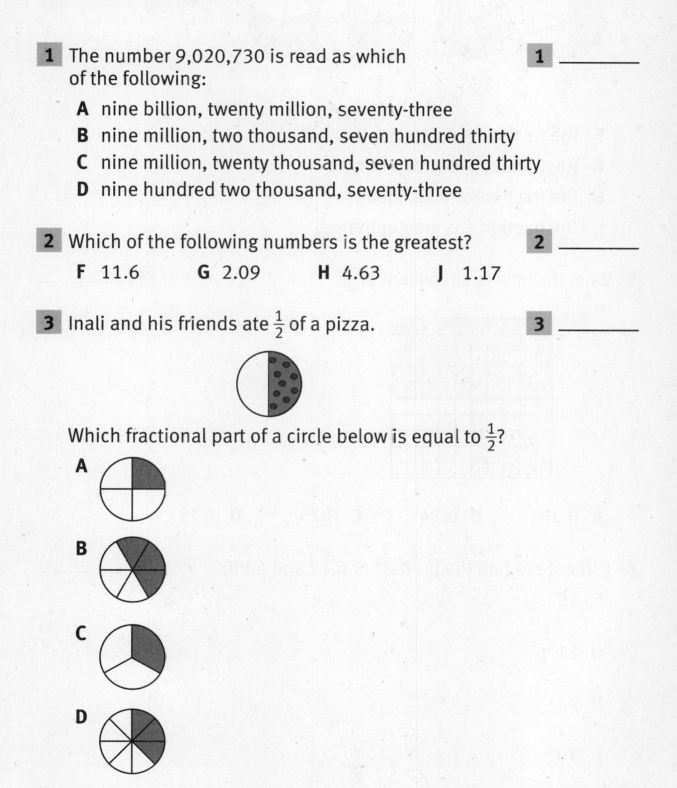

Which fractional part of a circle below is equal to $\frac{1}{2}$?

   A

   B

   C

   D

Diagnostic and Placement Tests

4 During basketball practice, Michael spends time shooting free throws. The figures below are shaded to show the number of shots made compared to the number of shots attempted at each practice. What can you conclude from the data?

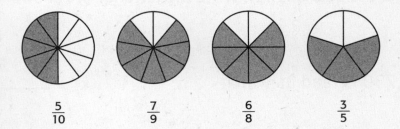

$$\frac{5}{10} \qquad \frac{7}{9} \qquad \frac{6}{8} \qquad \frac{3}{5}$$

F The fraction $\frac{5}{10}$ is greater than $\frac{3}{5}$.

G The fraction $\frac{7}{9}$ is greater than $\frac{3}{5}$.

H The fractions are all equal.

J The fraction $\frac{3}{5}$ is greater than $\frac{5}{10}$.

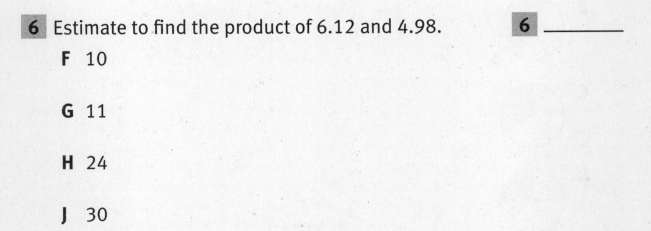

5 What decimal is equivalent to $\frac{3}{4}$?

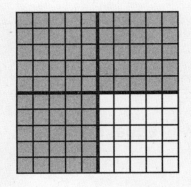

A 0.25 **B** 0.34 **C** 0.75 **D** 1.33

6 Estimate to find the product of 6.12 and 4.98.

F 10

G 11

H 24

J 30

4 _____

5 _____

6 _____

7 The menu below shows the prices at Lunchtime Café. Lucita orders a turkey sandwich, salad, and juice. What operation should she use to determine the cost of her meal?

Lunchtime Cafe	
Item	Cost
Turkey Sandwich	$4.50
Ham Sandwich	$4.35
Salad	$2.10
Fruit Cup	$2.50
Juice	$1.90

A addition

B subtraction

C multiplication

D division

8 Each student in fifth grade donates 4 cans of food to the food bank. There are 285 fifth-grade students. Which of the following shows the number of cans donated and the correct justification for the number?

F 71, because 285 divided by 4 is approximately 71

G 289, because 285 plus 4 is 289

H 1,120, because 280 times 4 is 1120

J 1,140, because 285 times 4 is 1140

9 Look at the table below. Which of the following has NOT been rounded correctly to the nearest hundred?

Population in 2005		
City	Exact Population	Estimated Population
Amarillo	183,021	183,000
Austin	690,252	690,300
Corpus Christi	280,002	280,000
Fort Worth	624,067	624,000

Source: U.S. Census Bureau

A Amarillo

B Austin

C Corpus Christi

D Fort Worth

10 Which completes the fact family for the following set of number sentences?

$$3 \times 6 = 18, \ 18 \div 3 = 6, \ 18 \div 6 = 3$$

F $3 \times 6 = 18$ **H** $6 \div 3 = 2$
G $6 \times 3 = 18$ **J** $6 \div 18 = \frac{1}{3}$

10 _____

11 Raven is asked to check the answer to the multiplication problem below. Which number sentence could she use to check her answer?

$$8 \times 7 = 54$$

A $54 + 8 = 62$ **C** $54 \times 8 = 7$
B $54 - 8 = 48$ **D** $54 \div 8 = 7$

11 _____

12 Each week, Melanie saves the same amount of money. After the third week, she has $30. After the fifth week, she has $50. After the seventh week, she has $70. Which operation could Melanie use to determine the amount she will have saved by the tenth week?

F Add 10 to the number of weeks.

G Add 20 to the numbers of weeks.

H Multiply 10 times the number of weeks.

J Multiply 20 times the number of weeks.

12 _____

13 Carmen created the following table of multiplication facts for 100. If the pattern continues, what is 100×12?

13 _____

#	× 100
1	100
2	200
3	300
4	400
5	500

A 120   **B** 210   **C** 1,200   **D** 2,100

14 Bennett created the table below. Which operation did he perform on the numbers in the left column to find the numbers in the right column?

x	y
1	9
2	10
3	11
4	12
5	13
6	14

F Add 8. **H** Multiply by 8.
G Add 9. **J** Multiply by 9.

15 Martin notices that certain pickup trucks have 6 wheels. Which table could he use to determine the number of wheels on five of these pickup trucks?

A

Trucks	1	2	3	4	5
Wheels	4	8	12	16	20

B

Trucks	1	2	3	4	5
Wheels	6	12	18	24	30

C

Trucks	1	2	3	4	5
Wheels	4	16	64	256	1024

D

Trucks	1	2	3	4	5
Wheels	6	36	216	1296	7776

16 Tamera is 4 years younger than her brother. Which number sentence could you use to determine Tamera's age, given her brother's age b?

F $b + 4$ **H** $b \times 4$
G $b - 4$ **J** $b \div 4$

17 Look at the four angles marked on the picture of a bicycle.

Which angle appears to be a right angle?

A angle 1   **B** angle 2   **C** angle 3   **D** angle 4

18 The polygon below has two right angles.

18 _____

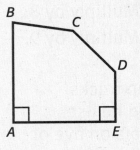

Which side of the polygon is parallel to side $\overline{AB}$?

F $\overline{BC}$ **H** $\overline{DE}$
G $\overline{CD}$ **J** $\overline{EA}$

19 On the graph below, △ABC has been rotated about the center to form △DEF. Which of the following statements can be made?

19 _____

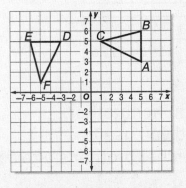

A △ABC is congruent to △DEF.

B △ABC is a right triangle.

C △ABC is a reflection of △DEF.

D △ABC is parallel to △DEF.

20 Which of the following figures shows a trapezoid and its reflection line?

20 _____

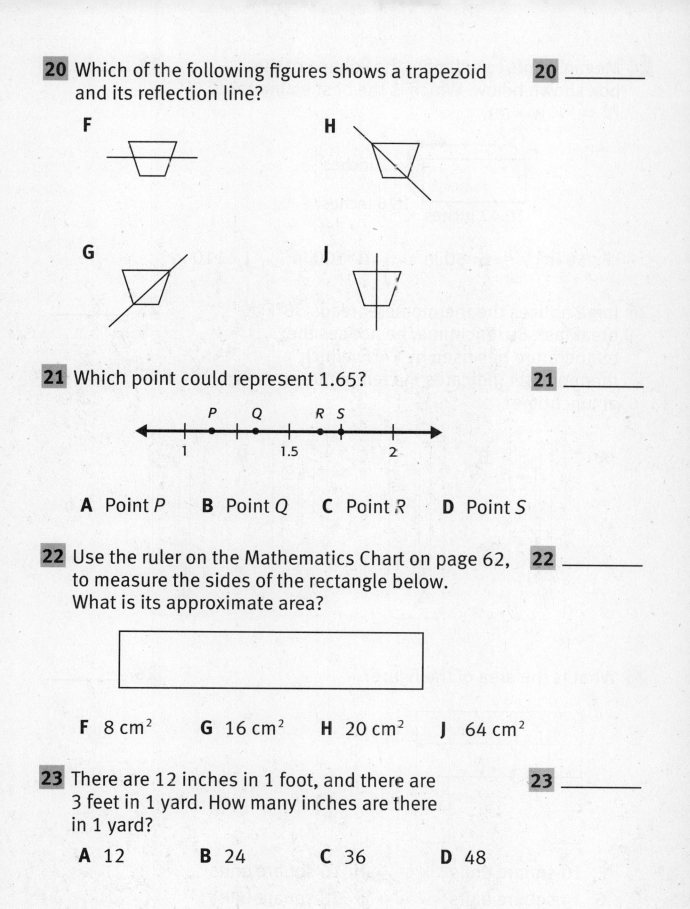

F

H

G

J

21 Which point could represent 1.65?

21 _____

P *Q* *R S*

1 1.5 2

A Point *P*   **B** Point *Q*   **C** Point *R*   **D** Point *S*

22 Use the ruler on the Mathematics Chart on page 62, to measure the sides of the rectangle below. What is its approximate area?

22 _____

F 8 cm²   **G** 16 cm²   **H** 20 cm²   **J** 64 cm²

23 There are 12 inches in 1 foot, and there are 3 feet in 1 yard. How many inches are there in 1 yard?

23 _____

A 12   **B** 24   **C** 36   **D** 48

24 Megan wants to estimate the volume of the box shown below. Which is the best estimate? ($V = l \times w \times h$)

24 _____

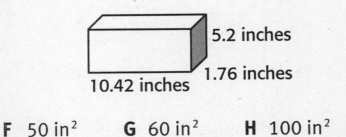

5.2 inches

1.76 inches

10.42 inches

F 50 in² **G** 60 in² **H** 100 in² **J** 110 in²

25 Jorge notices the thermometer reads 38°F at breakfast. By lunchtime, he notices the temperature has risen by 14°F. Which thermometer indicates the temperature at lunchtime?

25 _____

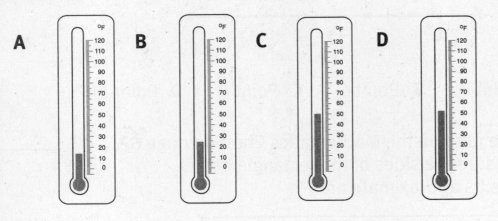

26 What is the area of the figure?

26 _____

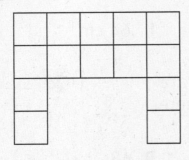

F 10 square units **H** 16 square units
G 14 square units **J** 28 square units

27 To win a prize, first choose a box and then choose a prize bag inside that box. There are 3 boxes and 2 prize bags in each box. There is a different prize in each bag. How many different prizes are there?

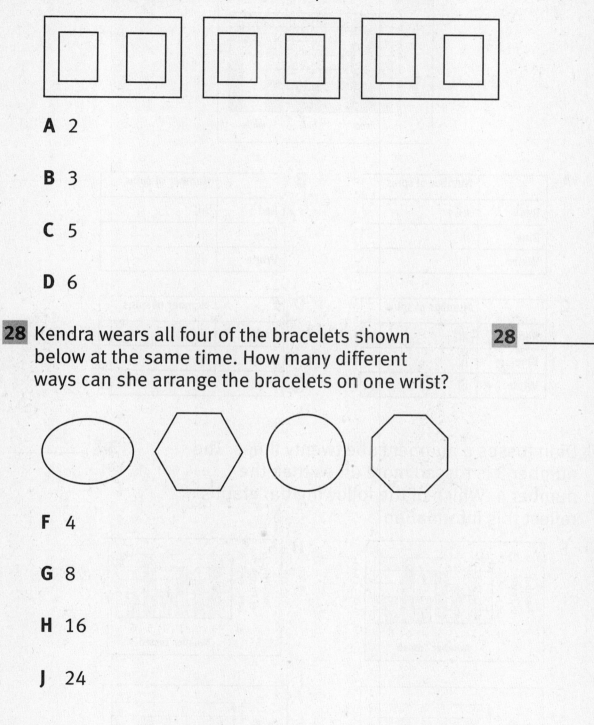

A 2

B 3

C 5

D 6

28 Kendra wears all four of the bracelets shown below at the same time. How many different ways can she arrange the bracelets on one wrist?

F 4

G 8

H 16

J 24

29 Adam spins a spinner 12 times. The results are shown in the bar graph below. Which tally chart shows these results?

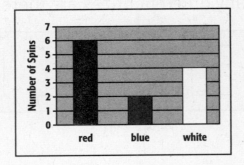

A

	Number of spins
Red	ЖII
Blue	II
White	IIII

B

	Number of spins
Red	ЖI
Blue	III
White	IIII

C

	Number of spins
Red	ЖI
Blue	III
White	III

D

	Number of spins
Red	ЖI
Blue	II
White	ЖI

30 Dion tosses a number cube twenty times. The number 3 is tossed more times than the number 4. Which of the following bar graphs reflect this information?

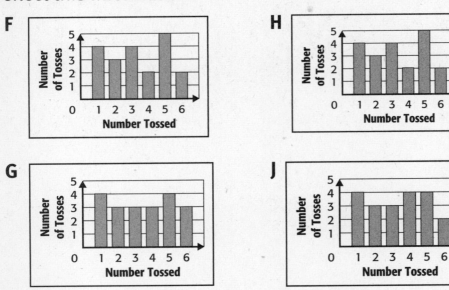

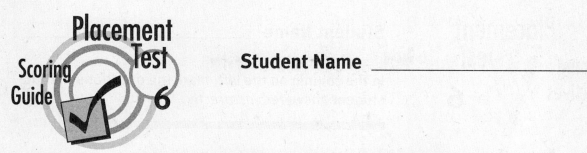

Placement Test 6

Scoring Guide

Student Name _____

For each part, mark the box under the number of correctly answered questions.

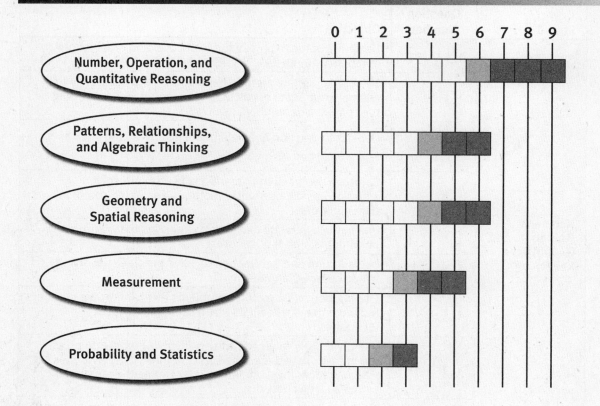

	0 1 2 3 4 5 6 7 8 9
Number, Operation, and Quantitative Reasoning	
Patterns, Relationships, and Algebraic Thinking	
Geometry and Spatial Reasoning	
Measurement	
Probability and Statistics	

Mark the total number correct below.

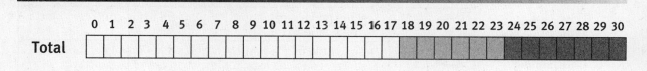

Total: 0 1 2 3 4 5 6 7 8 9 10 11 12 13 14 15 16 17 18 19 20 21 22 23 24 25 26 27 28 29 30

Key: Consider this student for...

☐ *Math Triumphs*

▨ Grade 6 Strategic Intervention—See page 77 for materials list.

▪ *Math Connects: Concepts, Skills, and Problem Solving, Course 1*

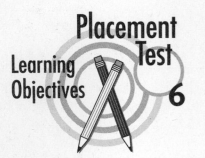

Placement Test
Learning Objectives
6

In the column on the left, mark the questions that the student answered *incorrectly*.

Strand	Question Number	Objective
Number, Operation, and Quantitative Reasoning	☐ 1	Use place value to read, write, compare, and order whole numbers through 999,999,999,999.
	☐ 2	Select appropriate methods and apply them accurately to estimate quotients or calculate them mentally, depending on the context and numbers involved.
	☐ 3	Generate a fraction equivalent to a given fraction such as $\frac{1}{2}$ and $\frac{3}{6}$ or $\frac{4}{12}$ and $\frac{1}{3}$.
	☐ 4	Compare two fractional quantities in problem-solving situations using a variety of methods, including common denominators
	☐ 5	Use models to relate decimals to fractions that name tenths, hundredths, and thousandths.
	☐ 6	Use addition and subtraction to solve problems involving whole numbers and decimals.
	☐ 7	Use multiplication to solve problems involving whole numbers (no more than three digits times two digits without technology).
	☐ 8	Use division to solving problems involving whole numbers (no more than two-digit divisors and three-digit dividends without technology), including interpreting the remainder within a given context.
	☐ 9	Model situations using addition and/or subtraction involving fractions with unlike denominators using concrete objects, pictures, words, and numbers.
Patterns, Relationships, and Algebraic Reasoning	☐ 10	Describe the relationship between sets of data in graphic organizers such as lists, tables, charts, and diagrams.
	☐ 11	Identify prime and composite numbers using concrete objects, pictorial models, and patterns in factor pairs.
	☐ 12	Identify prime and composite numbers using concrete objects, pictorial models, and patterns in factor pairs.
	☐ 13	Describe the relationship between sets of data in graphic organizers such as lists, tables, charts, and diagrams.
	☐ 14	Select from and use diagrams and equations such as $y = 5 + 3$ to represent meaningful problem situations.
	☐ 15	Select from and use diagrams and equations such as $y = 5 + 3$ to represent meaningful problem situations.

Strand	Question Number	Objective
Geometry and Spatial Reasoning	☐ 16	Identify essential attributes including parallel, perpendicular, and congruent parts of two- and three-dimensional geometric figures.
	☐ 17	Identify essential attributes including parallel, perpendicular, and congruent parts of two- and three-dimensional geometric figures.
	☐ 18	Students add and subtract fractions and decimals to solve problems, including problems involving measurement.
Geometry and Spatial Reasoning	☐ 19	Identify the transformation that generates on figure from the other when given two congruent figures on a Quadrant I coordinate grid.
	☐ 20	Quantify volume by finding the total number of same-sized units of volume that they need to fill the space without gaps or overlaps.
	☐ 21	Locate and name points on a coordinate grid using ordered pairs of whole numbers.
Measurement	☐ 22	Perform simple conversions within the same measurement system (SI (metric) or customary).
	☐ 23	Select and use appropriate units and formulas to measure length, perimeter, area, and volume.
	☐ 24	Connect models for perimeter, area, and volume within their respective formulas.
	☐ 25	Select and use appropriate units and formulas to measure length, perimeter, area, surface area, and volume.
	☐ 26	Solve problems involving changes in temperature.
	☐ 27	Solve problems involving elapsed time.
Probability and Statistics	☐ 28	Use fractions to describe the results of an experiment.
	☐ 29	List all possible outcomes of a probability experiment, such as tossing a coin.
	☐ 30	Use experimental results to make predictions.

Diagnostic and Placement Tests

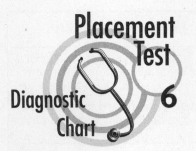

Placement Test
Diagnostic Chart 6

Student Performance Level	Number of Questions Correct	Suggestions for Intervention and Remediation
Intensive Intervention	0–17	Use *Math Triumphs* to accelerate the achievement of students who are two or more years below grade level. Students should follow a personalized remediation plan. A variety of materials and instructional methods are recommended. For example, instruction and practice should be provided in print, technology, and hands-on lessons.
Strategic Intervention	18–23	Use the additional Intervention and Remediation materials listed on the next page. This list of materials can provide helpful resources for students who struggle in the traditional mathematics program. Strategic intervention allows students to continue to remain in the *Math Connects* program, while receiving the differentiated instruction they need. Teaching Tips and other resources are also listed in the Teacher Edition.
Grade 6	24 or more	Use *Math Connects*. This student does not require overall intervention. However, based on the student's performance on the different sections, intervention may be required. For example, a student who missed 2 or more questions in the Measurement section may require extra assistance as you cover these skills throughout the year.

A Special Note About Intervention

When using diagnostic tests, teachers should always question the reason behind the students' scores. Students can struggle with mathematics concepts for a variety of reasons. Personalized instruction is recommended for English language learners, students with specific learning disabilities, students with certain medical conditions, or for those who struggle with traditional instructional practice. Teachers should always consider the needs of the individual student when determining the best approach for instruction and program placement.

Intervention/Remediation Materials Grade 6

Print Materials

Reteach Masters	A brief explanation, along with examples and exercises, for every lesson in the Student Edition. (Two pages for Problem-Solving Lessons and one page per lesson for all other lessons.) These masters are included in the Chapter Resource Masters.
Skills Practice Masters	Additional practice in computational and application exercises for each lesson in the Student Edition. These masters are included in the Chapter Resource Masters.
Homework Practice Masters	Additional practice in computational and spiral review exercises for each lesson in the Student Edition. These masters are included in the Chapter Resource Masters.
Study Guide and Intervention Workbook	A consumable version of the Study Guide and Intervention Masters for each lesson.
Skills Practice Workbook	A consumable version of the Skills Practice Workbook Masters for each lesson.
Practice Workbook	A consumable version of the Practice Masters for each lesson.
Prerequisite Skills Workbook	Arithmetic study guide and practice pages for each of the prerequisite skills that review basic math concepts.

Technology Products

ExamView® Assessment Suite	Networkable software includes a Worksheet Builder to make worksheets and tests, a Student Module to take tests on-screen, and a Management System to keep student records.
MindJogger Videoquizzes	Chapter review provided in a game-show format.
Vocabulary PuzzleMaker Software	Improves students' mathematics vocabulary using crossword puzzles, scrambles, and word searches.
Problem-Solving Practice Masters	Additional practice in application exercises for each lesson in the Student Edition.
Interactive Classroom	A custom classroom teacher-tool incorporating a variety of assets including Additional Examples, Check Your Progress, and 5-Minute Checks.

Mathematics Chart

LENGTH	CAPACITY AND VOLUME
Metric	**Metric**
1 kilometer = 1000 meters	1 liter = 1000 milliliters
1 meter = 100 centimeters	
1 centimeter = 10 millimeters	**Customary**
	1 gallon = 4 quarts
Customary	1 gallon = 128 ounces
1 mile = 1760 yards	1 quart = 2 pints
1 mile = 5280 feet	1 pint = 2 cups
1 yard = 3 feet	1 cup = 8 ounces
1 foot = 12 inches	

MASS AND WEIGHT	TIME
Metric	1 year = 365 days
1 kilogram = 1000 grams	1 year = 12 months
1 gram = 1000 milligrams	1 year = 52 weeks
	1 week = 7 days
Customary	1 day = 24 hours
1 ton = 2000 pounds	1 hour = 60 minutes
1 pound = 16 ounces	1 minute = 60 seconds

Centimeters

Mathematics Chart

Perimeter		Area	
rectangle	$P = 2\ell + 2w$ or $P = 2(\ell + w)$	rectangle	$A = \ell w$ or $A = bh$
		triangle	$A = \frac{1}{2}bh$ or $A = \frac{bh}{2}$
		trapezoid	$A = \frac{1}{2}(b_1 + b_2)h$ or $A = \frac{(b_1 + b_2)h}{2}$
		circle	$A = \pi r^2$

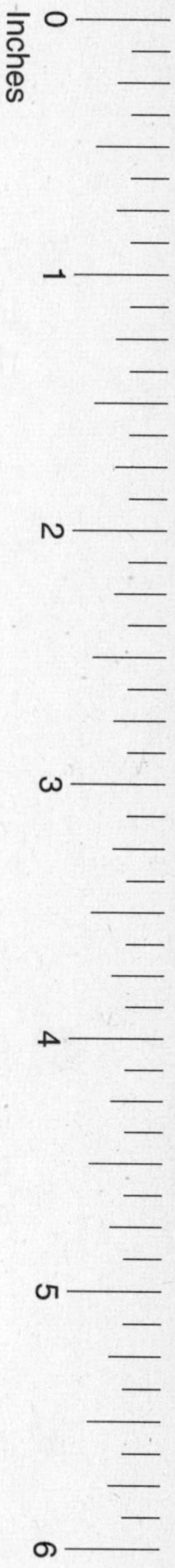

0
Inches

1

2

3

4

5

6

Diagnostic and Placement Tests

Diagnostic and Placement Grade 6

Name _____

Date _____

This test contains 30 multiple-choice questions. Work each problem in the space on this page. Select the best answer. Write the letter of the answer on the blank at the right.

1 Last year, 2,080,015 people attended the state fair. What is this number written in word form?

    A two billion, eighty million, fifteen

    B two million, eight thousand, fifteen

    C two million, eighty thousand, fifteen

    D two hundred eighty thousand, fifteen

1 _____

2 The table below shows the length of the hiking trails at a local park. Aaron hikes half of the blue trail. Estimate to find the distance he hiked.

2 _____

Hiking Trails	
Trail	**Length (miles)**
Red	1.09
Blue	1.87
Green	1.10
Yellow	1.28

    F 0.5 mile   **H** 1 mile   **G** 1.5 miles   **J** 2 miles

3 Darla and Catalina collect stuffed animals. Darla says $\frac{2}{3}$ of her collection is teddy bears. The fraction of stuffed cats in Catalina's collection is equivalent to the fraction of teddy bears in Darla's collection. What is the fraction of stuffed cats in Catalina's collection?

3 _____

    A $\frac{3}{4}$ **B** $\frac{9}{12}$ **C** $\frac{10}{15}$ **D** $\frac{16}{18}$

4 Marlene and Jason each took an online test. Marlene answered $\frac{3}{5}$ of the questions correctly. Jason answered a greater fraction of the questions correctly. Which of the following fractions could represent the fraction Jason answered correctly?

4 _____

    F $\frac{2}{3}$ **G** $\frac{6}{10}$ **H** $\frac{1}{2}$ **J** $\frac{3}{8}$

5 The model below shows $\frac{28}{100}$ shaded. Which of the following decimals is equivalent to $\frac{28}{100}$?

A 2.8   **B** 2.08   **C** 0.28   **D** 0.028

6 Candace is knitting a scarf. The scarf is 4.6 feet long. If she knits another 1.75 feet, how long will the scarf be?

F 6.35 feet   **G** 5.81 feet   **H** 5.35 feet   **J** 2.85 feet

7 The art teacher has 46 boxes of crayons. Each box has 8 crayons. How many crayons are there altogether?

A 248   **B** 288   **C** 328   **D** 368

8 Ms. Ayala had 152 pencils. She divided the number of pencils equally among 13 students. She kept the leftover pencils in her desk. What is the greatest number of pencils Ms. Ayala could have given each student?

F 9   **G** 10   **H** 11   **J** 12

9 Josie draws a rectangle. She colors $\frac{3}{8}$ of the rectangle red and $\frac{1}{4}$ of the rectangle blue. How much of the whole rectangle does she color?

A $\frac{1}{8}$ **B** $\frac{1}{2}$ **C** $\frac{5}{8}$ **D** $\frac{3}{4}$

10 Tia, Veronica, Pam, and Lily are sisters. Tia is 8 years old and she is 2 years older than Pam. Pam is 5 years younger than Veronica and Veronica is 4 years younger than Lily. Which list has the sisters in order from youngest to oldest?

F Tia, Veronica, Pam, Lily

G Lily, Veronica, Tia, Pam

H Tia, Pam, Veronica, Lily

J Pam, Tia, Veronica, Lily

Diagnostic and Placement Tests

11 Eva's age is a prime number. Which of the following could be Eva's age?

    A 8 years old   **C** 13 years old

    B 9 years old   **D** 15 years old

11 _____

12 Mrs. Levit arranged chairs for the school assembly in equal rows, with more than one chair in each row. Which of the following could NOT be the number of chairs she arranged?

    F 27   **G** 73   **H** 81   **J** 99

12 _____

13 The table below shows the cost for different numbers of tickets.

13 _____

Number of Tickets	2	4	6	8	10
Cost	12	24	36	48	60

Based on the information in the table, which of the following statements is true?

    A Each ticket costs $2.

    B Each ticket costs $6.

    C The more tickets you buy the less each ticket costs.

    D The more tickets you buy the greater each ticket costs.

14 Edmundo bought 4 trading cards yesterday. He bought some more trading cards today. Now he has 12 trading cards. If n represents the number of trading cards Edmundo bought today, which equation is correct?

14 _____

    F $4 + 12 = n$ **H** $n + 12 = 4$

    G $4 + n = 12$ **J** $n + 4 = 16$

15 Mr. Izquierdo is joining a gym. There is a $150 registration fee and a monthly fee of $28. Which number sentence shows the total cost c for Mr. Izquierdo to join the gym for a year?

15 _____

    A $(\$150 + \$28) \times 12 = c$ **C** $(\$150 \times 12) + \$28 = c$

    B $\$150 \times (\$28 + 12) = c$ **D** $\$150 + (\$28 \times 12) = c$

16 The polygon below has two right angles. Which side of the polygon is parallel to side $\overline{AB}$?

16 _____

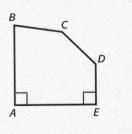

    F $\overline{BC}$ **G** $\overline{CD}$ **H** $\overline{DE}$ **J** $\overline{EA}$

17 A rectangular prism is shown below. How many faces does a rectangular prism have?

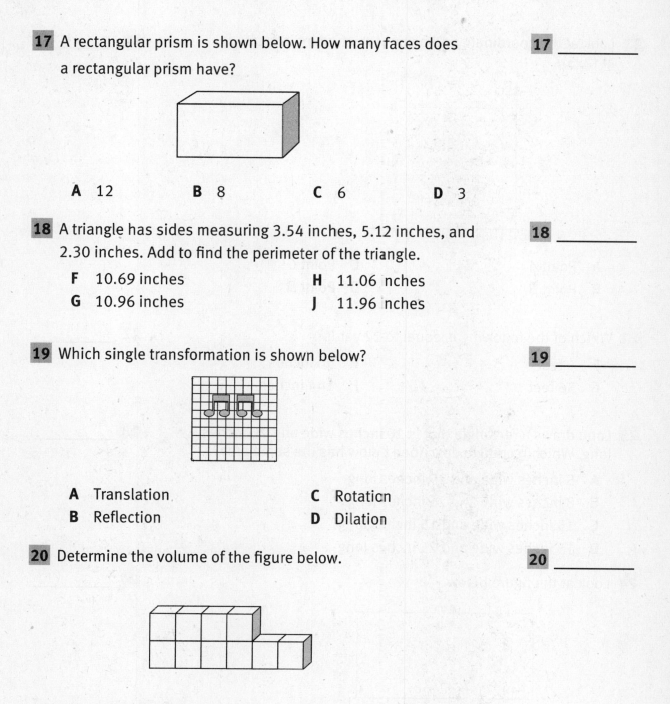

    A 12   **B** 8   **C** 6   **D** 3

18 A triangle has sides measuring 3.54 inches, 5.12 inches, and 2.30 inches. Add to find the perimeter of the triangle.

    F 10.69 inches   **H** 11.06 nches
    G 10.96 inches   **J** 11.96 nches

19 Which single transformation is shown below?

    A Translation   **C** Rotaticn
    B Reflection   **D** Dilation

20 Determine the volume of the figure below.

    F 5 cubic units   **H** 16 cub c units
    G 10 cubic units   **J** 20 cub c units

17 _____

18 _____

19 _____

20 _____

Diagnostic and Placement Tests

21 Look at the coordinate grid below. Which point is located at (2, 5)?

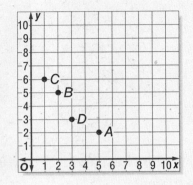

    A Point *A*   **C** Point *C*

    B Point *B*   **D** Point *D*

22 Which of the following is equal to 12 yards?

    F 4 feet   **H** 36 inches

    G 36 feet   **J** 144 inches

23 Lanu draws a rectangle that is 10 inches wide and 20 inches long. Which rectangle described below has the same area?

    A 5 inches wide and 25 inches long

    B 8 inches wide and 25 inches long

    C 15 inches wide and 15 inches long

    D 15 inches wide and 25 inches long

24 Look at the figure below.

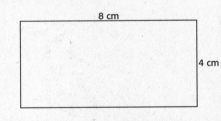

Which equation below represents the area *A* of the rectangle in square centimeters?

    F $32 = A \times 8$ **H** $A = (2 \times 4) + (2 \times 8)$

    G $A = 8 \times 4$ **J** $A = (4 \times A)$

25 A box has a square base with each side measuring 8 inches. The height of the box is 4 inches. What is the surface area of the box in cubic inches?

    A 96 square inches   **C** 256 square inches

    B 192 square inches   **D** 612 square inches

26 The thermometer below shows the temperature at noon. When Xavier looked at the thermometer this morning it was 12°F colder. What was the temperature this morning?

F   41°F

G   44°F

H   56°F

J   68°F

26 _____

27 The dance competition started at 10:45 A.M. Five hours and 25 minutes later the awards were presented. Which clock shows the time at which the awards presentation started?

27 _____

A 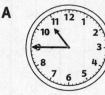   B    C   D

28 Booker has a bag of marbles. There are 10 blue marbles, 6 yellow marbles, and 4 red marbles. Booker reaches into the bag without looking and picks a marble. What is the probability that he picks a red marble?

F $\frac{1}{3}$ G $\frac{1}{4}$ H $\frac{1}{5}$ J $\frac{1}{20}$

28 _____

29 Mrs. Esperanza's math class is playing a game using two spinners. One spinner has the colors red, blue, and green. The other spinner has the numbers 1, 2, 3, 4, 5, 6, 7, and 8. How many possible outcomes are there?

A   11   B   16   C   21   D   24

29 _____

30 Trent has a math quiz every Friday. The table below shows his quiz scores. What is the mode of Trent's scores?

30 _____

Trent's Math Quiz Scores						
Quiz	1	2	3	4	5	6	7
Score	97	88	78	77	82	57	88

F   97   G   88   H   82   J   81

For each part, mark the box under the number of correctly answered questions.

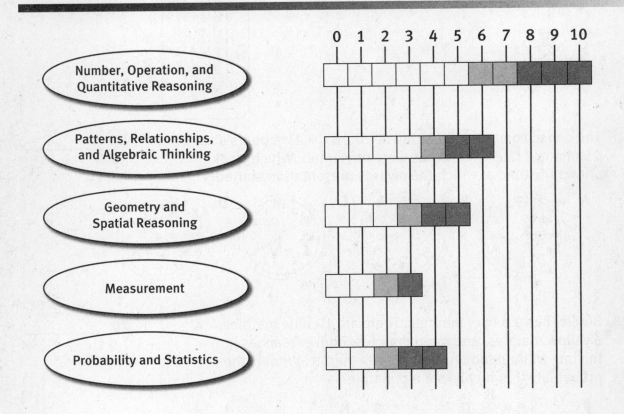

Mark the total number correct below.

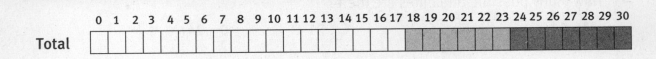

Key: Consider this student for...

□ *Math Triumphs*

▨ Grade 7 Strategic Intervention—See page 90 for materials list.

▨ *Math Connects: Concepts, Skills, and Problem Solving, Course 2*

Placement Test 7
Learning Objectives

Student Name _____

In the column on the left, mark the questions that the student answered *incorrectly*.

Strand	Question Number	Objective
Number, Operation, and Quantitative Reasoning	☐ 1	Compare and order non-negative rational numbers.
	☐ 2	Use integers to represent real-life situations.
	☐ 3	Write prime factorizations using exponents.
	☐ 4	Identify factors of a positive integer, common factors, and the greatest common factor of a set of positive integers.
	☐ 5	Identify multiples of a positive integer and common multiples and the least common multiple of a set of positive integers.
	☐ 6	Use the meanings of fractions, multiplication and division, and the inverse relationship between multiplication and division to make sense of procedures for multiplying and dividing fractions.
	☐ 7	Use addition and subtraction to solve problems involving fractions and decimals.
	☐ 8	Use multiplication and division of whole numbers to solve problems including situations involving equivalent ratios and rates.
	☐ 9	Estimate and round to approximate reasonable results and to solve problems where exact answers are not required.
	☐ 10	Understand that expressions in different forms can be equivalent, and they can rewrite an expression to represent a quantity in a different way.
Patterns, Relationships, and Algebraic Reasoning	☐ 11	Use ratios to describe proportional situations.
	☐ 12	Represent ratios and percents with concrete models, fractions, and decimals.
	☐ 13	Use ratios to make predictions in proportional situations.
	☐ 14	Use tables and symbols to represent and describe proportional and other relationships such as those involving conversions, arithmetic sequences (with a constant rate of change), perimeter and area
	☐ 15	Use tables of data to generate formulas representing relationships involving perimeter, area, volume of a rectangular prism, etc.
	☐ 16	Formulate equations from problem situations described by linear relationships.
	☐ 17	Solve simple one-step equations by using number sense, properties of operations, and the idea of maintaining equality on both sides of an equation.

Strand	Question Number	Objective
Geometry and Spatial Reasoning	☐ 18	Identify relationships involving angles in triangles and quadrilaterals.
	☐ 19	Identify relationships involving angles in triangles and quadrilaterals.
Geometry and Spatial Reasoning	☐ 20	Describe the relationship between the radius, diameter, and circumference of a circle.
	☐ 21	Locate and name points on a coordinate plane using ordered pairs of non-negative irrational numbers.
Measurement	☐ 22	Estimate measurements (including circumference) and evaluate reasonableness of results.
	☐ 23	Select and use appropriate units, tools, or formulas to measure and to solve problems involving length (including perimeter), area, time, temperature, volume, and weight.
	☐ 24	Measure angles.
	☐ 25	Convert measures within the same measurement system (customary and metric) based on relationships between units.
Probability and Statistics	☐ 26	Construct sample spaces using lists and tree diagrams.
	☐ 27	Find the probabilities of a simple event and its complement and describe the relationship between the two.
	☐ 28	Select and use an appropriate representation for displaying different graphical representations of the same data including line plot, line graph, bar graph, and stem and leaf plot.
	☐ 29	Identify mean (using concrete objects and pictorial models), median, mode, and range of a set of data.
	☐ 30	Solve problems by collecting, organizing, displaying, and interpreting data.

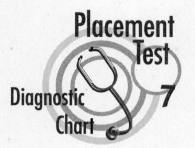

Student Performance Level	Number of Questions Correct	Suggestions for Intervention and Remediation
Intensive Intervention	0–17	Use *Math Triumphs* to accelerate the achievement of students who are two or more years below grade level. Students should follow a personalized remediation plan. A variety of materials and instructional methods are recommended. For example, instruction and practice should be provided in print, technology, and hands-on lessons.
Strategic Intervention	18–23	Use the additional Intervention and Remediation materials listed on the next page. This list of materials can provide helpful resources for students who struggle in the traditional mathematics program. Strategic intervention allows students to continue to remain in the *Math Connects* program, while receiving the differentiated instruction they need. Teaching Tips and other resources are also listed in the Teacher Edition.
Grade 7	24 or more	Use *Math Connects*. This student does not require overall intervention. However, based on the student's performance on the different sections, intervention may be required. For example, a student who missed 1 or more questions in the Measurement section may require extra assistance as you cover these skills throughout the year.

A Special Note About Intervention

When using diagnostic tests, teachers should always question the reason behind the students' scores. Students can struggle with mathematics concepts for a variety of reasons. Personalized instruction is recommended for English language learners, students with specific learning disabilities, students with certain medical conditions, or for those who struggle with traditional instructional practice. Teachers should always consider the needs of the individual student when determining the best approach for instruction and program placement.

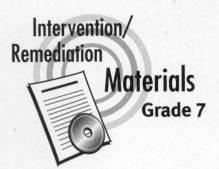

Intervention/ Remediation Materials
Grade 7

Print Materials	
Reteach Masters	A brief explanation, along with examples and exercises, for every lesson in the Student Edition. (Two pages for Problem-Solving Lessons and one page per lesson for all other lessons.) These masters are included in the Chapter Resource Masters.
Skills Practice Masters	Additional practice in computational and application exercises for each lesson in the Student Edition. These masters are included in the Chapter Resource Masters.
Homework Practice Masters	Additional practice in computational and spiral review exercises for each lesson in the Student Edition. These masters are included in the Chapter Resource Masters.
Study Guide and Intervention Workbook	A consumable version of the Study Guide and Intervention Masters for each lesson.
Skills Practice Workbook	A consumable version of the Skills Practice Workbook Masters for each lesson.
Practice Workbook	A consumable version of the Practice Masters for each lesson.
Prerequisite Skills Workbook	Arithmetic study guide and practice pages for each of the prerequisite skills that review basic math concepts.

Technology Products	
ExamView® Assessment Suite	Networkable software includes a Worksheet Builder to make worksheets and tests, a Student Module to take tests on-screen, and a Management System to keep student records.
MindJogger Videoquizzes	Chapter review provided in a game-show format.
Vocabulary PuzzleMaker Software	Improves students' mathematics vocabulary using crossword puzzles, scrambles, and word searches.
Problem-Solving Practice Masters	Additional practice in application exercises for each lesson in the Student Edition.
Interactive Classroom	A custom classroom teacher-tool incorporating a variety of assets including Additional Examples, Check Your Progress, and 5-Minute Checks.

Mathematics Chart

LENGTH	CAPACITY AND VOLUME
Metric	**Metric**
1 kilometer = 1000 meters	1 liter = 1000 milliliters
1 meter = 100 centimeters	
1 centimeter = 10 millimeters	**Customary**
	1 gallon = 4 quarts
Customary	1 gallon = 128 fluid ounces
1 mile = 1760 yards	1 quart = 2 pints
1 mile = 5280 feet	1 pint = 2 cups
1 yard = 3 feet	1 cup = 8 fluid ounces
1 foot = 12 inches	
MASS AND WEIGHT	**TIME**
Metric	1 year = 365 days
1 kilogram = 1000 grams	1 year = 12 months
1 gram = 1000 milligrams	1 year = 52 weeks
	1 week = 7 days
Customary	1 day = 24 hours
1 ton = 2000 pounds	1 hour = 60 minutes
1 pound = 16 ounces	1 minute = 60 seconds

Inches
0
1
2
3
4
5
6

Mathematics Chart

PERIMETER		AREA	
square	$P = 4s$	square	$A = s^2$
rectangle	$P = 2\ell + 2w$ or $P = 2(\ell + w)$	rectangle	$A = \ell w$ or $A = bh$
		triangle	$A = \frac{1}{2} bh$ or $A = \frac{bh}{2}$
		trapezoid	$A = \frac{1}{2}(b_1 + b_2)h$ or $A = \frac{(b_1 + b_2)h}{2}$
		circle	$A = \pi r^2$

CIRCUMFERENCE		VOLUME	
circle	$C = 2\pi r$ or $C = \pi d$	cube	$V = s^3$
		rectangular prism	$V = lwh$

PI

$\pi \approx 3.14$ or $\pi \approx \frac{22}{7}$

Diagnostic and Placement Grade 7

Name _____

Date _____

This test contains 30 multiple-choice questions. Work each problem in the space on this page. Select the best answer. Write the letter of the answer on the blank at the right.

1 Which of the following has the least value?

$$6\tfrac{1}{5}, \tfrac{59}{8}, 6.1, 7$$

    A $6\tfrac{1}{5}$ **C**   6.1

    B $\tfrac{59}{8}$ **D**   7

1 _____

2 Miranda and Tamera are on the same basketball team. Miranda scored 6 points in both the first and third periods of the basketball game. She scored 8 points in the second and fourth periods. Tamera scored 14 points in the first and third periods. Which of the following statements is true?

    F   Miranda scored more points during the first period than Tamera.

    G   Tamera scored fewer points than Miranda in the third period.

    H   Both Miranda and Tamera scored the same amount of points during the game.

    J   Both Miranda and Tamera scored 56 points each during the game.

2 _____

3 What is the prime factorization of 18?

    A 3×6 **C** 2×3^3

    B 2×9 **D** 2×3^2

3 _____

4 Kono divides the numerator and denominator of $\tfrac{48}{72}$ by the same number to simplify the fraction in one step. By what number does he divide?

    F   2   **H**   16

    G   12   **J**   24

4 _____

5 In January, Aleta has band practice every fourth day and swimming lessons every third day. If both programs end January 31, how many days in January will Aleta have both band practice and swimming lessons?

    A   1 day   **C**   3 days

    B   2 days   **D**   4 days

5 _____

6 In simplest form, what is the quotient of $\frac{1}{6} \div \frac{2}{9}$?

   F $\frac{1}{27}$ **H** $\frac{9}{12}$

   G $\frac{2}{54}$ **J** $\frac{3}{4}$

7 Nate has $6\frac{3}{5}$ yards of fabric. He uses $3\frac{1}{2}$ yards of fabric to make a pillow. How much fabric does he have left?

   A $3\frac{1}{10}$ yards   **C** $3\frac{2}{3}$ yards

   B $3\frac{1}{5}$ yards   **D** $4\frac{1}{10}$ yards

8 On a map, 3 inches represent an actual distance of 42 miles. If the actual distance between two cities is 322 miles, how many inches apart will the two cities be on the map?

   F   8 inches   **H**   23 inches
   G   14 inches   **J**   107 inches

9 On the first floor of a middle school, there are 9 classrooms that have 27 desks each. On the second floor, there are 14 classrooms that have 24 desks each. Which of the following is a reasonable estimate of the total number of desks in the middle school?

   A   about 400 desks   **C**   about 800 desks
   B   about 500 desks   **D**   about 900 desks

10 Which expression is equivalent to $5x + 2 - x + 10$?

   F $4x + 12$ **H** $4x - 8$
   G $6x + 12$ **J** $6x - 8$

11 For every 12 slices of pizza sold at Ping's Pizza Shop, 3 slices are pepperoni, 4 are sausage, and the rest are cheese. What is the ratio of pepperoni to cheese?

A 3:12   C 3:4

B 3:5   D 5:3

11 _____

12 Kara is training for a 5-kilometer race. On the first day of training, she runs 0.75 kilometer. What percent of the total distance does she run the first day of training?

F 5%   H 15%

G 10%   J 25%

12 _____

13 Tyler earned $68 for babysitting 8 hours. If Tyler is paid the same rate, how much will he earn for babysitting 12 hours?

A $8.50   C $102

B $80   D $816

13 _____

14 A triangle has a height that is 5 units shorter than its base. If b represents the base and h represents the height, which of the following equations represent the area of the triangle?

F $A = \frac{1}{2}(b - 5)$ H $A = \frac{1}{2}b(b - 5)$

G $A = \frac{1}{2}(h - 5)$ J $A = \frac{1}{2}(b - 5)h$

14 _____

15 The volume of a rectangular prism is 36 in³. The length of the rectangle is 2 inches and the height is 3 inches. Which of the following equations will help you find the width of the rectangular prism?

15 _____

Length	Width	Height	Volume
2	3	3	18
2	4	3	24
2	5	3	30
2	w	3	36

A $w = 36 - 6$ C $w = 36 \div 6$

B $w = 6 \div 36$ D $w = 36 \times 6$

Diagnostic and Placement Tests

16 Which equation shows the relationship between the x- and y-values in the table to the right?

x	y
2	4
4	6
6	8
7	9
10	12

16 _____

F $y = x - 2$

G $x = y + 2$

H $y = x + 2$

J $y = \frac{x}{2}$

17 What is the solution to the equation $3t - 10 = 8$?

17 _____

A $t = 3$

B $t = 6$

C $t = 8$

D $t = 9$

18 Diane draws an obtuse, isosceles triangle with one of the angles measuring 35°. What is the measure of the obtuse angle in her triangle?

18 _____

F 35°   **G** 55°   **H** 110°   **J** 145°

19 The measure of $\angle B$ in parallelogram $ABCD$ is 75°. What is the measure of $\angle A$?

19 _____

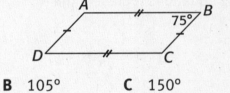

A 75°   **B** 105°   **C** 150°   **D** 210°

20 The circumference of a circle is 20π. What is the radius of this circle?

20 _____

F 2   **G** 10   **H** 20   **J** 40

21 The map below shows where four of Vincente's friends live. Which friend lives at point (2, 4)?

21 _____

A Aesha   **B** Carter   **C** Jenny   **D** Josh

22 Lucas attends 8 classes each day. If each class is about 45 minutes long, about how long will Lucas have been in school when he starts his fourth class of the day?

    F about 2 hours   **H** about 4 hours

    G about 3 hours   **J** about 5 hours

23 A rectangular sandbox has a length of 60 inches, a width of 40 inches, and a depth of 6 inches. What is the volume?

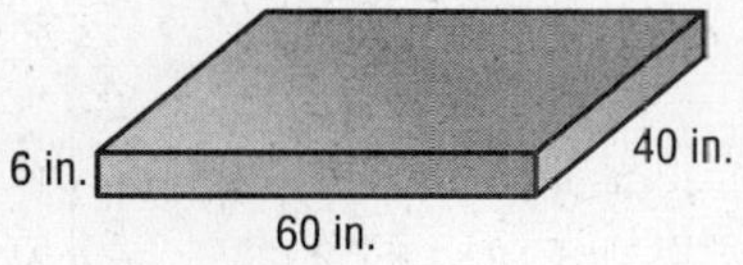

6 in.   40 in.

60 in.

    A 240 cubic inches   **C** 2,400 cubic inches

    B 1,440 cubic inches   **D** 14,400 cubic inches

24 Which of the following is closest to the measure of the angle shown below?

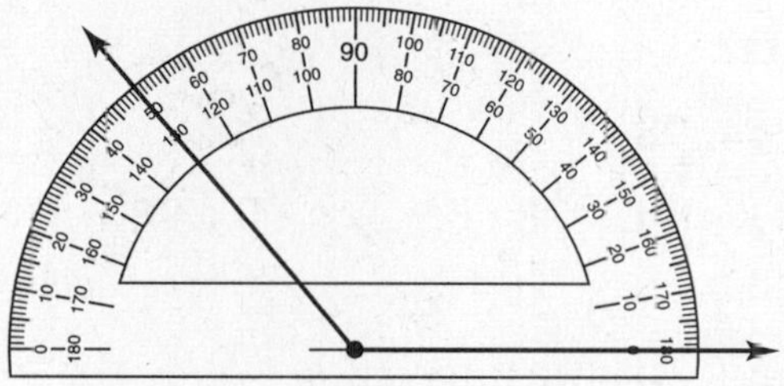

    F 50°   **G** 80°   **H** 130°   **J** 180°

25 A package weighs $2\frac{3}{4}$ pounds. What is the weight of the package in ounces?

    A 35 ounces   **C** 43.7 ounces

    B 36.8 ounces   **D** 44 ounces

26 To win a prize, a player picks a door and then a box behind the door. There are 3 doors and 4 boxes behind each door. How many prizes can be won if each box has a different prize?

    F 3   **G** 4   **H** 7   **J** 12

27 There are 10 marbles in a bag: 1 blue, 4 yellow, 3 red, and 2 white. If you choose a marble at random, which is the probability that you will NOT choose white?

    A 20%   **B** 25%   **C** 75%   **D** 80%

28 Kahlid spins a spinner 10 times. The results are shown in the tally chart below. Which of the following graphs show these results?

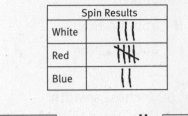

Spin Results	
White	|||
Red	|||||
Blue	||

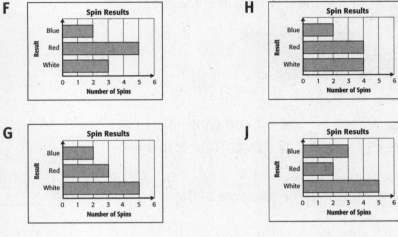

F

Spin Results

G

Spin Results

H

Spin Results

J

Spin Results

29 What is the median of these data?

67, 98, 78, 75, 83, 44, 98

A 44   **B** 75   **C** 78   **D** 98

30 After every run, Gabe's track coach records how many minutes it took Gabe to run a mile. The graph below shows Gabe's times. How many times did Gabe run before he was able to complete a mile in less than 10 minutes?

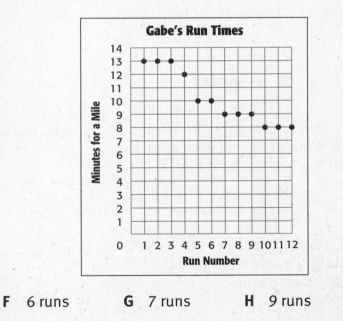

F 6 runs   **G** 7 runs   **H** 9 runs   **J** 10 runs

28 _____

29 _____

30 _____

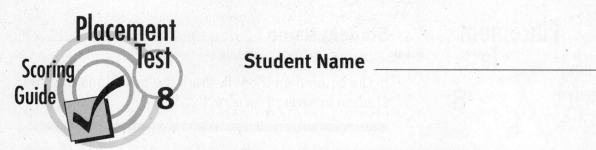

Placement Test 8
Scoring Guide

Student Name _____

For each part, mark the box under the number of correctly answered questions.

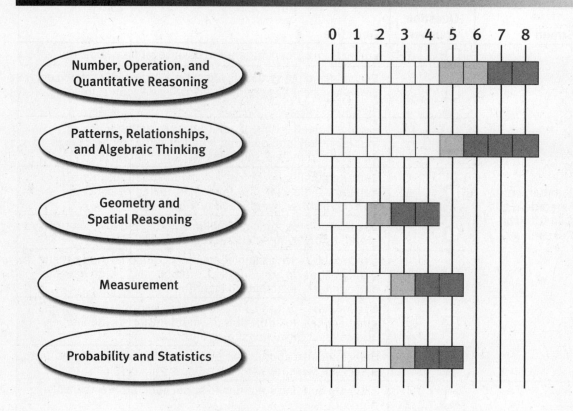

	0	1	2	3	4	5	6	7	8
Number, Operation, and Quantitative Reasoning									
Patterns, Relationships, and Algebraic Thinking									
Geometry and Spatial Reasoning									
Measurement									
Probability and Statistics									

Mark the total number correct below.

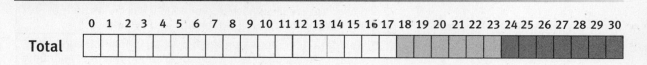

Total — 0 1 2 3 4 5 6 7 8 9 10 11 12 13 14 15 16 17 18 19 20 21 22 23 24 25 26 27 28 29 30

Key: Consider this student for...

☐ *Math Triumphs*

▨ Grade 8 Strategic Intervention—See page 103 for materials list.

▮ *Math Connects: Concepts, Skills, and Problem Solving, Course 3*

Placement Test 8

Learning Objectives

Student Name _____

In the column on the left, mark the questions that the student answered *incorrectly*.

Strand	Question Number	Objective
Number, Operation, and Quantitative Reasoning	☐ 1	Compare and order integers and positive rational numbers.
	☐ 2	Use ratio and proportionality to solve a wide variety of percent problems, including problems involving discounts, interest, taxes, tips and percent increase or decrease.
	☐ 3	Extend understanding of addition, subtraction, multiplication, and division, together with their properties, to all rational numbers, including negatives integers.
	☐ 4	Represent multiplication and division situations involving fractions and decimals with models, including concrete objects, pictures, words, and numbers.
	☐ 5	Use addition, subtraction, multiplication, and division to solve problems involving fractions and decimals.
	☐ 6	Use models, such as concrete objects, pictorial models, and number lines, to add, subtract, multiply and divide integers and connect the actions to algorithms.
	☐ 7	Use models, such as concrete objects, pictorial models, and number lines, to add, subtract, multiply and divide integers and connect the actions to algorithms.
	☐ 8	Select and use appropriate operations to solve problems and justify the selections.
Patterns, Relationships, and Algebraic Reasoning	☐ 9	Estimate and find solutions to application problems involving percent.
	☐ 10	Estimate and find solutions to application problems involving proportional relationships such as similarity, scaling, unit costs, and related measurement units.
	☐ 11	Estimate and find solutions to application problems involving proportional relationships such as similarity, scaling, unit costs, and related measurement units.
	☐ 12	Find surface areas and develop and justify formulas for the surface areas and volumes of prisms and cylinders.
	☐ 13	Graph data to demonstrate relationships in familiar concepts such as conversions, perimeter, area, circumference, volume, and scaling.
	☐ 14	Use words and symbols to describe the relationship between the terms in an arithmetic sequence (with a constant rate of change) and their positions in the sequence.
	☐ 15	Use words and symbols to describe the relationship between the terms in an arithmetic sequence (with a constant rate of change) and their positions in the sequence.
	☐ 16	Use concrete and pictorial models to solve equations and use symbols to record the actions.

Strand	Question Number	Objective
Geometry and Spatial Reasoning	☐ 17	Use angle measurements to classify pairs of angles as complementary or supplementary.
	☐ 18	Use properties to classify triangles and quadrilaterals.
	☐ 19	Locate and name points on a coordinate plane using ordered pairs of integers.
	☐ 20	Make a net (two-dimensional model) of the surface of a three-dimensional figure.
Measurement	☐ 21	Estimate measurements and solve application problems involving length (including perimeter and circumference) and area of polygons and other shapes.
	☐ 22	Estimate measurements and solve application problems involving length (including perimeter and circumference) and area of polygons and other shapes.
	☐ 23	Estimate measurements and solve application problems involving length (including perimeter and circumference) and area of polygons and other shapes.
	☐ 24	Connect models for volume of prisms (triangular and rectangular) and cylinders to formulas of prisms (triangular and rectangular) and cylinders.
	☐ 25	Estimate measurements and solve applications problems involving volume of prisms (rectangular and triangular) and cylinders.
Probability and Statistics	☐ 26	Construct sample spaces for simple or composite experiments.
	☐ 27	Find the probability of independent events.
	☐ 28	Select and use an appropriate representation for presenting and representations among collected data including line plot, line graph, bar graph, stem and leaf plot, circle graph, and Venn diagrams, and justify the selection.
	☐ 29	Describe a set of data using mean, median, mode, and range.
	☐ 30	Choose among the mean, median, mode, or range to describe a set of data and justify the choice for a particular situation.

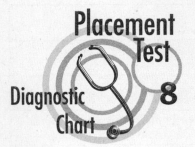

Placement Test
Diagnostic
Chart
8

Student Performance Level	Number of Questions Correct	Suggestions for Intervention and Remediation
Intensive Intervention	0–17	Use *Math Triumphs* to accelerate the achievement of students who are two or more years below grade level. Students should follow a personalized remediation plan. A variety of materials and instructional methods are recommended. For example, instruction and practice should be provided in print, technology, and hands-on lessons.
Strategic Intervention	18–23	Use the additional Intervention and Remediation materials listed on the next page. This list of materials can provide helpful resources for students who struggle in the traditional mathematics program. Strategic intervention allows students to continue to remain in the *Math Connects* program, while receiving the differentiated instruction they need. Teaching Tips and other resources are also listed in the Teacher Edition.
Grade 6	24 or more	Use *Math Connects*. This student does not require overall intervention. However, based on the student's performance on the different sections, intervention may be required. For example, a student who missed 1 or more questions in the Measurement section may require extra assistance as you cover these skills throughout the year.

A Special Note About Intervention

When using diagnostic tests, teachers should always question the reason behind the students' scores. Students can struggle with mathematics concepts for a variety of reasons. Personalized instruction is recommended for English language learners, students with specific learning disabilities, students with certain medical conditions, or for those who struggle with traditional instructional practice. Teachers should always consider the needs of the individual student when determining the best approach for instruction and program placement.

Intervention/ Remediation Materials
Grade 8

Print Materials

Reteach Masters	A brief explanation, along with examples and exercises, for every lesson in the Student Edition. (Two pages for Problem-Solving Lessons and one page per lesson for all other lessons.) These masters are included in the Chapter Resource Masters.
Skills Practice Masters	Additional practice in computational and application exercises for each lesson in the Student Edition. These masters are included in the Chapter Resource Masters.
Homework Practice Masters	Additional practice in computational and spiral review exercises for each lesson in the Student Edition. These masters are included in the Chapter Resource Masters.
Study Guide and Intervention Workbook	A consumable version of the Study Guide and Intervention Masters for each lesson.
Skills Practice Workbook	A consumable version of the Skills Practice Workbook Masters for each lesson.
Practice Workbook	A consumable version of the Practice Masters for each lesson.
Prerequisite Skills Workbook	Arithmetic study guide and practice pages for each of the prerequisite skills that review basic math concepts.

Technology Products

ExamView® Assessment Suite	Networkable software includes a Worksheet Builder to make worksheets and tests, a Student Module to take tests on-screen and a Management System to keep student records.
MindJogger Videoquizzes	Chapter review provided in a game-show format.
Vocabulary PuzzleMaker Software	Improves students' mathematics vocabulary using crossword puzzles, scrambles, and word searches.
Problem-Solving Practice Masters	Additional practice in application exercises for each lesson in the Student Edition.
Interactive Classroom	A custom classroom teacher-tool incorporating a variety of assets including Additional Examples, Check Your Progress, and 5-Minute Checks.

Mathematics Chart

LENGTH	CAPACITY AND VOLUME
Metric	**Metric**
1 kilometer = 1000 meters	1 liter = 1000 milliliters
1 meter = 100 centimeters	
1 centimeter = 10 millimeters	**Customary**
	1 gallon = 4 quarts
Customary	1 gallon = 128 ounces
1 mile = 1760 yards	1 quart = 2 pints
1 mile = 5280 feet	1 pint = 2 cups
1 yard = 3 feet	1 cup = 8 ounces
1 foot = 12 inches	

MASS AND WEIGHT	TIME
Metric	1 year = 365 days
1 kilogram = 1000 grams	1 year = 12 months
1 gram = 1000 milligrams	1 year = 52 weeks
	1 week = 7 days
Customary	1 day = 24 hours
1 ton = 2000 pounds	1 hour = 60 minutes
1 pound = 16 ounces	1 minute = 60 seconds

Centimeters

20 19 18 17 16 15 14 13 12 11 10 9 8 7 6 5 4 3 2 1 0

Mathematics Chart

PERIMETER		AREA	
square	$P = 4s$	square	$A = s^2$
rectangle	$P = 2\ell + 2w$ or $P = 2(\ell + w)$	rectangle	$A = \ell w$ or $A = bh$
		triangle	$A = \frac{1}{2}bh$ or $A = \frac{bh}{2}$
		trapezoid	$A = \frac{1}{2}(b_1 + b_2)h$ or $A = \frac{(b_1 + b_2)h}{2}$
		circle	$A = \pi r^2$

CIRCUMFERENCE		VOLUME	
circle	$C = 2\pi r$ or $C = \pi d$	cube	$V = s^3$
		retangular prism	$V = lwh$ or $V = Bh*$
		triangular prism	$V = Bh*$
		cylinder	$V = \pi r^2 h$ or $V = Bh*$

B represents the area of the base of a solid figure.

PI

$\pi \approx 3.14$ or $\pi \approx \frac{22}{7}$

0
Inches
1
2
3
4
5
6

Diagnostic and Placement Tests

Diagnostic and Placement Grade 8

Name _____

Date _____

This test contains 30 multiple-choice questions. Work each problem in the space on this page. Select the best answer. Write the letter of the answer on the blank at the right.

1 Which set of numbers is in order from greatest to least?

1 _____

   A   4, $\frac{1}{4}$, $\frac{2}{3}$, 0.04, 40   **C**   40, 4, $\frac{2}{3}$, $\frac{1}{4}$, 0.04

   B   0.04, $\frac{1}{4}$, $\frac{2}{3}$, 4, 40   **D** $\frac{1}{4}$, $\frac{2}{3}$, 0.04, 4, 40

2 Charlene bought her friends lunch. The bill came to $52.80 before Charlene added an 18% service tip. How much did she add for the service tip?

2 _____

   F $4.75   **H** $9.50

   G $5.70   **J** $10.20

3 Randy is playing a number game. Beginning with the number 8, he adds 4, multiples by 5, and then divides by −10. He then subtracts 2. What number does he find at the end of the game?

3 _____

   A   −8   **B**   −6   **C**   6   **D**   8

4 Which multiplication is shown by the picture below?

4 _____

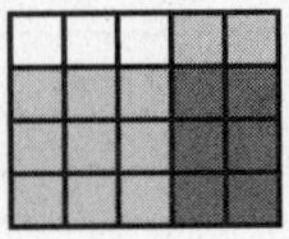

   F $\frac{1}{5} \times \frac{1}{4}$ **H** $\frac{2}{20} \times \frac{3}{20}$

   G $\frac{2}{5} \times \frac{3}{5}$ **J** $\frac{2}{5} \times \frac{3}{4}$

5 Olivia orders 4 ham sandwiches at the deli. The total amount was $30.52. How much did each sandwich cost?

5 _____

   A $7.63   **B** $7.83   **C** $12.63   **D** $122.08

6 The table below shows the charges for a taxi ride in a city.

6 _____

Charges for Each Taxi Ride	
Charges	**Rate**
Mileage Charge	$0.75 Each Mile
City Gas Tax	$0.10 Each Mile
Tourist Charge	$2.50

If a taxi ride is m miles, which expression can be used to find the total charge of the ride?

  F $2.50m + 0.75$ **H** $0.10m + 3.25$

  G $0.75m + 2.50$ **J** $0.85m + 2.50$

7 Michael's age is 5 years younger than Jordan. Jordan is 4 years younger than Keanu. Keanu is 17 years old. How old is Michael?

7 _____

  A Michael is 12 years old, because he is 5 years younger than Keanu.

  B Michael is 22 years old, because he is 5 years older than Keanu.

  C Michael is 8 years old, because he is 5 years younger than Jordan, and Jordan is 13 years old.

  D Michael is 18 years old, because he is 5 years older than Jordan, and Jordan is 13 years old.

8 Jeb's weight w is $\frac{1}{3}$ of Iago's weight a. Which equation could be used to find Jeb's weight?

8 _____

  F $w = a - \frac{1}{3}$ **H** $w = \frac{1}{3} + a$

  G $w = \frac{1}{3}a$ **J** $w = a \div \frac{1}{3}$

9 The school band sold 200 tickets to their concert. If 90 of the tickets were adult tickets, what percent of the tickets sold were adult tickets?

9 _____

  A 18%   **C** 55%

  B 45%   **D** 90%

10 A car travels 528 miles on 16 gallons of gas. At the same rate, how many gallons of gas are needed to travel 165 miles?

10 _____

  F 4   **G** 5   **H** 6   **J** 7

Diagnostic and Placement Tests

11 An electrician charges $30 for a house visit and $55 for each hour of work. If Mrs. Firewalks was charged $222.50 for work, which can be used to find the number of hours that the electrician worked?

11 _____

    A Subtract 55 from 222.50 and then divide the difference by 30.

    B Subtract 30 from 222.50 and then divide the difference by 55.

    C Divide 222.50 by 55.

    D Divide 222.50 by 30.

12 The height of a box is 6 inches. The length of the box is 14 inches and the width of the box is 4 inches.

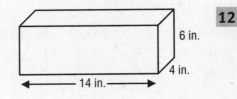

12 _____

Which equation could be used to find the surface area of the box?

    F $s = 2 \cdot (14 \cdot 6) + 2 \cdot (4 \cdot 6)$ **H** $s = 2 \cdot (14 \cdot 4) + 2 \cdot (14 \cdot 6) + 2 \cdot (6 \cdot 4)$

    G $s = (14 \cdot 4) + (14 \cdot 6) + (6 \cdot 4)$ **J** $s = (14 \cdot 4) \cdot (14 \cdot 6) \cdot (6 \cdot 4)$

13 The table shows circles and their corresponding diameters. Which of the following graphs show the correct relationship between the radius and the area of each circle?

13 _____

Circles	
Circle	**Diameter (feet)**
R	2
S	4
T	8
U	12

A

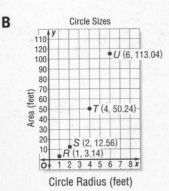

C

B

D

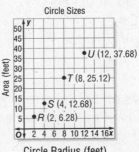

14 Look at the sequence in the table.

Position	Value of Term
1	3
2	7
3	11
4	15
5	19
n	

Which expression can find the nth term in the sequence where n represents the position of the term?

F $n + 3$ **H** $4n + 2$

G $4n - 1$ **J** $3n - 2$

15 Which statement best describes the pattern shown below?

66, 62, 58, 54, 50, 46, 42, 38

A Divide by 4 to get the next term

B Add 4 to get the next term

C Subtract 4 to get the next term

D Multiply by 4 to get the next term

16 The picture models the equation $5x + 2 = 3x + 6$.

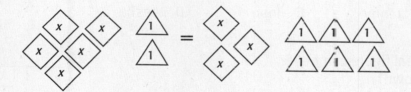

What value of x makes the equation true?

F $x = 1$ **H** $x = 4$

G $x = 2$ **J** $x = 6$

17 $\angle A$ and $\angle B$ are supplementary angles. If the measure of $\angle A$ is 33°, what is the measure of $\angle B$?

A 17°   **B** 57°   **C** 137°   **D** 147°

Diagnostic and Placement Tests

18 Which picture below is an obtuse isosceles triangle?

18 _____

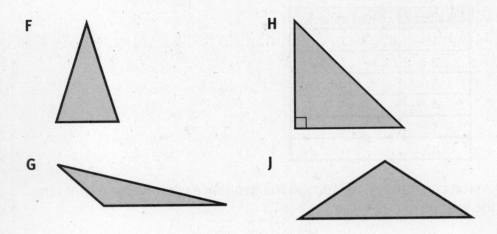

19 The map below shows where four of Nahimana's friends live.

19 _____

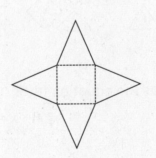

Which friend lives at the point $(-4, 2)$?

   A Carter   **B** Jenny   **C** Josh   **D** Aesha

20 What three-dimensional figure can be made from the net shown?

20 _____

   F Triangular pyramid
   G Cube
   H Rectangular pyramid
   J Rectangular prism

21 The length of a rectangle is 3 times the width. The perimeter is 48 centimeters. What is the area?

21 _____

   A 108 cm^2 **C** 222.75 cm^2
   B 141.75 cm^2 **D** 432 cm^2

22 A homeowner wants to cover the floor of a patio with square tiles that are the same size. She knows the area of each tile. What additional information does she need in order to find the number of tiles that she needs?

22 _____

    F The price of each tile

    G The perimeter of the patio

    H The area of the patio

    J The perimeter of each tile

23 In the figure below, *ABCD* is a parallelogram.

23 _____

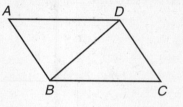

If the area of triangle *ABD* is 64 square centimeters, what is the area of *ABCD*?

    A 16 square centimeters   **C** 64 square centimeters

    B 32 square centimeters   **D** 128 square centimeters

24 What is the volume of the cylinder shown below?

24 _____

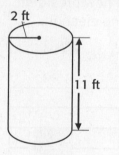

    F 44 ft^3 **H** 138.16 ft^3

    G 69.08 ft^3 **J** 276.32 ft^3

25 What is the difference in the volume of the two triangular prisms shown below?

25 _____

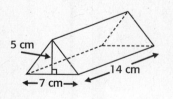
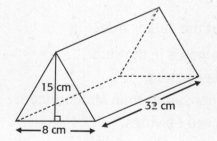

    A 32 cm^3 **C** 1,675 cm^3

    B 158 cm^3 **D** 3,350 cm^3

26 Juan needs to choose an outfit from his closet. He can choose from a red, green, or blue T-shirt and he can choose from a pair of blue, tan, or black pants. Which table shows all possible outfits if Juan picked one shirt and one pair of pants at random?

F

Outfits	
Shirts	Pants
red	blue
green	black
blue	tan

G

Outfits	
Shirts	Pants
red	blue
green	blue
blue	blue
red	black
green	black
blue	black
red	tan
green	tan
blue	tan

H

Outfits	
Shirts	Pants
red	blue
green	black
blue	tan
red	blue
green	black
blue	tan
red	blue
green	black
blue	tan

J

Outfits	
Shirts	Pants
red	blue
green	black
blue	tan
red	blue
green	black
blue	tan

27 A jar contains 4 green marbles, 2 pink marbles, and 3 striped marbles. One marble is picked at random and then replaced. Then another marble is drawn at random again. What is the probability that both marbles are striped?

A $\frac{1}{81}$ **B** $\frac{1}{9}$ **C** $\frac{1}{3}$ **D** $\frac{1}{2}$

28 All the members of a garden club vote for a new president. The bar graph below shows the results of the election.

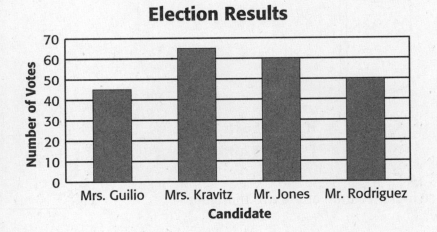

Which statement about the data is true?

F There are 220 members in the club.

G Mr. Jones won the election.

H Mrs. Guilio had more votes than Mr. Rodriguez.

J Mrs. Kravitz received 60 votes.

29 The basketball team's scores for 5 games are listed below.

29 _____

$$35, 48, 24, 31, 47$$

What is the mean of the scores?

A 24 **B** 35 **C** 37 **D** 185

30 A walker records her walking times for 1 mile over several weeks. The mean, median, mode, and range of her times are shown in the table below.

30 _____

Walking Times	
Measure of Data	**Time**
mean	17 minutes, 30 seconds
median	19 minutes
mode	18 minutes, 20 seconds
range	7 minutes, 2 seconds

Which measure of data tells the time that she walked most often?

F Range **G** Median **H** Mode **J** Mean

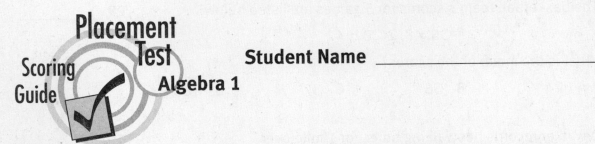

Placement Test
Scoring Guide
Algebra 1

Student Name _____

For each part, mark the box under the number of correctly answered questions.

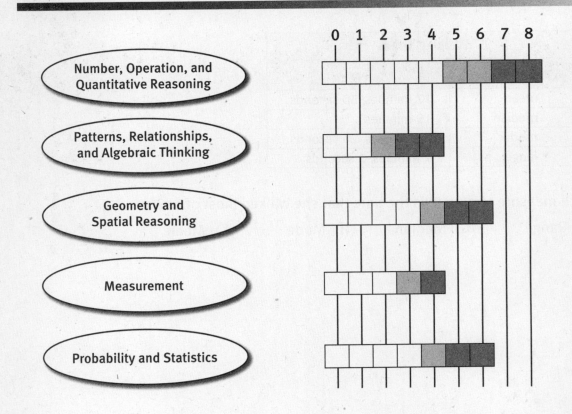

Mark the total number correct below.

Key: Consider this student for...

☐ *Glencoe Pre-Algebra*

▨ Algebra 1 Strategic Intervention—See page 118 for materials list.

▨ *Glencoe Algebra 1*

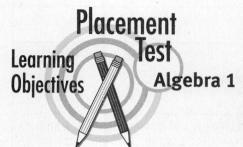

Placement Test

Learning Objectives

Algebra 1

Student Name _____

In the column on the left, mark the questions that the student answered *incorrectly*.

Strand	Question Number	Objective
Number, Operation, and Quantitative Reasoning	☐ 1	Compare and order rational numbers in various forms including integers, percents, and positive and negative fractions and decimals.
	☐ 2	Approximate (mentally and with calculators) the value of irrational numbers as they arise from problems situations (such as π, $\sqrt{2}$).
	☐ 3	Express numbers in scientific notation, including negative exponents, in appropriate problems situations.
	☐ 4	Express numbers in scientific notation, including negative exponents, in appropriate problems situations.
	☐ 5	Select appropriate operations to solve problems involving rational numbers and justify the selections.
	☐ 6	Select appropriate operations to solve problems involving rational numbers and justify the selections.
	☐ 7	Use appropriate operations to solve problems involving rational numbers in problem situations.
	☐ 8	Use multiplication by a constant factor (unit rate) to represent proportional relationships.
Patterns, Relationships, and Algebraic Reasoning	☐ 9	Compare and contrast proportional and non-proportional linear relationships.
	☐ 10	Translate among verbal, tabular, graphical, and algebraic representations of functions, and describe how such aspects of a function as slope and *y*-intercept appear in different representations.
	☐ 11	Estimate and find solutions to application problems involving percents and other proportional relationships such as similarity and rates.
	☐ 12	Solve systems of two linear equations in two variables and relate the systems to pairs of lines that intersect, are parallel, or are the same, in the plane.
	☐ 13	Find and evaluate an algebraic expression to determine any term in an arithmetic sequence (with a constant rate of change.
Geometry and Spatial Reasoning	☐ 14	Generate similar figures using dilations including enlargements and reductions.
	☐ 15	Graph dilations, reflections, and translations on a coordinate plane.
	☐ 16	Use facts about the angles created when a transversal cuts parallel lines to explain why the sum of the measures of the angles in a triangle is 180 degrees, and they apply this fact about triangles to find unknown measures of angles.
	☐ 17	Use geometric concepts and properties to solve problems in fields such as art and architecture.

Strand	Question Number	Objective
Geometry and Spatial Reasoning	☐ 18	Use geometric concepts and properties to solve problems in fields such as art and architecture.
	☐ 19	Locate and name points on a coordinate plane using ordered pairs of rational numbers.
Measurement	☐ 20	Find lateral and total surface area of prisms, pyramids, and cylinders using concrete models and nets (two-dimensional models).
	☐ 21	Estimate measurements and use formulas to solve application problems involving lateral and total surface area and volume.
	☐ 22	Use the Pythagorean Theorem to solve real-life problems.
	☐ 23	Use proportional relationships in similar two-dimensional figures or similar three-dimensional figures to find missing measurements.
	☐ 24	Describe the resulting effects on perimeter and area when dimensions of a shape are changed proportionally.
Probability and Statistics	☐ 25	Find the probability of dependent and independent events.
	☐ 26	Use theoretical probabilities and experimental results to make predictions and decisions.
	☐ 27	Select the appropriate measure of central tendency or range to describe a set of data and justify the choice for a particular situation.
	☐ 28	Draw conclusions and make predictions analyzing trends in scatterplots.
	☐ 29	Select and use an appropriate representation for presenting and displaying relationships among collected data including line plots, line graphs, stem and leaf plots, histograms, and Venn diagrams, with and without the use of technology.
	☐ 30	Evaluate methods of sampling to determine validity of an inference made from a set of data.

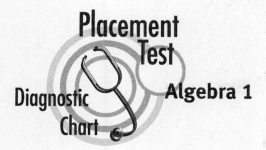

Placement Test

Diagnostic Chart

Algebra 1

Student Performance Level	Number of Questions Correct	Suggestions for Intervention and Remediation
Intensive Intervention	0–17	Use *Glencoe Pre-Algebra* to accelerate the achievement of students who are below grade level. Students should follow a personalized remediation plan. A variety of materials and instructional methods are recommended. For example, instruction and practice should be provided in print, technology, and hands-on lessons.
Strategic Intervention	18–23	Use the additional Intervention and Remediation materials listed on the next page. This list of materials can provide helpful resources for students who struggle in the traditional mathematics program. Strategic intervention allows students to continue to remain in the *Math Connects* program, while receiving the differentiated instruction they need. Teaching Tips and other resources are also listed in the Teacher Edition.
Algebra 1	24 or more	Use *Glencoe Algebra 1*. This student does not require overall intervention. However, based on the student's performance on the different sections, intervention may be required. For example, a student who missed 3 or more questions in the Measurement section may require extra assistance as you cover these skills throughout the year.

A Special Note About Intervention

When using diagnostic tests, teachers should always question the reason behind the students' scores. Students can struggle with mathematics concepts for a variety of reasons. Personalized instruction is recommended for English language learners, students with specific learning disabilities, students with certain medical conditions, or for those who struggle with traditional instructional practice. Teachers should always consider the needs of the individual student when determining the best approach for instruction and program placement.

Intervention/Remediation Materials
Algebra 1

Print Materials

Quick Review Math Handbook	A comprehensive reference of important mathematical terms and concepts to help build math literacy. Also available in Spanish.
Study Guide and Intervention Masters	A brief explanation, along with examples and exercises, for every lesson in the Student Edition. These masters are included in the Chapter Resource Masters.
Skills Practice Masters	Additional practice in computational and application exercises for each lesson in the Student Edition. These masters are included in the Chapter Resource Masters.
Practice Masters	Additional practice in computational and spiral review exercises for each lesson in the Student Edition. These masters are included in the Chapter Resource Masters.
Study Guide and Intervention Workbook	A consumable version of the Study Guide and Intervention Masters for each lesson.
Skills Practice Workbook	A consumable version of the Skills Practice Workbook Masters for each lesson.
Practice Workbook	A consumable version of the Practice Masters for each lesson.
Prerequisite Skills Workbook: Remediation and Intervention	Arithmetic study guide and practice pages for each of the prerequisite skills that review basic math concepts.

Technology Products

ExamView Pro® Assessment Suite	Networkable software includes a Worksheet Builder to make worksheets and tests, a Student Module to take tests on-screen, and a Management System to keep student records.
Mathematics Super DVDs	Includes: MindJogger Plus, a chapter review provided in a game-show format, and What's Math Got to Do With It? Real Life Math Videos that show students how math is used in everyday situations through engaging videos.
Problem-Solving Practice Masters	Additional practice in application exercises for each lesson in the Student Edition.
Interactive Classroom	A custom classroom teacher-tool incorporating a variety of assets including Additional Examples, Check Your Progress, and 5-Minute Checks.

Mathematics Chart

LENGTH	CAPACITY AND VOLUME
Metric	**Metric**
1 kilometer = 1000 meters	1 liter = 1000 milliliters
1 meter = 100 centimeters	
1 centimeter = 10 millimeters	**Customary**
	1 gallon = 4 quarts
Customary	1 gallon = 128 ounces
1 mile = 1760 yards	1 quart = 2 pints
1 mile = 5280 feet	1 pint = 2 cups
1 yard = 3 feet	1 cup = 8 ounces
1 foot = 12 inches	
MASS AND WEIGHT	**TIME**
Metric	1 year = 365 days
1 kilogram = 1000 grams	1 year = 12 months
1 gram = 1000 milligrams	1 year = 52 weeks
	1 week = 7 days
Customary	1 day = 24 hours
1 ton = 2000 pounds	1 hour = 60 minutes
1 pound = 16 ounces	1 minute = 60 seconds

Inches
0
1
2
3
4
5
6

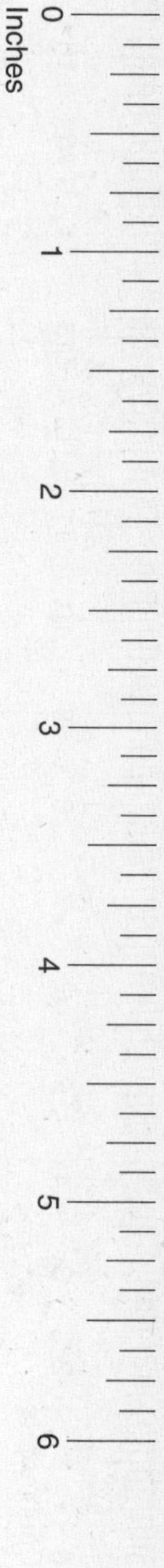

Mathematics Chart

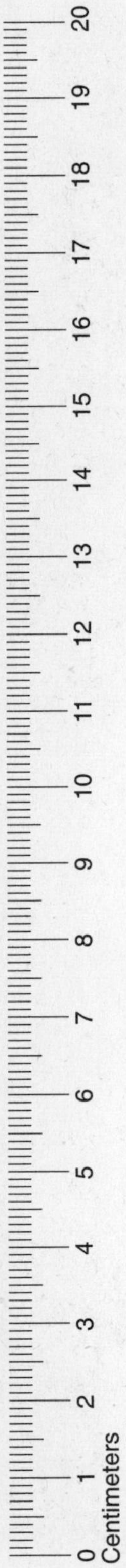

PERIMETER

square	$P = 4s$
rectangle	$P = 2\ell + 2w$ or
	$P = 2(\ell + w)$

AREA

square	$A = s^2$
rectangle	$A = \ell w$ or $A = bh$
triangle	$A = \frac{1}{2} bh$ or $A = \frac{bh}{2}$
trapezoid	$A = \frac{1}{2}(b_1 + b_2)h$ or
	$A = \frac{(b_1 + b_2)h}{2}$
circle	$A = \pi r^2$

CIRCUMFERENCE

circle	$C = 2\pi r$ or $C = \pi d$

B *represents the area of the base of a solid figure.*

P *represents the Perimeter of the Base of a three-dimensional figure.*

VOLUME

cube	$V = s^3$
retangular prism	$V = lwh$ or
	$V = Bh$
triangular prism	$V = Bh$
cylinder	$V = \pi r^2 h$ or
	$V = Bh$

SURFACE AREA

cube (total)	$S = 6s^2$
prism (lateral)	$S = Ph$
prism (total)	$S = Ph + 2B$
pyramid (lateral)	$S = \frac{1}{2} P\ell$
pyramid (total)	$S = \frac{1}{2} P\ell + B$
cylinder (lateral)	$S = 2\pi rh$
cylinder (total)	$S = 2\pi rh + 2\pi r^2$ or
	$S = 2\pi r(h + r)$

PI

$\pi \approx 3.14$ or $\pi \approx \frac{22}{7}$

PYTHAGOREAN THEOREM

$a^2 + b^2 = c^2$

SIMPLE INTEREST FORMULA

$I = prt$

20
19
18
17
16
15
14
13
12
11
10
9
8
7
6
5
4
3
2
1
0
Centimeters

Diagnostic and Placement
Algebra 1

Name _____

Date _____

This test contains 30 multiple-choice questions. Work each problem in the space on this page. Select the best answer. Write the letter of the answer on the blank at the right.

1 Which set of numbers is ordered from least to greatest?

   A $\frac{3}{8}; \frac{1}{2}; 1; \sqrt{2}; 4$

   B $\frac{3}{8}; \frac{1}{2}; \sqrt{2}; 1, 4$

   C $4; \sqrt{2}; 1; \frac{1}{2}; \frac{3}{8}$

   D $\frac{1}{2}; \frac{3}{8}; 1; 4; \sqrt{2}$

1 _____

2 The area of a square is 8 square meters. Which of these is closest to the length of one side of the square?

   F 2 square meters

   G 2.8 square meters

   H 3.5 square meters

   J 4 square meters

2 _____

3 Light travels at a speed of about 2.998×10^8 meters per second. Express this number in standard notation.

   A 299,800,000

   B 0.00002998

   C 0.0000002998

   D 29,980,000

3 _____

4 A thunderstorm cloud holds about 6,200,000,000 raindrops. Which of the following shows this number in scientific notation?

   F 0.62×10^{10}

   G 6.2×10^9

   H 6.2×10^8

   J 62.0×10^8

4 _____

5 Jake goes to the grocery store and buys 3 apples, 2 cans of soup, and 1 box of cereal. The apples cost $0.89 each; the soup costs $2.98 per can; and the box of cereal costs $4.99. Write an equation that represents the total cost c of Jake's purchases.

   A $c = (3 + 0.89) + (2 + 2.98) + 4.99$

   B $c = (3 + 0.89) \times (3 + 2.98) + 4.99$

   C $c = (3 \times 0.89) + (2 \times 2.98) + 4.99$

   D $c = (3 \times 0.89) \times (2 \times 2.98) \times 4.99$

5 _____

6 Mr. Thomas wants to buy a boat. He must make 48 monthly payments to pay back the amount he borrowed, plus interest. His monthly payment is $161.85. What other information is necessary to determine the amount of money Mr. Thomas borrowed from the bank?

    F How much Mr. Thomas makes per month

    G The interest rate the bank charges

    H How much the boat costs

    J How much the value of the boat will increase

7 Barb walked 1.3 miles to her friend's house and then $\frac{3}{4}$ mile to the library. How far did Barb walk in all?

    A $1\frac{9}{40}$ miles   **C** $2\frac{1}{20}$ miles

    B $1\frac{3}{7}$ miles   **D** $2\frac{1}{10}$ miles

8 On average, a dog runs 5.5 times faster than a child. Which equation can be used to find s, the speed of a dog, given r, the speed of the child?

    F $s = 5.5r$ **H** $s = r + 5.5$

    G $s = \frac{5.5}{r}$ **J** $s = \frac{r}{5.5}$

9 Ricky jogs 5 laps around a track in 8 minutes. Which of the following would be the same number of laps per minute?

    A 7 laps in 9.6 minutes   **C** 12 laps in 19.2 minutes

    B 10 laps in 15.6 minutes   **D** 8 laps in 20 minutes

10 What is the slope and y-intercept of the equation $6x - 1 = 3y - 10$?

    F $m = 2, b = 3$ **H** $m = 3, b = 4$

    G $m = 2, b = -3$ **J** $m = 6, b = 9$

11 Aleta went to dinner. The bill was $36. She gave the waiter a 15% tip. What was the total amount Aleta spent on the food and the tip?

    A $36.15   **C** $38.40

    B $37.50   **D** $41.40

12 What is true concerning the lines graphed by the system of
equations shown below?

$$\begin{cases} 8x + 6 = 2y \\ 12x - 3 = 3y \end{cases}$$

12 _____

F   The lines intersect.   **H**   The lines are parallel.

G   The lines are perpendicular.   **J**   The lines are the same.

13 Which algebraic expression can be used to find the
nth term in the following sequence?

13 _____

$$6, 10, 14, 18, 22, \ldots$$

A $n + 4$ **B** $6n + 4$ **C** $6n$ **D** $4n + 2$

14 A photo with a length of 3 inches and a width of 5 inches is
enlarged to poster size. The poster and the photo are similar.
The length of the poster is 21 inches. What is the width of
the poster?

14 _____

F   7.2 inches   **H**   19 inches

G   12.6 inches   **J**   35 inches

15 Rectangle *ABCD* is shown on the coordinate grid below.
Which of the following graphs represent the translation
of Rectangle *ABCD* over the following: $(x, y) \rightarrow (x+1, y-2)$?

15 _____

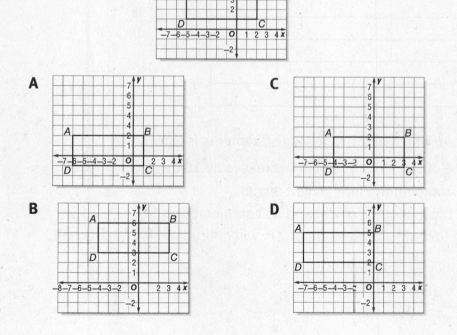

16 A rectangle is cut along its diagonal. The measure of ∠A is 55°.
What is the measure of ∠B?

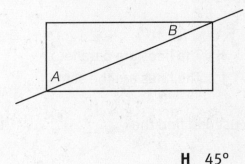

F   125°   H   45°

G   105°   J   35°

17 A farmer wants to fence in part of her land so that her
chickens will have their own little area. If she only has
28 feet of fence, what is the area of the largest pen that
she can build?

A   48 square feet   C   196 square feet

B   49 square feet   D   784 square feet

18 Jason is experimenting with different ramps to replace
the stair step into his house. The table below shows the
measure of a given angle *m* and its complement.

Measure of ∠m	Measure of ∠m's Complement
5°	85°
15°	75°
25°	65°
35°	55°
45°	45°

Based on the table, which of the following statements is true?

F   The measure of ∠m's complement decreases by 10 degrees.

G   ∠m and its complement form a right angle.

H   The sum of the measures of ∠m and its complement is 90.

J   Subtracting 90 from the measure of ∠m will determine its complement.

19 Robin's neighborhood is mapped out on the graph below.

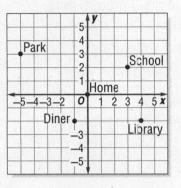

Which ordered pair shows the location of the library?

   A (4, 2)   **B** (4, −2)   **C** (−2, −4)   **D** (−2, 4)

20 The figure below is a net of a rectangular prism with a length of 14 yards, a width of 12 yards, and a height of 4 yards.

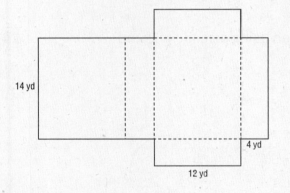

What is the surface area of the prism?

   F 180 square yards   **H** 600 square yards
   G 672 square yards   **J** 544 square yards

21 A cylindrical water tower is 24 feet high and has a diameter of 20 feet. Approximately how many cubic feet of water could the tower hold?

   A 2,400 cubic feet   **C** 9,600 cubic feet
   B 7,500 cubic feet   **D** 30,200 cubic feet

Diagnostic and Placement Tests

22 The delivery ramp at the Corner Café is a right triangle. The hypotenuse is 4 meters long. One leg is 3 meters long. What is the length of the other leg?

22 _____

    F $\sqrt{7}$ meters   **H** 3.5 meters

    G $\sqrt{12}$ meters   **J** 5 meters

23 The triangles below are similar triangles. Find the value of x and y.

23 _____

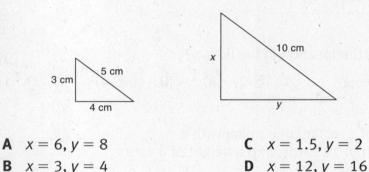

    A $x = 6, y = 8$ **C** $x = 1.5, y = 2$

    B $x = 3, y = 4$ **D** $x = 12, y = 16$

24 The following figures are formed using a semicircle and a rectangle.

24 _____

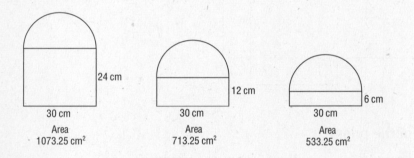

Based on this pattern, what will be the area of the next figure?

    F 266.625 cm² because the next figure will decrease in area by $\frac{1}{2}$ the previous figure.

    G 173.25 cm² because the next figure will decrease in area by 360 cm².

    H 353.25 cm² because the next figure will decrease in area by 180 cm².

    J 433.25 cm² because the next figure will decrease in area by 90 cm².

25 Four cards numbered 1, 5, 8, and 9 are placed in a bag. A card is drawn at random and then replaced. Then a card is drawn at random again. What is the probability that both cards drawn have the number 9?

25 _____

    A $\frac{1}{16}$ **B** $\frac{1}{9}$ **C** $\frac{1}{4}$ **D** $\frac{1}{2}$

26 Twelve members of a band purchased one beverage each during a break at practice. Exactly 5 of the 12 members bought bottled water. At this rate, how many band members would you expect to buy bottled water, if all 168 band members purchase a beverage?

26 _____

    F 12   **G** 70   **H** 98   **J** 138

27 A company has five employees. Their annual earnings, in dollars, are shown below.

27 _____

24,000	24,000	28,000	30,000	125,000

Which of the following measures best represents the typical annual earnings of an employee of the company?

    A mean   **C** mode

    B median   **D** range

28 The scatter plot below shows the yearly advertising expenditures and the relative sales for a small company. What can be concluded from this data?

28 _____

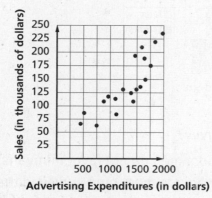

Advertising Expenditures (in dollars)

    F As advertising increases, sales tend to decrease.

    G As advertising increases, sales tend to increase.

    H As advertising increases, sales remain the same.

    J As advertising increases, sales always increase.

29 Last month, Enrico gave 25% of his salary to charity, put 25% into savings, spent 20% on food, spent 20% on rent, and spent the remaining amount on vacation. Which pie graph best shows how Enrico used his salary last month?

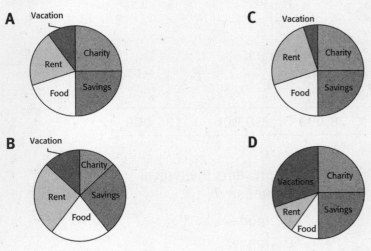

30 A survey is taken to determine which type of vehicle is most popular. The data is shown in the bar graph below.

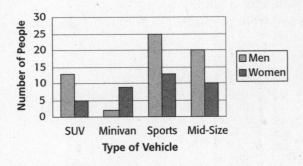

What can you conclude about the survey?

   F The survey is biased because most men do not favor minivans.

   G The survey is biased because there are more men surveyed than women.

   H The survey is not biased because sports cars are most popular among both men and women.

   J The survey is not biased because all car types are favored by both men and women.

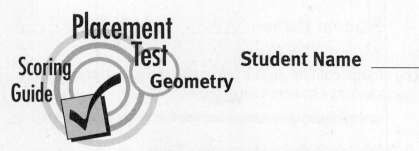

Placement Test
Scoring Guide
Geometry

Student Name _____

For each part, mark the box under the number of correctly answered questions.

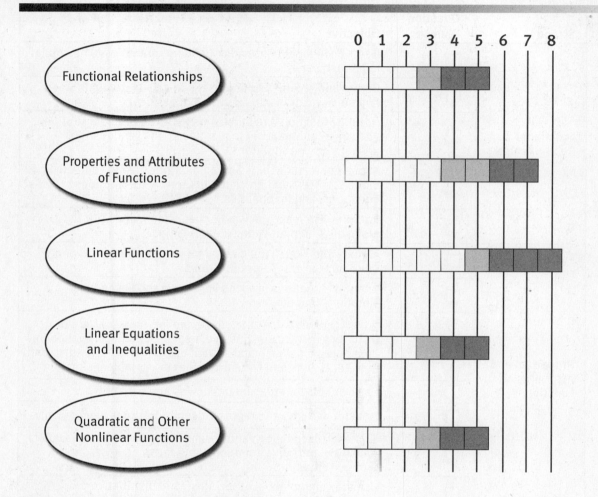

Mark the total number correct below.

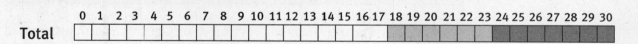

Key: Consider this student for...

☐ *Glencoe Algebra 1*

▨ **Geometry Strategic Intervention—See page 133 for materials list.**

▨ *Glencoe Geometry*

Placement Test
Learning Objectives — Geometry

In the column on the left, mark the questions that the student answered *incorrectly*.

Strand	Question Number	Objective
Functional Relationships	☐ 1	Describe independent and dependent quantities in functional relationships.
	☐ 2	Gather and record data and use data sets to determine functional relationships between quantities.
	☐ 3	Describe functional relationships for given problem situations and write equations or inequalities to answer questions arising from the situations.
	☐ 4	Represent relationships among quantities using concrete models, tables, graphs, diagrams, verbal descriptions, equations, and inequalities.
	☐ 5	Interpret and make decisions, predictions, and critical judgments from functional relationships.
Properties and Attributes of Functions	☐ 6	Identify and sketch the general forms of linear ($y = x$) and quadratic ($y = x^2$) parent functions.
	☐ 7	Interpret situations in terms of given graphs or creates situations that fit given graphs.
	☐ 8	Collect and organize data, make and interpret scatterplots (including recognizing positive, negative, or no correlation for data approximating linear situations), and model, predict, and make decisions and critical judgments in problem situations.
	☐ 9	Use symbols to represent unknowns and variables.
	☐ 10	Look for patterns and represent generalizations algebraically.
	☐ 11	Find specific function values, simplify polynomial expressions, transform and solve equations, and factor as necessary in problem situations.
	☐ 12	Use the commutative, associative, and distributive properties to simplify algebraic expressions.
Linear Functions	☐ 13	Determine the domain and range for linear functions in given situations.
	☐ 14	Use, translate, and make connections among algebraic, tabular, graphical, or verbal descriptions of linear functions.
	☐ 15	Develop the concept of slope as rate of change and determine slopes from graphs, tables, and algebraic representations.
	☐ 16	Interpret that meaning of slope and intercepts in situations using data, symbolic representations, or graphs.
	☐ 17	Investigate, describe, and predict the effects of changes in m and b on the graph of $y = mx + b$.

Strand	Question Number	Objective
Linear Functions	☐ 18	Graph and write equations of lines given characteristics such as two point, a point and a slope, or a slope and y-intercept.
	☐ 19	Determine the intercepts of graphs of linear functions and zeros of linear functions from graphs, tables, and algebraic representations.
	☐ 20	Relate direct variation to linear functions and solve problems involving proportional change.
Linear Equations and Inequalities	☐ 21	Analyze situations involving linear functions and formulate linear equations or inequalities to solve problems.
	☐ 22	Investigate methods for solving linear equations and inequalities using concrete models, graphs, and the properties of equality, select a method, and solve the equations and inequalities.
	☐ 23	Interpret and determine the reasonableness of solutions to linear equations and inequalities.
	☐ 24	Analyze situations and formulate systems of linear equations in two unknowns to solve problems.
	☐ 25	Solve systems of linear equations using concrete models, graphs, tables, and algebraic methods.
Quadratic and Other Nonlinear Functions	☐ 26	Determine the domain and range for quadratic functions in given situations.
	☐ 27	Investigate, describe, and predict the effects of changes in a on the graph of $y = ax^2 + c$.
	☐ 28	Investigate describe and predict the effects of changes in c on the graph of $y = ax^2 + c$.
	☐ 29	Solve quadratic equations using concrete models, tables, graphs, and algebraic methods.
	☐ 30	Use patterns to generate the laws of exponents and apply them in problem-solving situations.

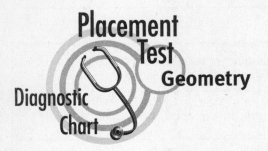

Placement Test
Geometry
Diagnostic Chart

Student Performance Level	Number of Questions Correct	Suggestions for Intervention and Remediation
Intensive Intervention	0–16	Use *Algebra 1* to accelerate the achievement of students who are below grade level. Students should follow a personalized remediation plan. A variety of materials and instructional methods are recommended. For example, instruction and practice should be provided in print, technology, and hands-on lessons.
Strategic Intervention	17–22	Use the additional Intervention and Remediation materials listed on the next page. This list of materials can provide helpful resources for students who struggle in the traditional mathematics program. Strategic intervention allows students to continue to remain in the *Math Connects* program, while receiving the differentiated instruction they need. Teaching Tips and other resources are also listed in the Teacher Edition.
Geometry	23 or more	Use *Geometry*. This student does not require overall intervention. However, based on the student's performance on the different sections, intervention may be required. For example, a student who missed 3 or more questions in the Linear Functions section may require extra assistance as you cover these skills throughout the year.

A Special Note About Intervention

When using diagnostic tests, teachers should always question the reason behind the students' scores. Students can struggle with mathematics concepts for a variety of reasons. Personalized instruction is recommended for English language learners, students with specific learning disabilities, students with certain medical conditions, or for those who struggle with traditional instructional practice. Teachers should always consider the needs of the individual student when determining the best approach for instruction and program placement.

Intervention/Remediation Materials
Geometry

Print Materials

Quick Review Math Handbook	A comprehensive reference of important mathematical terms and concepts to help build math literacy. Also available in Spanish.
Study Guide and Intervention Masters	A brief explanation, along with examples and exercises, for every lesson in the Student Edition. These masters are included in the Chapter Resource Masters.
Skills Practice Masters	Additional practice in computational and application exercises for each lesson in the Student Edition. These masters are included in the Chapter Resource Masters.
Practice Masters	Additional practice in computational and spiral review exercises for each lesson in the Student Edition. These masters are included in the Chapter Resource Masters.
Study Guide and Intervention Workbook	A consumable version of the Study Guide and Intervention Masters for each lesson.
Skills Practice Workbook	A consumable version of the Skills Practice Workbook Masters for each lesson.
Practice Workbook	A consumable version of the Practice Masters for each lesson.
Prerequisite Skills Workbook: Remediation and Intervention	Arithmetic study guide and practice pages for each of the prerequisite skills that review basic math concepts.

Technology Products

ExamView Pro® Assessment Suite	Networkable software includes a Worksheet Builder to make worksheets and tests, a Student Module to take tests on-screen, and a Management System to keep student records.
Mathematics Super DVDs	Includes: MindJogger Plus, a chapter review provided in a game-show format, and What's Math Got to Do With It? Real Life Math Videos that show students how math is used in everyday situations through engaging videos.
Problem-Solving Practice Masters	Additional practice in application exercises for each lesson in the Student Edition.
Interactive Classroom	A custom classroom teacher-tool incorporating a variety of assets including Additional Examples, Check Your Progress, and 5-Minute Checks.

Mathematics Chart

LENGTH	CAPACITY AND VOLUME
Metric	**Metric**
1 kilometer = 1000 meters	1 liter = 1000 milliliters
1 meter = 100 centimeters	
1 centimeter = 10 millimeters	**Customary**
	1 gallon = 4 quarts
Customary	1 gallon = 128 fluid ounces
1 mile = 1760 yards	1 quart = 2 pints
1 mile = 5280 feet	1 pint = 2 cups
1 yard = 3 feet	1 cup = 8 ounces
1 foot = 12 inches	
MASS AND WEIGHT	**TIME**
Metric	1 year = 365 days
1 kilogram = 1000 grams	1 year = 12 months
1 gram = 1000 milligrams	1 year = 52 weeks
	1 week = 7 days
Customary	1 day = 24 hours
1 ton = 2000 pounds	1 hour = 60 minutes
1 pound = 16 ounces	1 minute = 60 seconds

Mathematics Chart

PERIMETER		AREA	
rectangle	$P = 2\ell + 2w$ or $P = 2(\ell + w)$	rectangle	$A = \ell w$ or $A = bh$
		triangle	$A = \frac{1}{2} bh$ or $A = \frac{bh}{2}$
CIRCUMFERENCE		trapezoid	$A = \frac{1}{2}(b_1 + b_2)h$ or $A = \frac{(b_1 + b_2)h}{2}$
circle	$C = 2\pi r$ or $C = \pi d$	regular polygon	$A = \frac{1}{2} aP$
		circle	$A = \pi r^2$

B represents the area of the base of a solid figure.

P represents the Perimeter of the Base of a three-dimensional figure.

SURFACE AREA		VOLUME	
cube (total)	$S = 6s^2$	prism or cylinder	$V = Bh$
prism (lateral)	$S = Ph$	pyramid or cone	$V = \frac{1}{3} Bh$
prism (total)	$S = Ph + 2B$	sphere	$V = \frac{4}{3} \pi r^3$
pyramid (lateral)	$S = \frac{1}{2}P\ell$		
pyramid (total)	$S = \frac{1}{2}P\ell + B$	**SPECIAL RIGHT TRIANGLES**	
cylinder (lateral)	$S = 2\pi rh$	30°, 60°, 90°	$x, x\sqrt{3}, 2x$
cylinder (total)	$S = 2\pi rh + 2\pi r^2$ or $S = 2\pi r(h + r)$	45°, 45°, 90°	$x, x, x\sqrt{2}$
cone (lateral)	$S = \pi r\ell$	**PYTHAGOREAN THEOREM**	
cone (total)	$S = \pi r\ell + \pi r^2$ or $S = \pi r(\ell + r)$	$a^2 + b^2 = c^2$	
sphere	$S = 4\pi r^2$		

DISTANCE FORMULA	$d = \sqrt{(x_2 - x_1)^2 + (y_2 - y_1)^2}$
SLOPE OF A LINE	$m = \frac{y_2 - y_1}{x_2 - x_1}$
MIDPOINT FORMULA	$M = \left(\frac{x_1 + x_2}{2}, \frac{y_1 + y_2}{2}\right)$
QUADRATIC FORMULA	$x = \frac{-b \pm \sqrt{b^2 - 4ac}}{2a}$
SLOPE-INTERCEPT FROM OF AN EQUATION	$y = mx + b$
POINT-SLOPE FORM OF AN EQUATION	$y - y_1 = m(x - x_1)$
STANDARD FORM OF AN EQUATION	$Ax + By = C$
SIMPLE INTEREST FORMULA	$I = prt$

0 Inches
1
2
3
4
5
6

Diagnostic and Placement Geometry

Name _____

Date _____

This test contains 30 multiple-choice questions. Work each problem in the space on this page. Select the best answer. Write the letter of the answer on the blank at the right.

1 Carla earns $9 per hour working at a clothing store. She is writing a function to show the relationship between her hours worked h, and her wages earned w. In Carla's function, what does the independent variable represent?

    A the number of hours worked

    B the wage earned in one hour

    C the total wages earned

    D the amount of time Carla must work to earn $1

1 _____

2 Which statement describes each ordered pair (x, y) in the table?

x	0	2	4	6
y	−2	2	14	34

    F y is 2 less than x.   **H** y is 2 less than twice x.

    G y is equal to x.   **J** y is 2 less than the square of x.

2 _____

3 The health club charges a $75 membership fee plus a $40 monthly fee. Wesley has $300 to spend on a health club membership. Which inequality can be used to find m, the number of months for which Wesley can afford to be a member of the health club?

    A $300 \geq 75 + 40m$ **C** $300 \leq 75 + 40m$

    B $300 \leq 75m + 40$ **D** $300 \geq 75m + 40$

3 _____

4 The number of cars sold in May m was 60 less than four times the number of cars sold in April a. Which equation shows the relationship between m and a?

    F $m = a - 60$ **H** $m = a^4 - 60$

    G $m = 60 - 4a$ **J** $m = 4a - 60$

4 _____

5 The graph below shows several ordered pairs for a linear function.

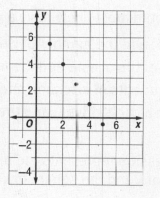

5 _____

Which is the best prediction of the value of *y* when *x* is 7?

A −1.5   **B** −2   **C** −2.5   **D** −3.5

6 Which of these shows the graphs of $y = x$ and $y = x^2$?

6 _____

F
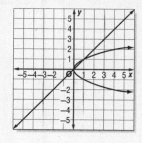

H
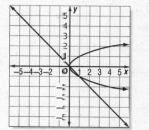

G
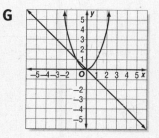

J
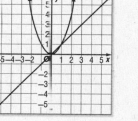

7 Which relationship is best shown by the graph?

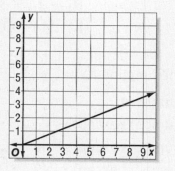

7 _____

A Oranges cost $0.50 per pound.

B A tree grows 2 inches every 5 months.

C The temperature of a cooler decreases 4 degrees every 10 minutes that it is open.

D A pool's water level increases at 5 gallons per minute.

8 Which relationship would most likely have a negative correlation?   **8** _____

    F the time elapsed, and the number of words typed

    G the temperature of the ocean, and the number of sunbathers on the beach

    H the number of students in a school, and the number of teachers in the school

    J the rate at which a car is driven, and the number of miles driven in one hour

9 Which algebraic expression represents the phrase   **9** _____
"6 less than the sum of x and the square of x?"

    A $x + x^2 - 6$ **C** $6 - x + x^2$

    B $x + \sqrt{x} - 6$ **D** $6 - (x + x^2)$

10 Which function describes the data in the table?   **10** _____

x	0	1	2	3
y	3	5	7	9

    F $y = x + 3$ **H** $y = 3x$

    G $y = 2x + 3$ **J** $y = 3x - 1$

11 Solve for x.   **11** _____
$12 - 14x = -72$

    A -36 **C** 36

    B -6 **D** 6

12 Which expression is equivalent to $-3(8 - 10)$?   **12** _____

    F $-24 - 30$ **H** $-24 + 30$

    G $-24 - 10$ **J** $24 - 30$

13 What is the domain of the function $f(x) = \frac{3}{x + 2}$?   **13** _____

    A the set of all real numbers

    B the set of all real numbers except $x = -2$

    C the set of all real numbers except $x = 0$

    D the set of all real numbers except $x = 2$

14 What is the equation of the line shown?

14 _____

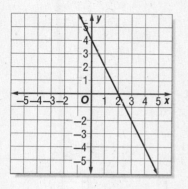

F $y = -2x + 4$ H $y = -2x - 4$

G $y = 4x - 2$ J $y = 4x + 2$

15 The table below defines a linear function. What is the slope of the line?

15 _____

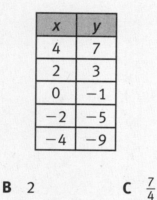

x	y
4	7
2	3
0	-1
-2	-5
-4	-9

A $\frac{1}{2}$ B 2   C $\frac{7}{4}$ D $\frac{11}{5}$

16 Which statement is NOT true for the graph below?

16 _____

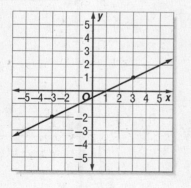

F The x-intercept is 1.   H The slope is $\frac{1}{2}$.

G The y-intercept is $-\frac{1}{2}$.   J The line contains the origin.

17 A student graphed the line $y = 3x + 2$ plotting and connecting points A, B, and C. How can the student use points A, B, and C to find the graph of $y = 3x - 5$?

    A Move each point down 5 units.

    B Move each point down 7 units.

    C Move each point left 3 units.

    D Move each point right 7 units.

17 _____

18 Which is an equation of the line that has a slope of $-\frac{1}{3}$ and passes through the point $(-5, 2)$?

    F $x - 3y = -11$ **H** $x + 3y = 1$

    G $x - 3y = 11$ **J** $x + 3y = 21$

18 _____

19 The graph shows part of the line $y = -\frac{1}{2}x + b$. What is the value of b?

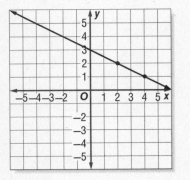

    A $-\frac{1}{2}$ **B** 2   **C** 3   **D** 6

19 _____

20 The weight of an object on the moon varies directly as its weight on earth. The constant of variation is 6. Which equation describes this relationship?

    F $y = 6x$ **H** $xy = 6$

    G $y = x + 6$ **J** $x + y = 6$

20 _____

21 Adam bought CDs for \$18 each and T-shirts for \$11 each. Altogether, he spent \$105. Which equation best represents Adam's purchase?

    A $4c + 3t = 105$ **C** $29ct = 105$

    B $18c + 11t = 105$ **D** $(18 + 11)(c + t) = 105$

21 _____

22 In which graph does the shaded area show the solutions to the inequality $3x - 2y \leq -6$?

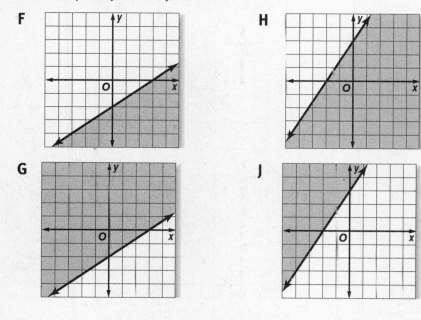

F

G

H

J

23 Which is NOT a reasonable solution to the inequality $2x \geq x$?

   A $x = -1$ **B** $x = 0$ **C** $x = 1$ **D** $x = 2$

24 Molly has $5.20 in dimes and quarters. The number of dimes is 3 more than the number of quarters. Which system of linear equations can be used to find d, the number of dimes, and q, the number of quarters?

   F $3q + d = 5.20$
       $q + d = 0.35$

   G $d = 3 + q$
       $0.10d + 0.25q = 5.20$

   H $(q + 3) + q = 5.20$
       $q + d = 0.35$

   J $q = 3 + d$
       $0.10d + 0.25q = 5.20$

25 Which shows the solution set of the following system of inequalities?

$$x - y \leq -1$$
$$x + 2y \leq 0$$

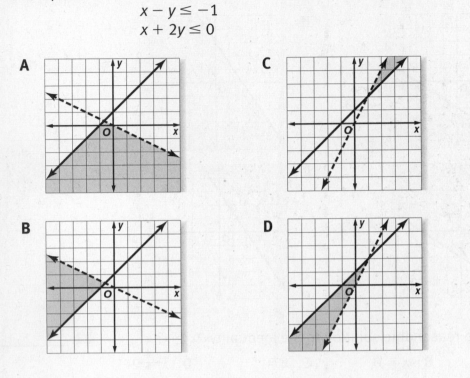

A

C

B

D

26 What is the range of the function $f(x) = 3x^2 - 7$?

    F $y \geq 7$ **G** $y \leq 7$ **H** $y \geq -7$ **J** $y \leq -7$

27 The graph of $y = ax^2$ and $y = bx^2$ are shown below. Which statement describes the relationship between a and b?

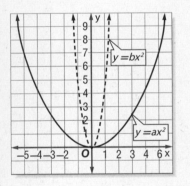

    A $a = b$

    B $a > b$

    C $a < b$

    D There is not enough information to determine the relationship.

28 The graph of $y = 2x^2$ is shown below.

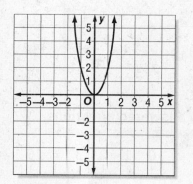

Which of the following shows the graph of $y = 2x^2 - 4$?

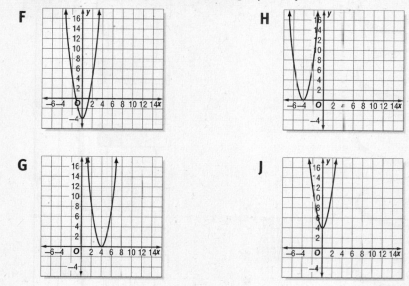

F

G

H

J

29 What are the solutions to the equation $2x^2 + 9x = 5$?

A $x = -1, x = \frac{5}{2}$

C $x = 5, x = -\frac{1}{2}$

B $x = 1, x = -\frac{5}{2}$

D $x = -5, x = \frac{1}{2}$

30 Simplify $\dfrac{\sqrt{a} \cdot b^2}{a^{\frac{3}{2}} b^5}$.

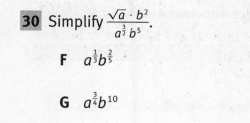

F $a^{\frac{1}{3}} b^{\frac{2}{5}}$

H $\dfrac{1}{ab^3}$

G $a^{\frac{3}{4}} b^{10}$

J $\dfrac{1}{a^{\frac{3}{4}} b^3}$

Diagnostic and Placement Tests

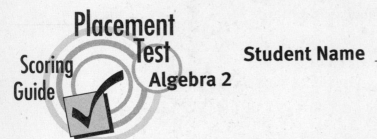

Placement Test
Scoring Guide
Algebra 2

Student Name _____

For each part, mark the box under the number of correctly answered questions.

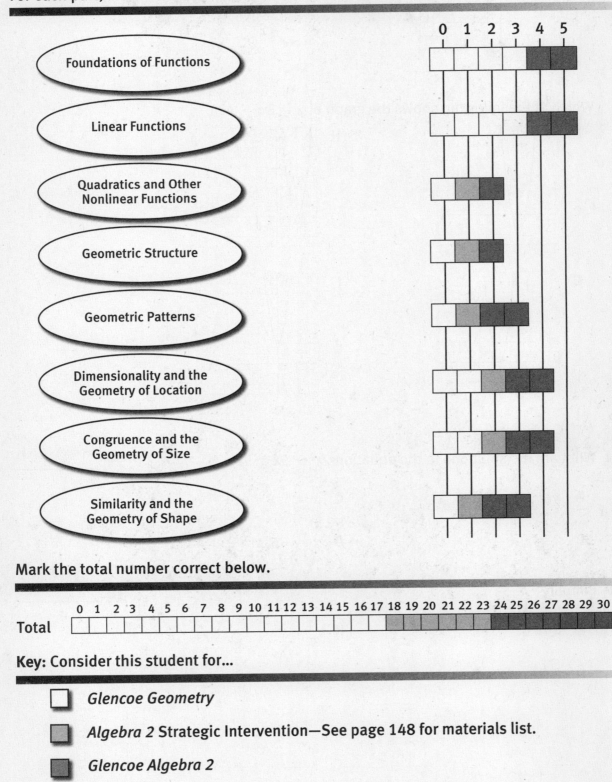

	0	1	2	3	4	5
Foundations of Functions						
Linear Functions						
Quadratics and Other Nonlinear Functions						
Geometric Structure						
Geometric Patterns						
Dimensionality and the Geometry of Location						
Congruence and the Geometry of Size						
Similarity and the Geometry of Shape						

Mark the total number correct below.

Total 0 1 2 3 4 5 6 7 8 9 10 11 12 13 14 15 16 17 18 19 20 21 22 23 24 25 26 27 28 29 30

Key: Consider this student for...

☐ *Glencoe Geometry*

▨ *Algebra 2* Strategic Intervention—See page 148 for materials list.

▮ *Glencoe Algebra 2*

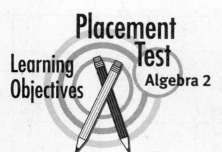

Placement Test
Learning Objectives
Algebra 2

In the column on the left, mark the questions that the student answered *incorrectly*.

Strand	Question Number	Objective
Foundations for Functions	☐ 1	Describe independent and dependent quantities in functional relationships.
	☐ 2	Gather and record data and use data sets to determine functional relationships between quantities.
	☐ 3	Identify and sketch the general forms of linear ($y = x$) and quadratic ($y = x^2$) parent functions.
	☐ 4	Use symbols to represent unknowns and variables.
	☐ 5	Find specific function values, simplify polynomial expressions, transform and solve equations, and factor as necessary in problem situations.
Linear Functions	☐ 6	Develop the concept of slope as rate of change and determine slopes from graphs, tables, and algebraic representations.
	☐ 7	Develop the concept of slope as rate of change and determine slopes from graphs, tables, and algebraic representations.
	☐ 8	Determine the intercepts of graphs of linear functions and zeros of linear functions from graphs, tables, and algebraic representations.
	☐ 9	Investigate methods for solving linear equations and inequalities using concrete models, graphs, and the properties of equality, select a method, and solve the equations and inequalities.
	☐ 10	Analyze situations and formulate systems of linear equations in two unknowns to solve problems.
Quadratic and Other Nonlinear Functions	☐ 11	Determine the domain and range for quadratic functions in given situations.
	☐ 12	Solve quadratic equations using concrete models, tables, graphs, and algebraic methods.
Geometric Structure	☐ 13	Use logical reasoning to prove statements are true and find counter examples to disprove statements that are false.
	☐ 14	Use inductive reasoning to formulate a conjecture.
Geometric Patterns	☐ 15	Use numeric and geometric patterns to develop algebraic expressions representing geometric properties.
	☐ 16	Use numeric and geometric patterns to make generalizations about geometric properties, including properties of polygons, ratios in similar figures and solids, and angle relationships in polygons and circles.
	☐ 17	Identify and apply patterns from right triangles to solve meaningful problems, including special right triangles (45-45-90 and 30-60-90) and triangles whose sides are Pythagorean triples.

Strand	Question Number	Objective
Dimensionality and the Geometry of Location	☐ 18	Describe and draw the intersection of a given plane with various three-dimensional geometric figures.
	☐ 19	Use nets to represent and construct three-dimensional geometric figures.
	☐ 20	Use orthographic and isometric views of three-dimensional geometric figures to represent and construct three-dimensional geometric figures and solve problems.
	☐ 21	Use slopes and equations of lines to investigate geometric relationships, including parallel lines, perpendicular lines, and special segments of triangles and other polygons.
	☐ 22	Derive and use formulas involving length, slope, and midpoint.
Congruence and the Geometry of Size	☐ 23	Find areas of regular polygons, circles, and composite figures.
	☐ 24	Find areas of sectors and arc lengths of circles using proportional reasoning.
	☐ 25	Find surface areas and volumes of prisms, pyramids, spheres, cones, cylinders, and composites of these figures in problem situations.
	☐ 26	Formulate and test conjectures about the properties and attributes of circles and the lines that intersect them based on explorations and concrete models.
	☐ 27	Justify and apply triangle congruence relationships.
Similarity and the Geometry of Shape	☐ 28	Use ratios to solve problems involving similar figures.
	☐ 29	Develop, apply, and justify triangle similarity relationships, such as right triangle ratios, trigonometric ratios, and Pythagorean triples using a variety of methods.
	☐ 30	Describe the effect on perimeter, area, and volume when one or more dimensions of a figure are changed and apply this idea in solving problems.

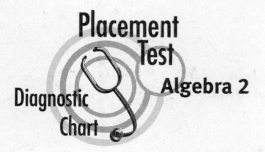

Student Performance Level	Number of Questions Correct	Suggestions for Intervention and Remediation
Intensive Intervention	0–5	Use *Glencoe Geometry* to accelerate the achievement of students who are below grade level. Students should follow a personalized remediation plan. A variety of materials and instructional methods are recommended. For example, instruction and practice should be provided in print, technology, and hands-on lessons.
Strategic Intervention	6–11	Use the additional Intervention and Remediation materials listed on the next page. This list of materials can provide helpful resources for students who struggle in the traditional mathematics program. Strategic intervention allows students to continue to remain in the *Math Connects* program, while receiving the differentiated instruction they need. Teaching Tips and other resources are also listed in the Teacher Edition.
Algebra 1	12 or more	Use *Glencoe Algebra 2*. This student does not require overall intervention. However, based on the student's performance on the different sections, intervention may be required. For example, a student who missed 1 or more questions in the Linear Functions section may require extra assistance as you cover these skills throughout the year.

A Special Note About Intervention

When using diagnostic tests, teachers should always question the reason behind the students' scores. Students can struggle with mathematics concepts for a variety of reasons. Personalized instruction is recommended for English language learners, students with specific learning disabilities, students with certain medical conditions, or for those who struggle with traditional instructional practice. Teachers should always consider the needs of the individual student when determining the best approach for instruction and program placement.

Intervention/Remediation Materials

Algebra 2

Print Materials

Quick Review Math Handbook	A comprehensive reference of important mathematical terms and concepts to help build math literacy. Also available in Spanish.
Study Guide and Intervention Masters	A brief explanation, along with examples and exercises, for every lesson in the Student Edition. These masters are included in the Chapter Resource Masters.
Skills Practice Masters	Additional practice in computational and application exercises for each lesson in the Student Edition. These masters are included in the Chapter Resource Masters.
Practice Masters	Additional practice in computational and spiral review exercises for each lesson in the Student Edition. These masters are included in the Chapter Resource Masters.
Study Guide and Intervention Workbook	A consumable version of the Study Guide and Intervention Masters for each lesson.
Skills Practice Workbook	A consumable version of the Skills Practice Workbook Masters for each lesson.
Practice Workbook	A consumable version of the Practice Masters for each lesson.
Prerequisite Skills Workbook: Remediation and Intervention	Arithmetic study guide and practice pages for each of the prerequisite skills that review basic math concepts.

Technology Products

ExamView Pro® Assessment Suite	Networkable software includes a Worksheet Builder to make worksheets and tests, a Student Module to take tests on-screen, and a Management System to keep student records.
Mathematics Super DVDs	Includes: MindJogger Plus, a chapter review provided in a game-show format, and What's Math Got to Do With It? Real Life Math Videos that show students how math is used in everyday situations through engaging videos.
Problem-Solving Practice Masters	Additional practice in application exercises for each lesson in the Student Edition.
Interactive Classroom	A custom classroom teacher-tool incorporating a variety of assets including Additional Examples, Check Your Progress, and 5-Minute Checks.

Mathematics Chart

LENGTH	CAPACITY AND VOLUME
Metric	**Metric**
1 kilometer = 1000 meters	1 liter = 1000 milliliters
1 meter = 100 centimeters	
1 centimeter = 10 millimeters	**Customary**
	1 gallon = 4 quarts
Customary	1 gallon = 128 fluid ounces
1 mile = 1760 yards	1 quart = 2 pints
1 mile = 5280 feet	1 pint = 2 cups
1 yard = 3 feet	1 cup = 8 ounces
1 foot = 12 inches	
MASS AND WEIGHT	**TIME**
Metric	1 year = 365 days
1 kilogram = 1000 grams	1 year = 12 months
1 gram = 1000 milligrams	1 year = 52 weeks
	1 week = 7 days
Customary	1 day = 24 hours
1 ton = 2000 pounds	1 hour = 60 minutes
1 pound = 16 ounces	1 minute = 60 seconds

0
Inches
1
2
3
4
5
6

Diagnostic and Placement Tests

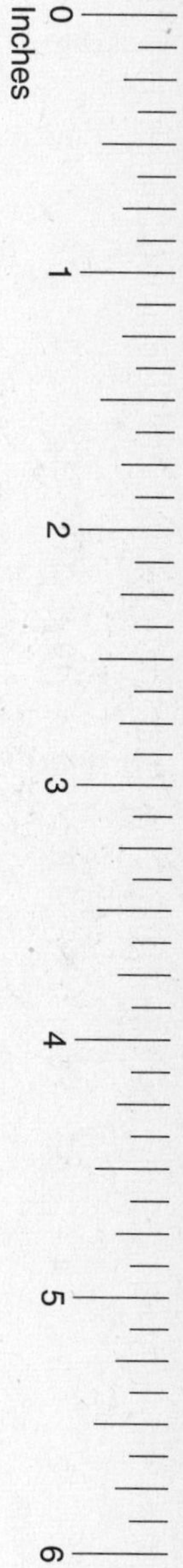

Mathematics Chart

PERIMETER	
rectangle	$P = 2\ell + 2w$ or $P = 2(\ell + w)$

CIRCUMFERENCE	
circle	$C = 2\pi r$ or $C = \pi d$

AREA	
rectangle	$A = \ell w$ or $A = bh$
triangle	$A = \frac{1}{2} bh$ or $A = \frac{bh}{2}$
trapezoid	$A = \frac{1}{2}(b_1 + b_2)h$ or $A = \frac{(b_1 + b_2)h}{2}$
regular polygon	$A = \frac{1}{2} aP$
circle	$A = \pi r^2$

B represents the area of the base of a solid figure.

P represents the Perimeter of the Base of a three-dimensional figure.

SURFACE AREA	
cube (total)	$S = 6s^2$
prism (lateral)	$S = Ph$
prism (total)	$S = Ph + 2B$
pyramid (lateral)	$S = \frac{1}{2}P\ell$
pyramid (total)	$S = \frac{1}{2}P\ell + B$
cylinder (lateral)	$S = 2\pi rh$
cylinder (total)	$S = 2\pi rh + 2\pi r^2$ or $S = 2\pi r(h + r)$
cone (lateral)	$S = \pi r\ell$
cone (total)	$S = \pi r\ell + \pi r^2$ or $S = \pi r(\ell + r)$
sphere	$S = 4\pi r^2$

VOLUME	
prism or cylinder	$V = Bh$
pyramid or cone	$V = \frac{1}{3} Bh$
sphere	$V = \frac{4}{3} \pi r^3$

SPECIAL RIGHT TRIANGLES	
30°, 60°, 90°	$x, x\sqrt{3}, 2x$
45°, 45°, 90°	$x, x, x\sqrt{2}$

PYTHAGOREAN THEOREM

$a^2 + b^2 = c^2$

DISTANCE FORMULA	$d = \sqrt{(x_2 - x_1)^2 + (y_2 - y_1)^2}$
SLOPE OF A LINE	$m = \frac{y_2 - y_1}{x_2 - x_1}$
MIDPOINT FORMULA	$M = \left(\frac{x_1 + x_2}{2}, \frac{y_1 + y_2}{2}\right)$
QUADRATIC FORMULA	$x = \frac{-b \pm \sqrt{b^2 - 4ac}}{2a}$
SLOPE-INTERCEPT FROM OF AN EQUATION	$y = mx + b$
POINT-SLOPE FORM OF AN EQUATION	$y - y_1 = m(x - x_1)$
STANDARD FORM OF AN EQUATION	$Ax + By = C$
SIMPLE INTEREST FORMULA	$I = prt$

Diagnostic and Placement Algebra 2

Name _____

Date _____

This test contains 30 multiple-choice questions. Work each problem in the space on this page. Select the best answer. Write the letter of the answer on the blank at the right.

1 The total cost c of buying b cans of beans can be found using the equation $c = \$0.79b$. What is represented by the dependent variable?

    A The total cost of b cans

    B The cost of 1 can

    C The number of cans purchased

    D The number of cans that can be purchased for $0.79

1 _____

2 Which equation describes the functional relationship shown in the table?

2 _____

x	-2	-1	0	1	2
y	-6	-3	0	-3	-6

    F $f(x) = 3|x|$ **H** $f(x) = |-3x|$

    G $f(x) = 3|-x|$ **J** $f(x) = -|3x|$

3 Which shows the graph of $y = x^2$?

3 _____

    A
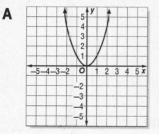

    C
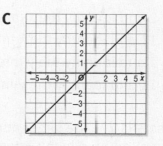

    B

    D
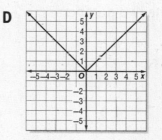

4 A certain oak tree is 12 feet taller than a certain pine tree. If the pine tree is p feet tall, which expression represents the height of the oak tree?

    F $12 + p$ **G** $12 - p$ **H** $p - 12$ **J** $12p$

4 _____

5 Simplify the expression $4(2x - 1) - 3(x + 5)$.

    A $3x - 19$ **C** $5x - 19$

    B $5x - 16$ **D** $9x - 2$

5 _____

6 What is the slope of a line that passes through $(4, -1)$ and $(2, 9)$?

    F $\frac{3}{7}$ **H** -5

    G $-\frac{5}{7}$ **J** -4

6 _____

7 Which is an equation of the line that has a slope of $\frac{1}{2}$ and passes through the point $(3, -1)$?

    A $x + 2y = 1$ **C** $x - 2y = 5$

    B $x + 2y = -1$ **D** $x - 2y = 8$

7 _____

8 What is the x-intercept of the graph of $3x - 4y = 12$?

    F -4 **G** -3 **H** 3 **J** 4

8 _____

9 Which of the following methods can be used to solve the linear equation $3x - 2 = 9$?

    A Graph $y = 3x - 2$ and identify the x-intercept.

    B Graph $y = 3x - 11$ and identify the x-intercept.

    C Graph $y = 3x - 2$ and identify the y-intercept.

    D Graph $y = 3x - 11$ and identify the y-intercept.

9 _____

10 The sum of two numbers is 27. The larger number is 6 more than twice the smaller number. Which system of equations can be used to find the two numbers?

    F $xy = 27$
        $y = 6 + x$

    G $x + y = 27$
         $y = 6 + x$

    H $x + y = 27$
         $y = 6 + 2x$

    J $xy = 27$
       $y = 6 + 2x$

10 _____

11 What is the range of the function $f(x) = x^2 + 6x + 9$?

11 _____

    A all real numbers

    B all real numbers greater than or equal to 0

    C all real numbers greater than or equal to 3

    D all real numbers greater than or equal to 9

12 What are the solutions of the equation $x^2 - 3x - 1 = 0$?

12 _____

    F $\dfrac{-3 + \sqrt{5}}{2}$ and $\dfrac{-3 - \sqrt{5}}{2}$ **H** $\dfrac{3 + \sqrt{5}}{2}$ and $\dfrac{3 - \sqrt{5}}{2}$

    G $\dfrac{-3 + \sqrt{13}}{2}$ and $\dfrac{-3 - \sqrt{13}}{2}$ **J** $\dfrac{3 + \sqrt{13}}{2}$ and $\dfrac{3 - \sqrt{13}}{2}$

13 Which of the following is a counterexample that disproves the statement $x^2 \geq x$?

13 _____

    A $x = -0.5$ **B** $x = 0.5$ **C** $x = 1.0$ **D** $x = 1.5$

14 Which of the following is an example of inductive reasoning?

14 _____

    F Every rectangle is a parallelogram. Every square is a rectangle. Therefore, every square is a parallelogram.

    G If $x > 3$, then $x^2 > y$. Therefore, $4^2 > y$.

    H Ted's bus arrived at his bus stop before 8:05 A.M. every morning for two weeks. Ted decides that his bus will arrive before 8:05 A.M. the next morning.

    J Keisha's uncle promises to give her $5 if she gets a grade of 85 or higher on her math test. Keisha gets a 93 on her math test. Then Keisha's uncle gives her $5.

15 The table below shows the number of diagonals in certain polygons. Which expression describes the number of diagonals in a polygon with n sides?

15 _____

Number of Sides	Number of Diagonals
3	0
4	2
5	5
6	9
7	14

    A $n(n - 3)$ **B** $\dfrac{n(n - 3)}{2}$ **C** $\dfrac{(n-3)}{2}$ **D** $\dfrac{n}{2}$

16 The table below shows the sum of the interior angle measures of certain polygons. According to the information in the table, which is the best prediction of the sum of the interior angle measures in an 11-gon?

Number of Sides	Sum of Interior Angle Measures
3	180°
4	360°
5	540°
6	720°

F 900°   **G** 1260°   **H** 1440°   **J** 1620°

17 Eleanor has a garden in the shape of a right isosceles triangle. Two sides of the triangle measure 10 feet long each. What is the length of the third side?

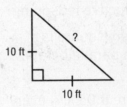

A 20 feet   **B** 10 √3 feet   **C** 15 feet   **D** 10 √2 feet

18 A plane intersects a right cylinder parallel to one of the cylinder's bases. What is the shape of the intersection?

F circle   **G** rectangle   **H** ellipse   **J** trapezoid

19 Which shows a net for the figure shown below?

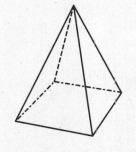

A

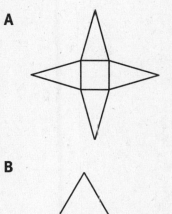

C

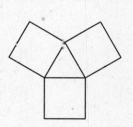

B

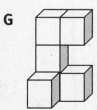

D

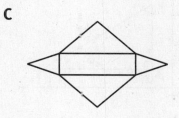

20 Which figure has the views shown?

Top   Front   Side

F

H

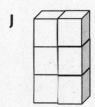

G

J

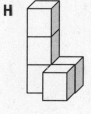

21 The line $y = mx + 7$ is perpendicular to the line $y = \frac{3}{4}x - 9$. What is m?

A $\frac{3}{4}$ **B** $-\frac{3}{4}$ **C** $\frac{4}{3}$ **D** $-\frac{4}{3}$

22 In the right triangle below, M is the midpoint of hypotenuse QR.

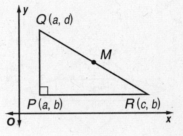

Which expression represents the distance from point P to point M?

F $\left(\frac{a+c}{2}\right) + \left(\frac{d+b}{2}\right)$ **H** $\left(\frac{c-a}{2}\right) + \left(\frac{b-d}{2}\right)$

G $\sqrt{\left(\frac{a+c}{2}\right)^2 + \left(\frac{d+b}{2}\right)^2}$ **J** $\sqrt{\left(\frac{c-a}{2}\right)^2 + \left(\frac{b-d}{2}\right)^2}$

23 Ed needs to paint the front wall on the building shown below. What is the area of the wall?

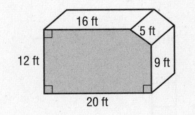

A 216 square feet   **C** 244 square feet

B 234 square feet   **D** 260 square feet

24 For the circle below, which expression can be used to find the area of the shaded region?

24 _____

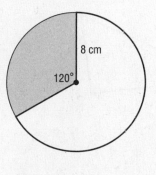

F $\frac{1}{3} \cdot 16\pi$ **G** $\frac{2}{3} \cdot 16\pi$ **H** $\frac{1}{3} \cdot 64\pi$ **J** $\frac{2}{3} \cdot 64\pi$

25 The volume of a cone is given by the formula $V = \frac{1}{3}\pi r^2 h$. What is the volume of the cone below, to the nearest whole number? Use 3.14 for π.

25 _____

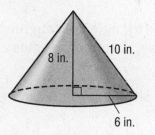

A 100 cubic inches   **C** 301 cubic inches
B 126 cubic inches   **D** 377 cubic inches

26 The radius of the circle below is 5 centimeters. Line segment AB is a diameter of the circle. What is the value of x to the nearest tenth?

26 _____

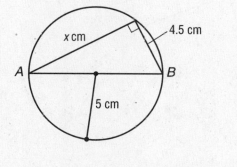

F 6.7   **G** 7.3   **H** 8.9   **J** 9.5

Based on the information in the diagram, which triangle congruence property can be used to justify that △ABC ≅ △FGH?

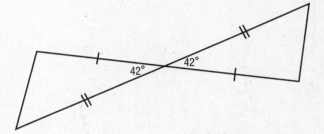

A   SSS (If three sides of one triangle are congruent to three sides of another triangle, then the triangles are congruent.)

B   SAS (If two sides and the included angle of one triangle are congruent to two sides and the included angle of another triangle, then the triangles are congruent.)

C   ASA (If two angles and the included side of one triangle are congruent to two angles and the included side of another triangle, then the triangles are congruent.)

D   AAS (If two angles and a side of one triangle are congruent to two angles and a side of another triangle, then the triangles are congruent).

28   A triangle undergoes an enlargement as shown in the diagram below. What is x?

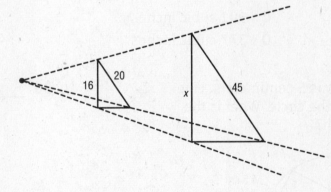

F   36

G   37

H   41

J   56.25

29 For the right triangle shown below, what is the tangent of ∠A?

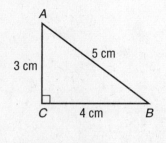

A $\tan A = \frac{3}{4}$ **B** $\tan A = \frac{4}{5}$ **C** $\tan A = \frac{5}{4}$ **D** $\tan A = \frac{4}{3}$

30 A scientist has two similar cylindrical beakers. Beaker A has radius 6 centimeters. Beaker B has radius 3 centimeters. Which answer correctly completes the statement?

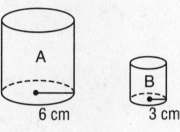

The volume of Beaker A is_____ times the volume of Beaker B.

F $\sqrt{2}$ **G** 2   **H** 2^2 **J** 2^3

Answers (Grade K)

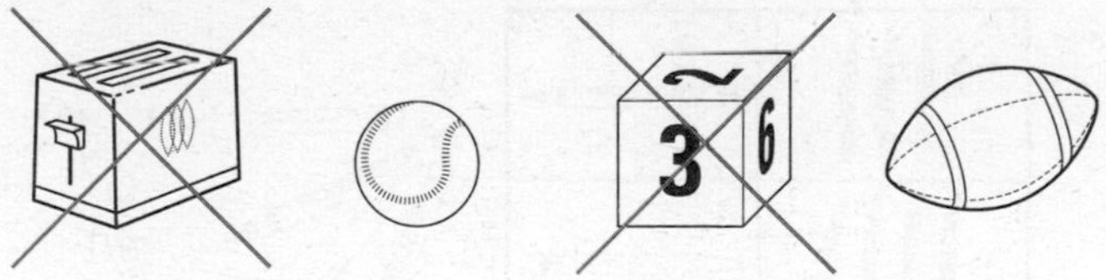

Diagnostic and Placement
Grade K

Name _____
Date _____

This test contains 15 questions. Work each problem in the space on this page. Select the best answer. Write the answer as directed.

1 Count the apples. Write the number. ____7____

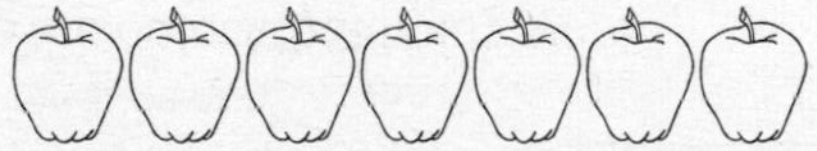

2 Put an X on the set of four cherries.

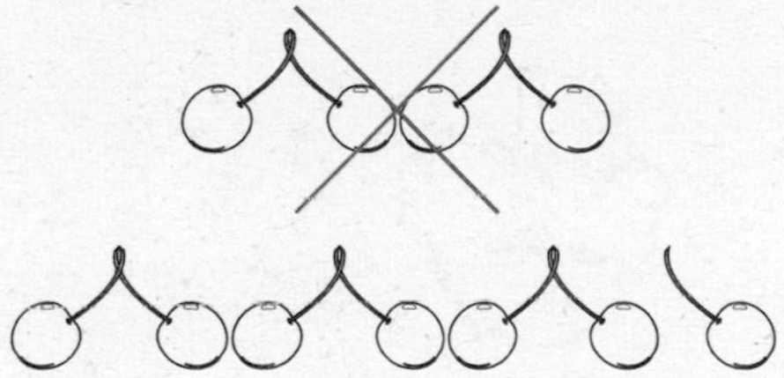

3 Circle the problem that fits the story. $2 + 1 = 3$

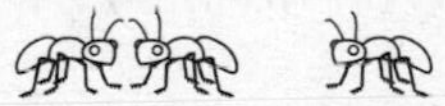

$$\begin{array}{r} 2 \\ -1 \\ \hline 1 \end{array} \qquad \boxed{\begin{array}{r} 2 \\ +1 \\ \hline 3 \end{array}}$$

4 Look at the first square. Circle the squares that are the same size.

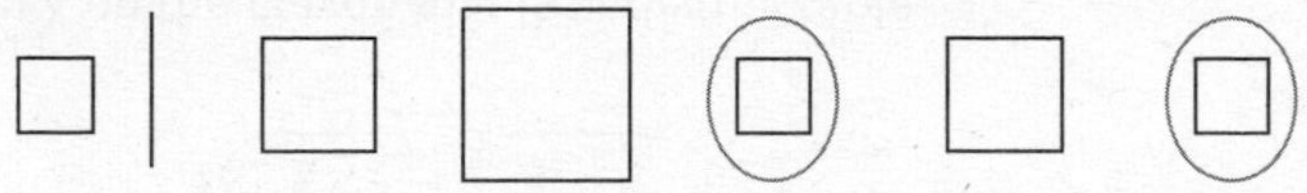

5 Circle the shape that comes next.

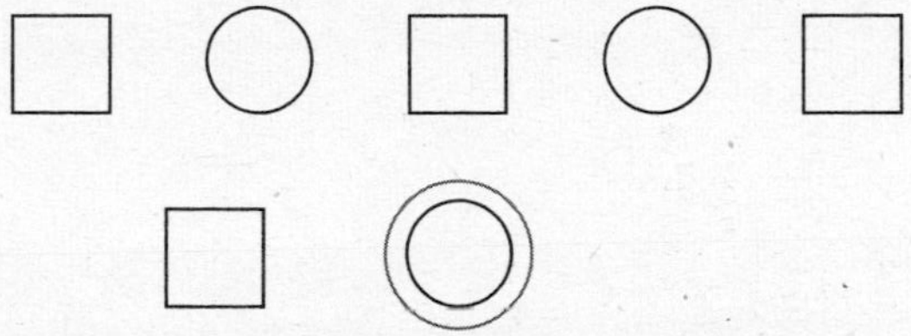

6 Look at the pattern. Circle the part that repeats.

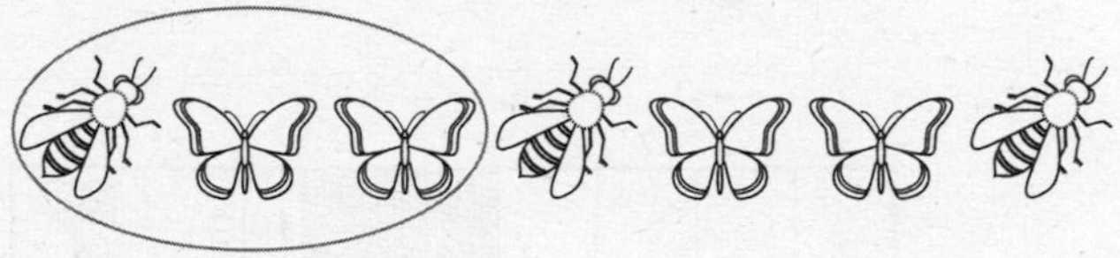

7 Look at the object. Color in the figure that matches the shape of the object.

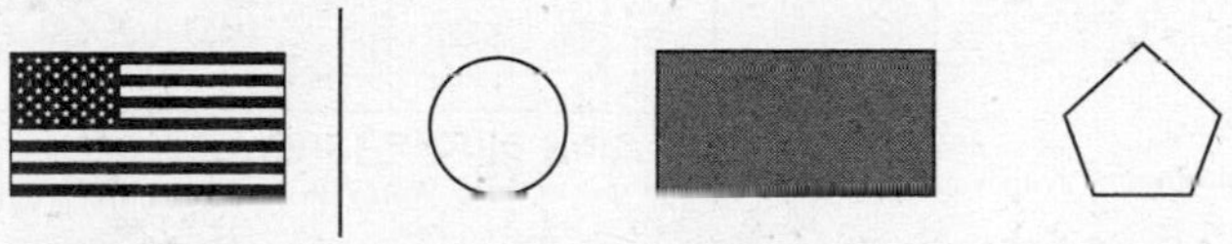

8 Put an X on the objects that can stack.

Answers (Grade K)

9 Put an X on the sailboat that is in the middle.

10 Put an X on the crayon that is under the table.

11 Put an X on the object that is next to the tree.

12 Circle the shorter object.

13 Circle the object that holds more.

14 Sort the crayons by color. Use tally marks to show how many crayons are in each group.

Number of Crayons

Crayons	Tally
	⦀⦀⦀
	⦀⦀⦀

15 Look at the group. Write how many of each pet.

Our Favorite Pets

	1	2	3	4	5	6
Cat						
Dog						
Bird						

3 ___   5 ___   2 ___

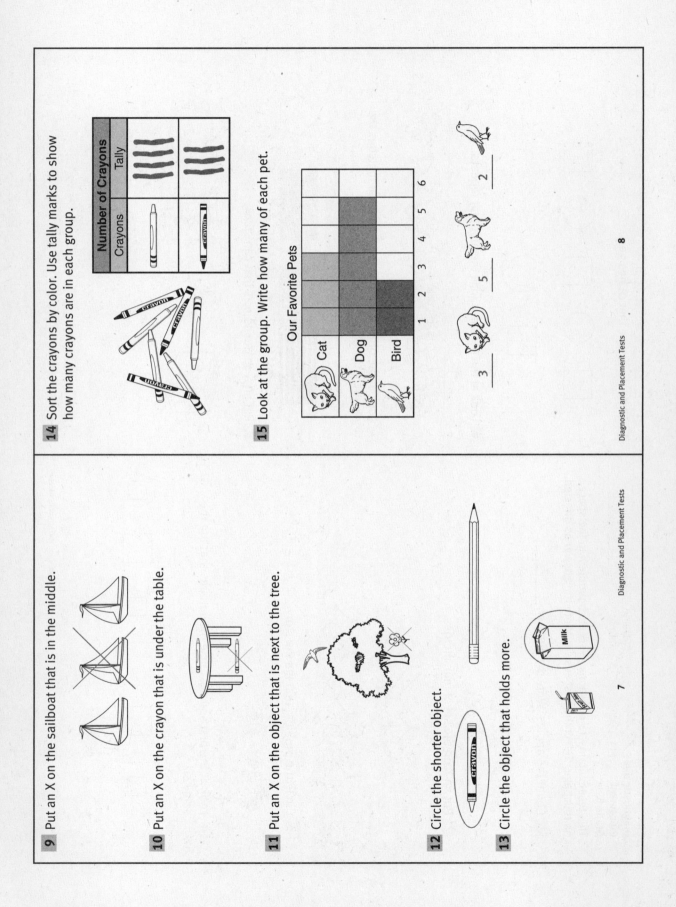

Answers (Grade 1)

Diagnostic and
Placement
Grade 1

Name _____
Date _____

This test contains 15 questions. Work each problem in the space on this page. Select the best answer. Circle the correct answer.

1 The number of hearts is _____ the number of triangles.

♥♥ ♥♥ ♥♥ ♥♥ ♥ ▲▲ ▲▲ ▲▲ ▲

(more than)
less than
equal to

2 How many diamonds?

◇◇◇◇◇ ◇◇◇◇◇ ◇◇◇◇

16   17   18   (19)

3 Circle the third fruit in the row.

4 Which picture shows a cookie split into 2 equal parts?

5 Write a number sentence that shows how many hats Maria bought in all.

_____
3 + 2 = 5 hats

Answers (Grade 1)

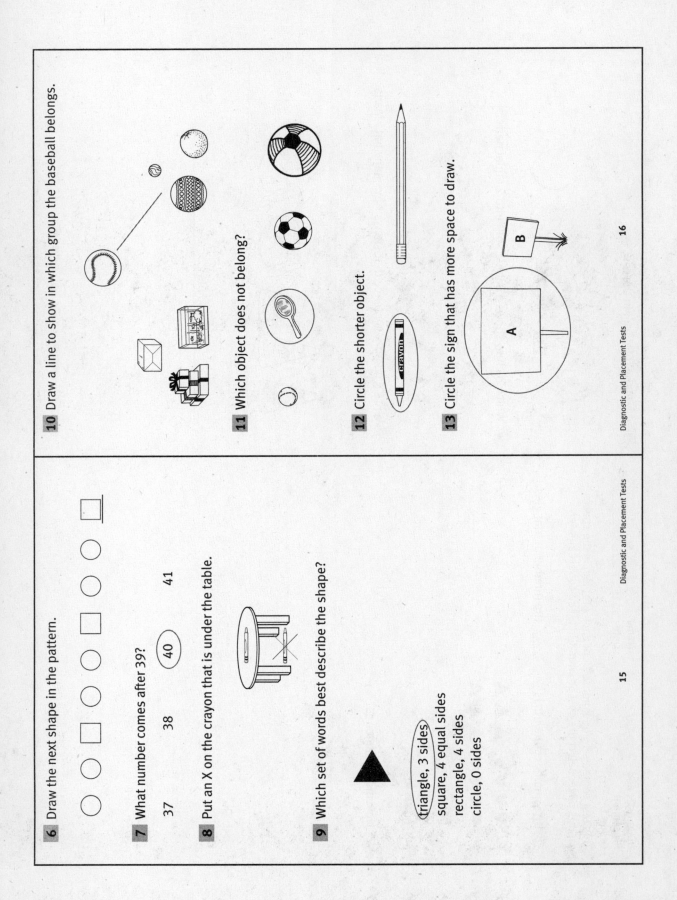

10 Draw a line to show in which group the baseball belongs.

11 Which object does not belong?

12 Circle the shorter object.

13 Circle the sign that has more space to draw.

6 Draw the next shape in the pattern.

7 What number comes after 39?

37   38   (40)   41

8 Put an X on the crayon that is under the table.

9 Which set of words best describe the shape?

(triangle, 3 sides)
square, 4 equal sides
rectangle, 4 sides
circle, 0 sides

A

B

15

16

Answers (Grade 1/Grade 2)

Diagnostic and Placement
Grade 2

Name _____
Date _____

This test contains 15 questions. Work each problem in the space on this page. Circle the best answer.

1 Which sign makes the number sentence 43 ◯ 34 true?

= + (>) <

2 If a pencil costs 15¢, what coins could Markel use to buy the pencil?

3 What number is modeled below?

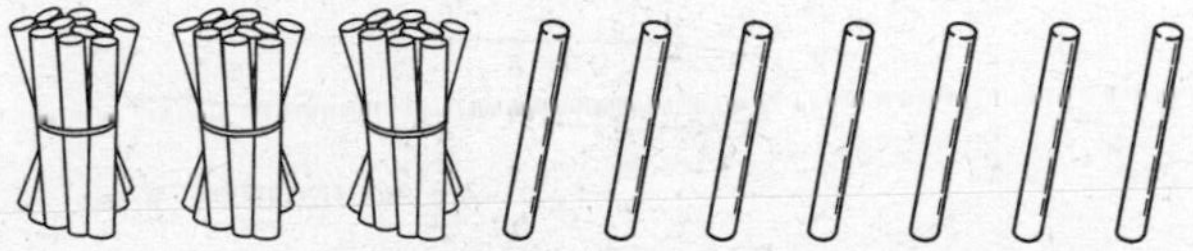

10   23   27   (37)

4 Which sentence describes the set of objects?

There are 9 shaded circles.
Four out of 9 circles are shaded.
Half of the circles are unshaded.
(Five out of 9 circles are shaded.)

14 Which is the heaviest?

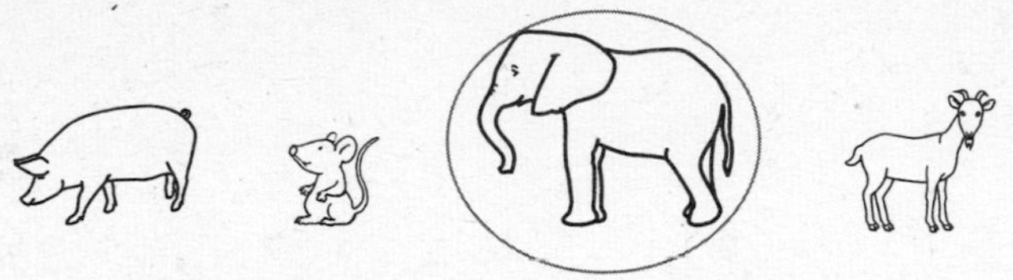

15 Look at the group. Write how many of each pet.

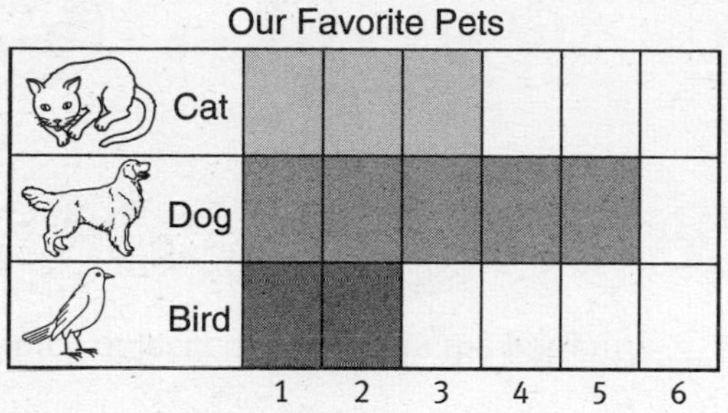

Our Favorite Pets

	1	2	3	4	5	6
Cat						
Dog						
Bird						

Cat 3   Dog 5   Bird 2

Answers (Grade 2)

5 Which number sentence tells how many more triangles than squares?

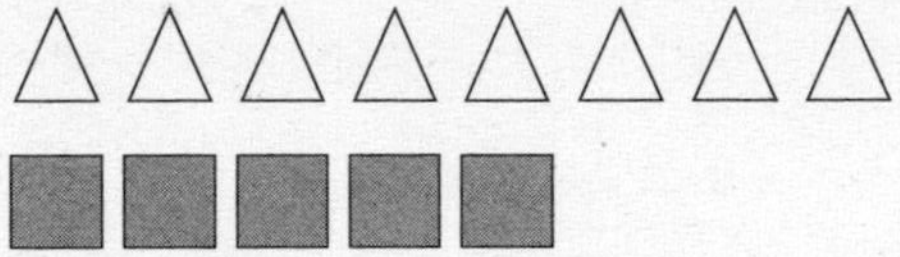

$8 - 5 = 3$
$8 - 3 = 5$
$5 - 8 = 3$
$5 + 8 = 13$

6 Which number sentence tells how many in all?

$8 + 6 = 14$
$4 + 3 = 7$
$8 - 6 = 2$
$4 - 3 = 1$

7 Which object comes next in the pattern?

8 What number makes the number sentence true?

$3 + 6 = \square + 3$

3   4   5   6

9 Which shape is a triangle?

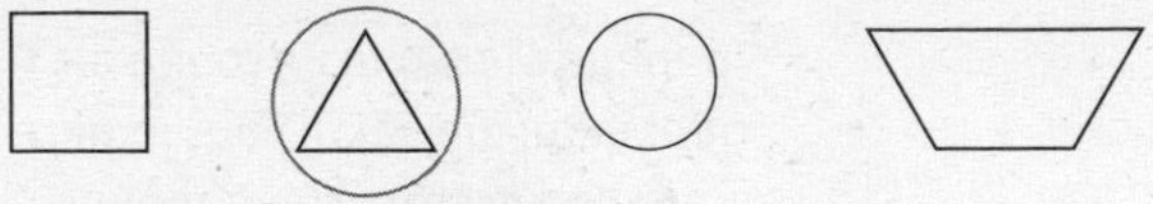

10 Which object has a face that is a circle?

Soup

Breakfast Cereal

11 List the items from longest to shortest.

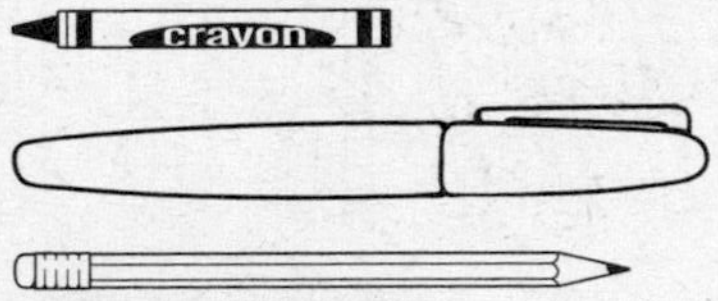

crayon

crayon, pencil, marker
pencil, marker, crayon
marker, pencil, crayon
crayon, marker, pencil

12 The triangles below can be combined to form which shape?

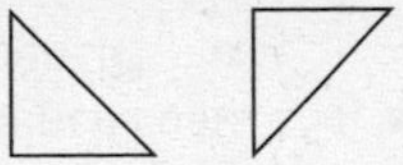

Answers (Grade 2)

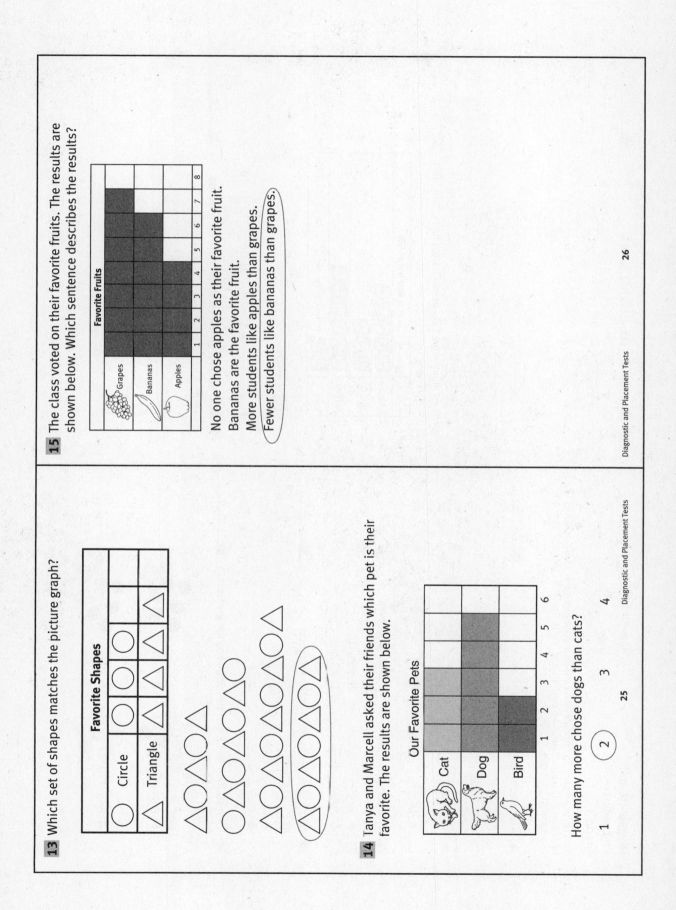

13 Which set of shapes matches the picture graph?

Favorite Shapes

Circle	○	○	○	
Triangle	△	△	△	△

△○△○△

○△○△○△○

△○△○△○△○

(△○△○△) ← circled

14 Tanya and Marcell asked their friends which pet is their favorite. The results are shown below.

Our Favorite Pets

Cat
Dog
Bird

1 2 3 4 5 6

How many more chose dogs than cats?

1   (2)   3   4

15 The class voted on their favorite fruits. The results are shown below. Which sentence describes the results?

Favorite Fruits

Grapes
Bananas
Apples

1 2 3 4 5 6 7 8

No one chose apples as their favorite fruit.

Bananas are the favorite fruit.

More students like apples than grapes.

(Fewer students like bananas than grapes.) ← circled

Answers (Grade 3)

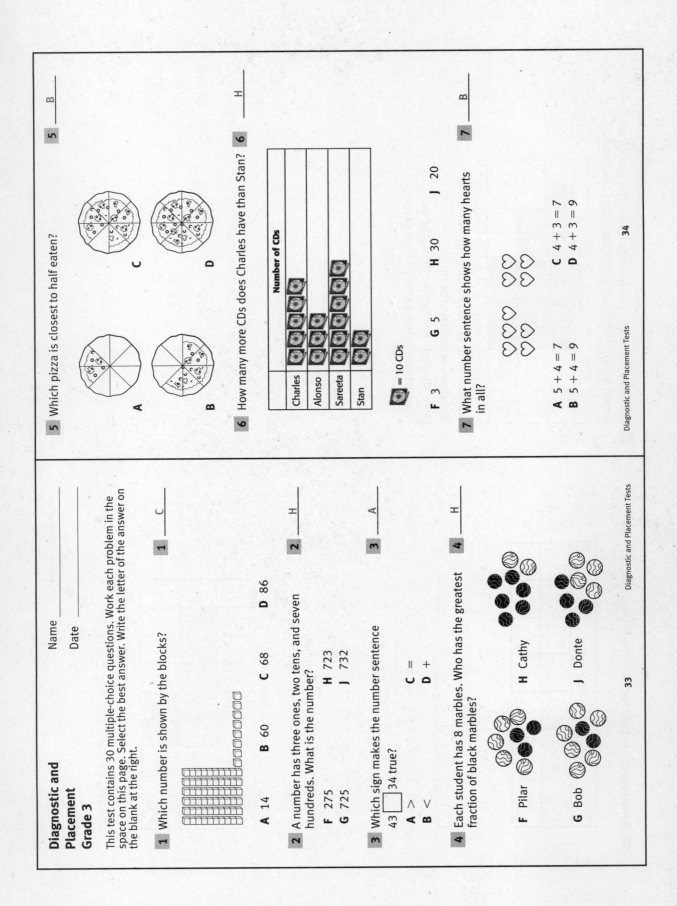

Diagnostic and Placement
Grade 3

Name _____
Date _____

This test contains 30 multiple-choice questions. Work each problem in the space on this page. Select the best answer. Write the letter of the answer on the blank at the right.

1 Which number is shown by the blocks?

1 ___ C

A 14   B 60   C 68   D 86

2 A number has three ones, two tens, and seven hundreds. What is the number?

2 ___ H

F 275   H 723
G 725   J 732

3 Which sign makes the number sentence 43 ☐ 34 true?

3 ___ A

A >
B <
C =
D +

4 Each student has 8 marbles. Who has the greatest fraction of black marbles?

4 ___ H

F Pilar   H Cathy
G Bob   J Donte

33   Diagnostic and Placement Tests

5 Which pizza is closest to half eaten?

5 ___ B

A   B   C   D

6 How many more CDs does Charles have than Stan?

6 ___ H

Number of CDs

Charles
Alonso
Sareeta
Stan

= 10 CDs

F 3   G 5   H 30   J 20

7 What number sentence shows how many hearts in all?

7 ___ B

A 5 + 4 = 7   C 4 + 3 = 7
B 5 + 4 = 9   D 4 + 3 = 9

34   Diagnostic and Placement Tests

Answers (Grade 3)

8 Molly has 6 stickers. She gives 3 stickers to her friend. Identify how many stickers Molly has now and the operation that you use to calculate it.

F 9; addition
G 3; subtraction
H 2; division
J 18; multiplication

8 _____ F

9 Mykia has 2 dimes, 3 nickels and 4 pennies. How much money does she have?

A $0.39   B $0.34   C $0.29   D $0.24

9 _____ A

10 Sam, Liana, Frank and Terrell went fishing. Each person caught four fish. How many fish were caught all together?

F 8   G 4   H 12   J 16

10 _____ J

11 Sanden purchased 4 packs of gum for $0.95 each. Estimate to find the total amount Sanden spent.

A $1.00   B $2.00   C $3.00   D $4.00

11 _____ D

12 A teacher had 20 pieces of chalk. He wanted to give each of his 5 students the same number of pieces. How many pieces of chalk should he give each student?

F 5   G 6   H 4   J 2

12 _____ H

13 Fumiko has 34 soccer cards. He gives 20 to his sister. Which number sentence shows how many soccer cards Fumiko has left?

A 34 + 20 = 64   C 54 − 20 = 34
B 34 − 20 = 14   D 20 + 14 = 34

13 _____ C

---

14 What is the missing number?
30, 32, 34, ____, 38, 40, 42

F 33   G 35   H 36   J 37

14 _____ H

15 Which of these can be used to check the answer to the problem below?

$$5 + 7 = 12$$

A 7 + 12 = 9   C 4 + 8 = 12
B 17 − 5 = 12   D 12 − 7 = 5

15 _____ D

16 Onatah noticed wagons have 4 wheels. Which table could she use to determine the number of wheels on four of these wagons?

F

Wagons	1	2	3	4
Wheels	4	6	8	10

G

Wagons	1	2	3	4
Wheels	4	8	12	16

H

Wagons	1	2	3	4
Wheels	4	8	16	20

J

Wagons	1	2	3	4
Wheels	4	8	16	32

16 _____ G

17 Look at the pattern in the table.

Starfish	1	2	3	4
Points	5	10	15	?

How many points do 4 starfish have?

A 16   B 20   C 25   D 30

17 _____ B

Answers (Grade 3)

22 ____ F

What number is located at Point *A* on the number line below?

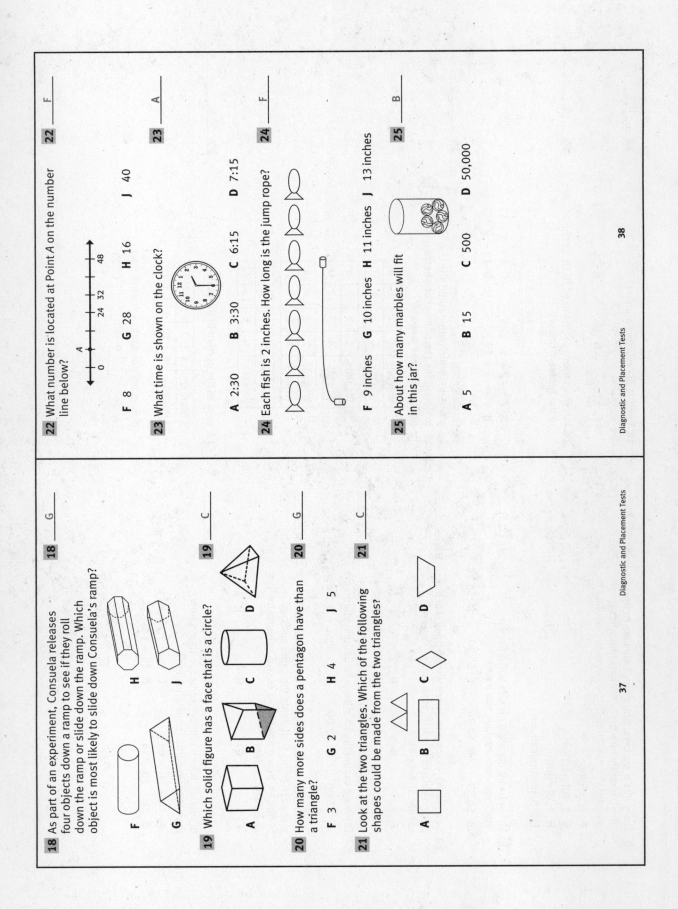

F 8   **G** 28   **H** 16   **J** 40

23 ____ A

What time is shown on the clock?

A 2:30   **B** 3:30   **C** 6:15   **D** 7:15

24 ____ F

Each fish is 2 inches. How long is the jump rope?

F 9 inches   **G** 10 inches   **H** 11 inches   **J** 13 inches

25 ____ B

About how many marbles will fit in this jar?

A 5   **B** 15   **C** 500   **D** 50,000

18 ____ G

As part of an experiment, Consuela releases four objects down a ramp to see if they roll down the ramp or slide down the ramp. Which object is most likely to slide down Consuela's ramp?

F   **G**   **H**   **J**

19 ____ C

Which solid figure has a face that is a circle?

A   **B**   **C**   **D**

20 ____ G

How many more sides does a pentagon have than a triangle?

F 3   **G** 2   **H** 4   **J** 5

21 ____ C

Look at the two triangles. Which of the following shapes could be made from the two triangles?

A   **B**   **C**   **D**

Answers (Grade 3)

26 _____ F _____

What is the area of this house?

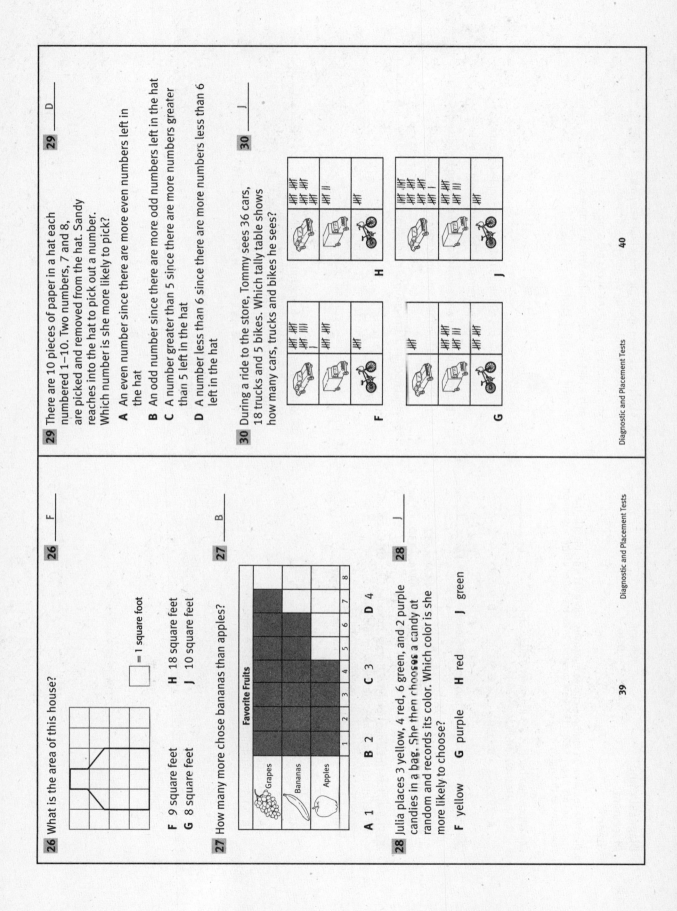

☐ = 1 square foot

F 9 square feet
G 8 square feet
H 18 square feet
J 10 square feet

27 _____ B _____

How many more chose bananas than apples?

Favorite Fruits

	1	2	3	4	5	6	7	8
Grapes								
Bananas								
Apples								

A 1   B 2   C 3   D 4

28 _____ J _____

Julia places 3 yellow, 4 red, 6 green, and 2 purple candies in a bag. She then chooses a candy at random and records its color. Which color is she more likely to choose?

F yellow   G purple   H red   J green

29 _____ D _____

There are 10 pieces of paper in a hat each numbered 1–10. Two numbers, 7 and 8, are picked and removed from the hat. Sandy reaches into the hat to pick out a number. Which number is she more likely to pick?

A An even number since there are more even numbers left in the hat

B An odd number since there are more odd numbers left in the hat

C A number greater than 5 since there are more numbers greater than 5 left in the hat

D A number less than 6 since there are more numbers less than 6 left in the hat

30 _____ J _____

During a ride to the store, Tommy sees 36 cars, 18 trucks and 5 bikes. Which tally table shows how many cars, trucks and bikes he sees?

F

G

H

J

Answers (Grade 4)

Diagnostic and Placement
Grade 4

Name _____
Date _____

This test contains 30 multiple-choice questions. Work each problem in the space on this page. Select the best answer. Write the letter of the answer on the blank at the right.

1 Which number has a 3 in the tens place and a 9 in the thousands place?

  A 2935   B 3592   C 9235   D 9253

1 ___C___

2 Which set of numbers is in order from least to greatest?

  F 4324, 4432, 4243, 4234   H 4243, 4234, 4324, 4432
  G 4432, 4324, 4243, 4234   J 4234, 4243, 4324, 4432

2 ___J___

3 Kiyoshi has three quarters, five dimes, and one nickel in her piggy bank. Identify Kiyoshi's total amount of money and the operation used to calculate it.

  A $1.10, addition   C $1.30, addition
  B $1.10, multiplication   D $1.30, multiplication

3 ___C___

4 Marley makes an apple pie and a blueberry pie to serve at Thanksgiving dinner. After dessert, she notices that $\frac{3}{8}$ of the apple pie remains and $\frac{1}{4}$ of the blueberry pie remains. Which statement is TRUE concerning Marley's observation?

  F More apple pie remained than blueberry pie because $\frac{3}{8} > \frac{1}{4}$.
  G More blueberry pie remained than apple pie because $\frac{3}{8} > \frac{1}{4}$.
  H More apple pie was eaten than blueberry pie because $\frac{3}{8} < \frac{1}{4}$.
  J Both pies had the same amount remaining because $\frac{3}{8} = \frac{1}{4}$.

4 ___F___

5 What fraction of the group of animals is cows?

  A $\frac{5}{2}$ B $\frac{2}{3}$ C $\frac{3}{5}$ D $\frac{2}{5}$

5 ___D___

6 Jordan buys twenty-four gumballs at the candy store. On the way home, he chews six gumballs and gives three to his sister. How many gumballs does Jordan have left when he gets home?

  F 13   G 14   H 15   J 16

6 ___H___

7 Which sign goes in the box to make the number sentence true?

$$42 \ \square \ 7 = 35$$

  A +   B –   C ×   D ÷

7 ___B___

Answers (Grade 4)

8 Drew owns 4 sheets of stickers. Each sheet has 12 stickers. Which number sentence shows how to find the total number of stickers Drew owns?

8 _____ H

F $12 + 4 = \square$

G $12 - 4 = \square$

H $12 \times 4 = \square$

J $12 \div 4 = \square$

9 Heather and Matt both collect rocks. Heather says that she has thirty-two rocks in her collection. Matt says that he has three times as many rocks as Heather does. Which number sentence could Heather use to find the number of rocks in Matt's collection?

9 _____ C

A $32 + 3$

B $32 - 3$

C 32×3

D $32 \div 3$

10 To enter a dog show, Tehya must weigh her Great Dane and record his weight rounded to the nearest ten pounds. Tehya's Great Dane weighs 123 pounds. Which weight should Tehya record for the dog show?

10 _____ G

F 100 pounds

G 120 pounds

H 125 pounds

J 130 pounds

11 The table below shows the number of crayons in each box. If every box has the same number of crayons, how many crayons will be in 8 boxes?

11 _____ C

Number of Boxes	Number of Crayons
1	8
2	16
3	24

A 8   **B** 32   **C** 64   **D** 72

12 A line of ants is moving across Denise's picnic blanket. She counts 6 legs on the first ant, 12 legs on the first two ants, and 18 legs on the first three ants. If Denise continues to count, how many legs will she count on the first 12 ants?

12 _____ J

F 24 legs   **G** 56 legs   **H** 60 legs   **J** 72 legs

13 Which completes the fact family for the following set of number sentences?

13 _____ A

$$4 \times 2 = 8, 2 \times 4 = 8, 8 \div 2 = 4$$

A $8 \div 4 = 2$ **C** $4 \div 2 = 2$

B $8 \div 2 = 4$ **D** $4 \div 8 = \frac{1}{2}$

Answers (Grade 4)

14 ____ H

Hector saves $5.00 of his allowance every week. After 12 weeks he has $60.00 saved. Which table could he use to show the amount of money he will save after 20 weeks?

F

Week	Money Saved
15	$65.00
16	$70.00
17	$75.00
18	$80.00
19	$85.00
20	$90.00

G

Week	Money Saved
15	$70.00
16	$75.00
17	$80.00
18	$85.00
19	$90.00
20	$95.00

H

Week	Money Saved
15	$75.00
16	$80.00
17	$85.00
18	$90.00
19	$95.00
20	$100.00

J

Week	Money Saved
15	$80.00
16	$85.00
17	$90.00
18	$95.00
19	$100.00
20	$105.00

15 ____ D

Bianca is building a tower with wooden blocks. She counts the number of blocks on each level and records it in the chart below.

Level	1	2	3	4	5
Blocks	20	16	12	8	4

Which statement describes the number of blocks on each level of her tower?

A Bianca adds 4 blocks with every level of the tower.
B Bianca adds 6 blocks with every level of the tower.
C Bianca subtracts 6 blocks with every level of the tower.
D Bianca subtracts 4 blocks with every level of the tower.

16 ____ F

Which best describes this figure?

F pentagon   **G** hexagon   **H** triangle   **J** octagon

51

17 ____ B

Which shape is this can of soup?

A sphere   **B** cylinder   **C** cone   **D** pyramid

18 ____ F

Which of the following boxes is congruent to the box shown below?

F   **G**   **H**   **J**

19 ____ C

How many lines of symmetry are there in the figure below?

A 0   **B** 1   **C** 5   **D** 10

20 ____ H

Identify a fraction equivalent to the fraction shown on the number line.

0 ——————— $\frac{1}{2}$ ——————— 1

F $\frac{1}{3}$ **G** $\frac{4}{6}$ **H** $\frac{3}{4}$ **J** $\frac{7}{8}$

21 ____ C

Look at the number line. Which point is located at $2\frac{3}{4}$?

2 ———A——B—C—D——— 3
        2.5

A A **B** B **C** C **D** D

52

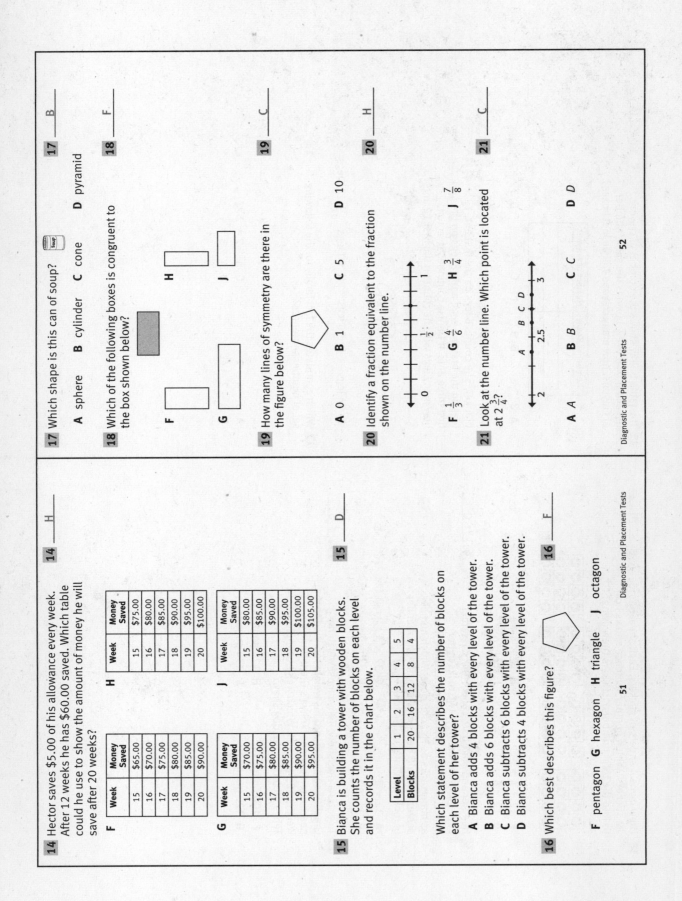

Answers (Grade 4)

22 Measure the length of the ribbon in centimeters. About how long is the ribbon?

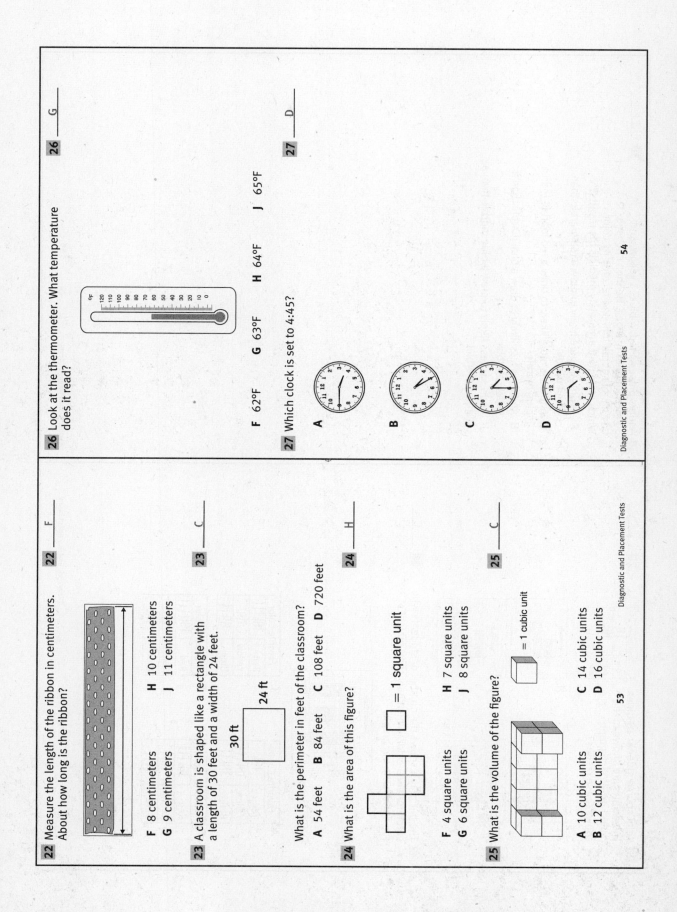

F 8 centimeters   H 10 centimeters
G 9 centimeters   J 11 centimeters

22 _____ F

23 A classroom is shaped like a rectangle with a length of 30 feet and a width of 24 feet.

30 ft   24 ft

What is the perimeter in feet of the classroom?
A 54 feet   B 84 feet   C 108 feet   D 720 feet

23 _____ C

24 What is the area of this figure?

☐ = 1 square unit

F 4 square units   H 7 square units
G 6 square units   J 8 square units

24 _____ H

25 What is the volume of the figure?

= 1 cubic unit

A 10 cubic units   C 14 cubic units
B 12 cubic units   D 16 cubic units

25 _____ C

26 Look at the thermometer. What temperature does it read?

F 62°F   G 63°F   H 64°F   J 65°F

26 _____ G

27 Which clock is set to 4:45?

A   B   C   D

27 _____ D

53

54

Answers (Grade 4)

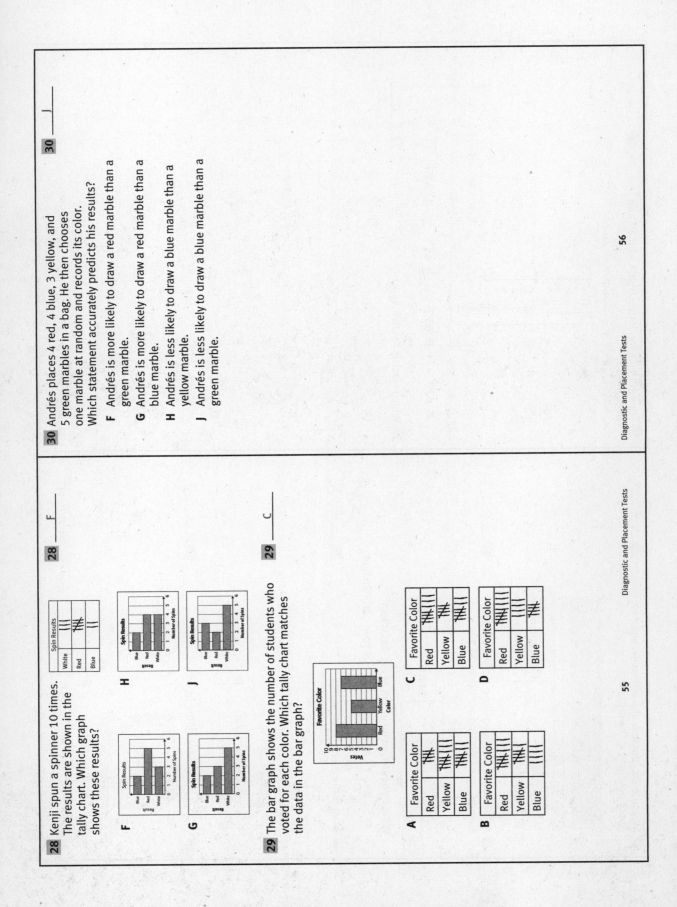

28 ___ F ___

Kenji spun a spinner 10 times. The results are shown in the tally chart. Which graph shows these results?

Spin Results	
White	|||
Red	╫╫
Blue	||

F

Spin Results

G

Spin Results

H

Spin Results

J

Spin Results

29 ___ C ___

The bar graph shows the number of students who voted for each color. Which tally chart matches the data in the bar graph?

Favorite Color

A

Favorite Color	
Red	╫╫ ||||
Yellow	╫╫ ||||
Blue	╫╫ ╫╫

B

Favorite Color	
Red	╫╫ ||||
Yellow	╫╫	
Blue	||||

C

Favorite Color	
Red	╫╫ ||||
Yellow	╫╫
Blue	╫╫	

D

Favorite Color	
Red	╫╫ ||||
Yellow	|||||
Blue	╫╫

30 ___ J ___

Andrés places 4 red, 4 blue, 3 yellow, and 5 green marbles in a bag. He then chooses one marble at random and records its color. Which statement accurately predicts his results?

F Andrés is more likely to draw a red marble than a green marble.

G Andrés is more likely to draw a red marble than a blue marble.

H Andrés is less likely to draw a blue marble than a yellow marble.

J Andrés is less likely to draw a blue marble than a green marble.

Answers (Grade 5)

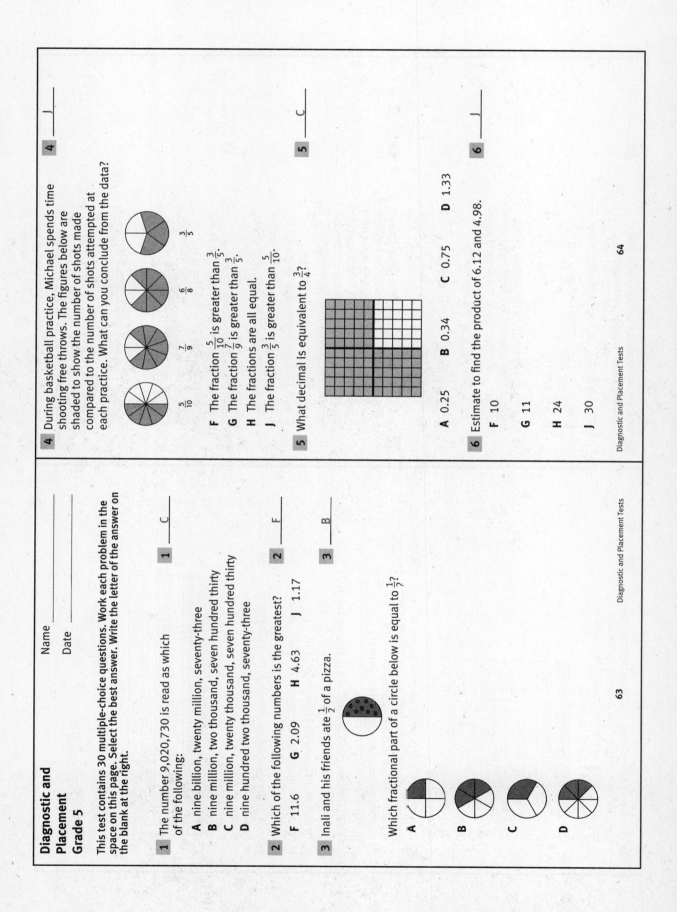

Diagnostic and Placement
Grade 5

Name _____

Date _____

This test contains 30 multiple-choice questions. Work each problem in the space on this page. Select the best answer. Write the letter of the answer on the blank at the right.

1 The number 9,020,730 is read as which of the following:

A nine billion, twenty million, seventy-three

B nine million, two thousand, seven hundred thirty

C nine million, twenty thousand, seven hundred thirty

D nine hundred two thousand, seventy-three

1 C

2 Which of the following numbers is the greatest?

F 11.6   G 2.09   H 4.63   J 1.17

2 F

3 Inali and his friends ate $\frac{1}{2}$ of a pizza.

Which fractional part of a circle below is equal to $\frac{1}{2}$?

A

B

C

D

3 B

4 During basketball practice, Michael spends time shooting free throws. The figures below are shaded to show the number of shots made compared to the number of shots attempted at each practice. What can you conclude from the data?

$\frac{5}{10}$ $\frac{7}{9}$ $\frac{6}{8}$ $\frac{3}{5}$

F The fraction $\frac{5}{10}$ is greater than $\frac{3}{5}$.

G The fraction $\frac{7}{9}$ is greater than $\frac{3}{5}$.

H The fractions are all equal.

J The fraction $\frac{3}{5}$ is greater than $\frac{5}{10}$.

4 J

5 What decimal is equivalent to $\frac{3}{4}$?

A 0.25   B 0.34   C 0.75   D 1.33

5 C

6 Estimate to find the product of 6.12 and 4.98.

F 10

G 11

H 24

J 30

6 J

Answers (Grade 5)

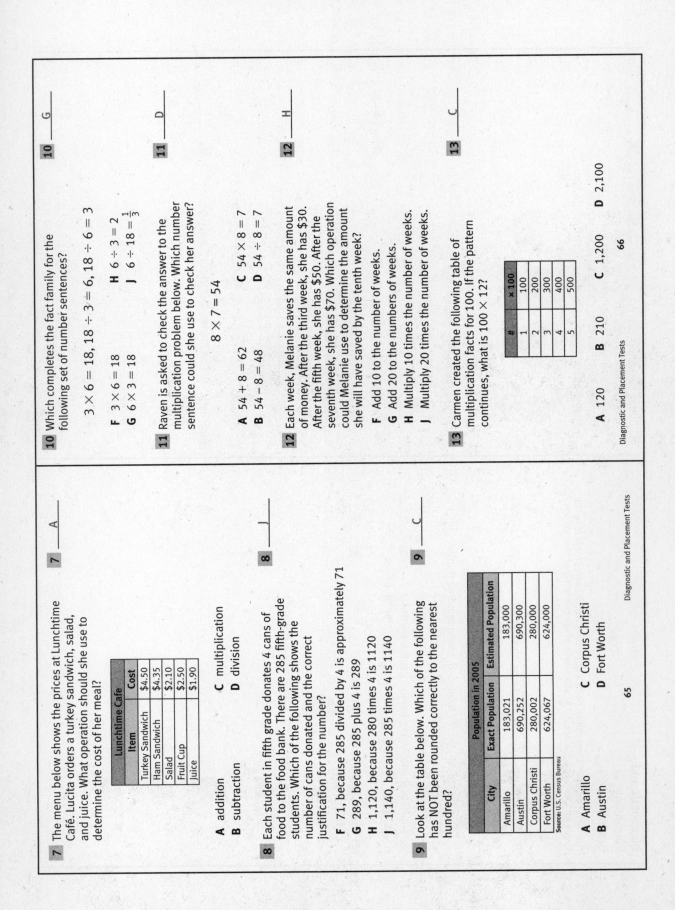

7 _____ A

The menu below shows the prices at Lunchtime Café. Lucita orders a turkey sandwich, salad, and juice. What operation should she use to determine the cost of her meal?

Lunchtime Cafe	
Item	Cost
Turkey Sandwich	$4.50
Ham Sandwich	$4.35
Salad	$2.10
Fruit Cup	$2.50
Juice	$1.90

A addition **C** multiplication
B subtraction **D** division

8 _____ J

Each student in fifth grade donates 4 cans of food to the food bank. There are 285 fifth-grade students. Which of the following shows the number of cans donated and the correct justification for the number?

F 71, because 285 divided by 4 is approximately 71
G 289, because 285 plus 4 is 289
H 1,120, because 280 times 4 is 1120
J 1,140, because 285 times 4 is 1140

9 _____ C

Look at the table below. Which of the following has NOT been rounded correctly to the nearest hundred?

Population in 2005		
City	Exact Population	Estimated Population
Amarillo	183,021	183,000
Austin	690,252	690,300
Corpus Christi	280,002	280,000
Fort Worth	624,067	624,000

Source: U.S. Census Bureau

A Amarillo **C** Corpus Christi
B Austin **D** Fort Worth

10 _____ G

Which completes the fact family for the following set of number sentences?

$$3 \times 6 = 18, 18 \div 3 = 6, 18 \div 6 = 3$$

F $3 \times 6 = 18$ **H** $6 \div 3 = 2$
G $6 \times 3 = 18$ **J** $6 \div 18 = \frac{1}{3}$

11 _____ D

Raven is asked to check the answer to the multiplication problem below. Which number sentence could she use to check her answer?

$$8 \times 7 = 54$$

A $54 + 8 = 62$ **C** $54 \times 8 = 7$
B $54 - 8 = 48$ **D** $54 \div 8 = 7$

12 _____ H

Each week, Melanie saves the same amount of money. After the third week, she has $30. After the fifth week, she has $50. After the seventh week, she has $70. Which operation could Melanie use to determine the amount she will have saved by the tenth week?

F Add 10 to the number of weeks.
G Add 20 to the numbers of weeks.
H Multiply 10 times the number of weeks.
J Multiply 20 times the number of weeks.

13 _____ C

Carmen created the following table of multiplication facts for 100. If the pattern continues, what is 100×12?

#	×100
1	100
2	200
3	300
4	400
5	500

A 120 **B** 210 **C** 1,200 **D** 2,100

Answers (Grade 5)

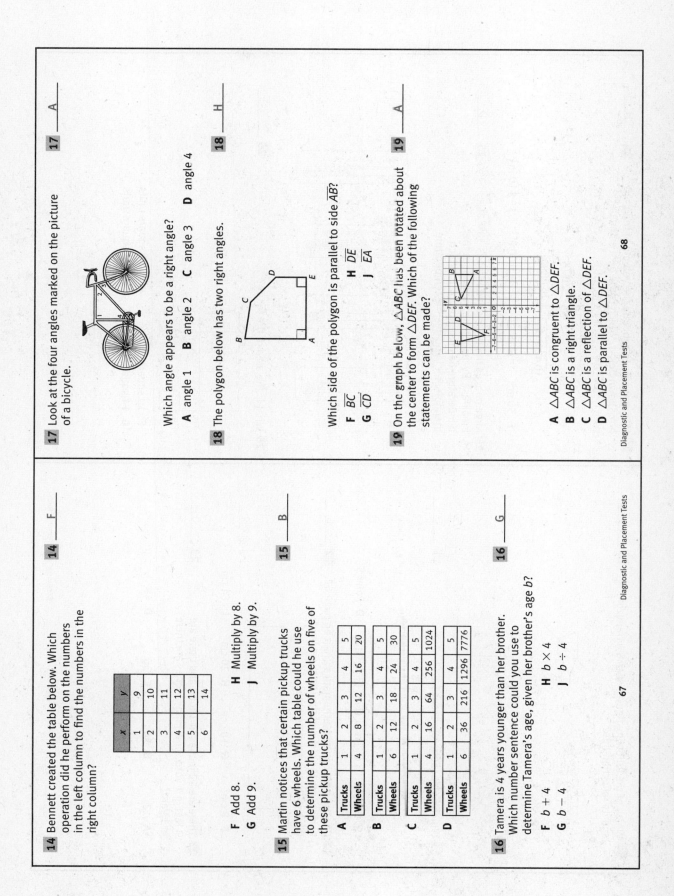

14 Bennett created the table below. Which operation did he perform on the numbers in the left column to find the numbers in the right column?

x	y
1	9
2	10
3	11
4	12
5	13
6	14

F Add 8.   **H** Multiply by 8.
G Add 9.   **J** Multiply by 9.

14 ____ F ____

15 Martin notices that certain pickup trucks have 6 wheels. Which table could he use to determine the number of wheels on five of these pickup trucks?

A

Trucks	1	2	3	4	5
Wheels	4	8	12	16	20

B

Trucks	1	2	3	4	5
Wheels	6	12	18	24	30

C

Trucks	1	2	3	4	5
Wheels	4	16	64	256	1024

D

Trucks	1	2	3	4	5
Wheels	6	36	216	1296	7776

15 ____ B ____

16 Tamera is 4 years younger than her brother. Which number sentence could you use to determine Tamera's age, given her brother's age *b*?

F $b + 4$ **H** $b \times 4$
G $b - 4$ **J** $b \div 4$

16 ____ G ____

17 Look at the four angles marked on the picture of a bicycle.

Which angle appears to be a right angle?
A angle 1   **B** angle 2   **C** angle 3   **D** angle 4

17 ____ A ____

18 The polygon below has two right angles.

Which side of the polygon is parallel to side $\overline{AB}$?
F $\overline{BC}$ **H** $\overline{DE}$
G $\overline{CD}$ **J** $\overline{EA}$

18 ____ H ____

19 On the graph below, △ABC has been rotated about the center to form △DEF. Which of the following statements can be made?

A △ABC is congruent to △DEF.
B △ABC is a right triangle.
C △ABC is a reflection of △DEF.
D △ABC is parallel to △DEF.

19 ____ A ____

Answers (Grade 5)

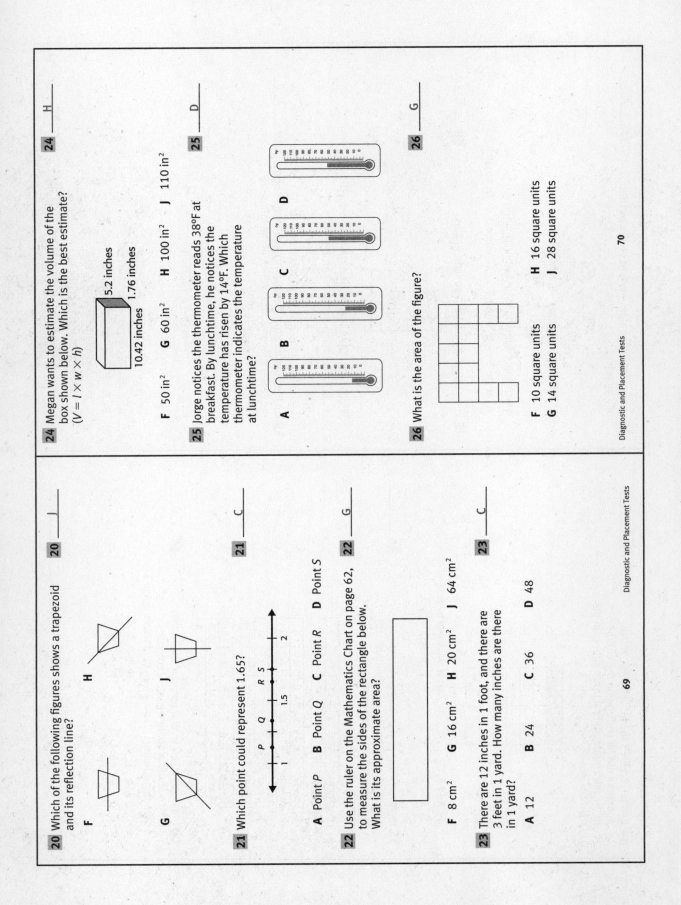

20 Which of the following figures shows a trapezoid and its reflection line?

F

H

G

J

20 ____ J ____

21 Which point could represent 1.65?

```
      P  Q    R  S
    |--•--•---•--•---•---|
    1       1.5        2
```

A Point P   **B** Point Q   **C** Point R   **D** Point S

21 ____ C ____

22 Use the ruler on the Mathematics Chart on page 62, to measure the sides of the rectangle below. What is its approximate area?

F 8 cm²   **G** 16 cm²   **H** 20 cm²   **J** 64 cm²

22 ____ G ____

23 There are 12 inches in 1 foot, and there are 3 feet in 1 yard. How many inches are there in 1 yard?

A 12   **B** 24   **C** 36   **D** 48

23 ____ C ____

24 Megan wants to estimate the volume of the box shown below. Which is the best estimate? ($V = l \times w \times h$)

5.2 inches
1.76 inches
10.42 inches

F 50 in²   **G** 60 in²   **H** 100 in²   **J** 110 in²

24 ____ H ____

25 Jorge notices the thermometer reads 38°F at breakfast. By lunchtime, he notices the temperature has risen by 14°F. Which thermometer indicates the temperature at lunchtime?

A   **B**   **C**   **D**

25 ____ D ____

26 What is the area of the figure?

F 10 square units   **H** 16 square units
G 14 square units   **J** 28 square units

26 ____ G ____

Answers (Grade 5)

27 To win a prize, first choose a box and then choose a prize bag inside that box. There are 3 boxes and 2 prize bags in each box. There is a different prize in each bag. How many different prizes are there? **27** ___D___

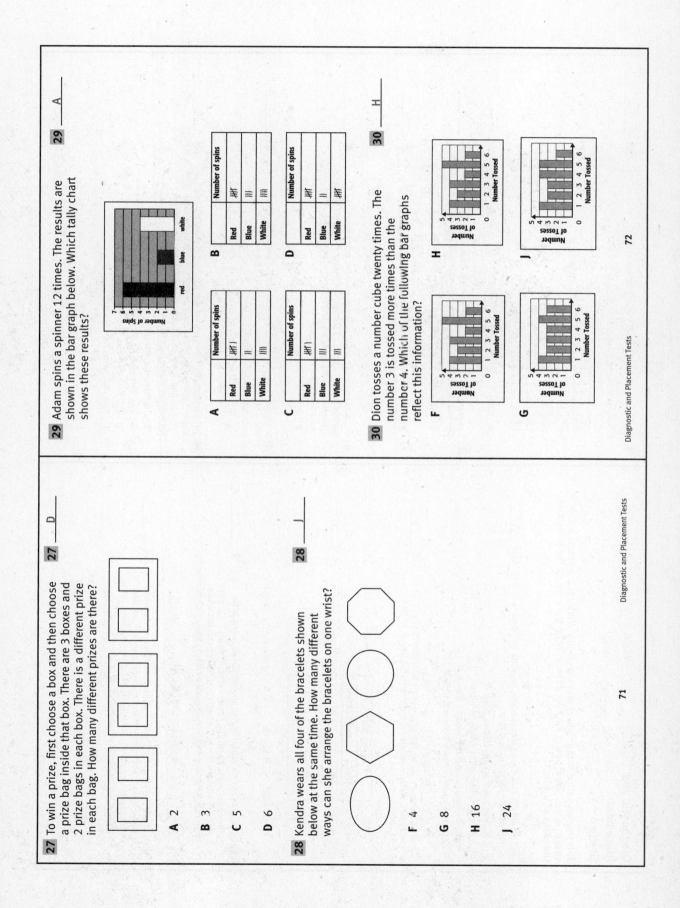

A 2

B 3

C 5

D 6

28 Kendra wears all four of the bracelets shown below at the same time. How many different ways can she arrange the bracelets on one wrist? **28** ___J___

F 4

G 8

H 16

J 24

29 ___A___

29 Adam spins a spinner 12 times. The results are shown in the bar graph below. Which tally chart shows these results?

A
Red	|||||
Blue	||
White	||||

Number of spins

B
Red	|||||
Blue	|||
White	||||

Number of spins

C
Red	|||||
Blue	|||
White	|||

Number of spins

D
Red	|||||
Blue	||
White	|||||

Number of spins

30 ___H___

30 Dion tosses a number cube twenty times. The number 3 is tossed more times than the number 4. Which of the following bar graphs reflect this information?

F

G

H

J

Answers (Grade 6)

Diagnostic and Placement

Grade 6

Name _____

Date _____

This test contains 30 multiple-choice questions. Work each problem in the space on this page. Select the best answer. Write the letter of the answer on the blank at the right.

1 Last year, 2,080,015 people attended the state fair. What is this number written in word form?

A two billion, eighty million, fifteen

B two million, eight thousand, fifteen

C two million, eighty thousand, fifteen

D two hundred eighty thousand, fifteen

1 ___ C

2 The table below shows the length of the hiking trails at a local park. Aaron hikes half of the blue trail. Estimate to find the distance he hiked.

Hiking Trails	
Trail	Length (miles)
Red	1.09
Blue	1.87
Green	1.10
Yellow	1.28

F 0.5 mile   G 1.5 miles   H 1 mile   J 2 miles

2 ___ H

3 Darla and Catalina collect stuffed animals. Darla says $\frac{2}{3}$ of her collection is teddy bears. The fraction of stuffed cats in Catalina's collection is equivalent to the fraction of teddy bears in Darla's collection. What is the fraction of stuffed cats in Catalina's collection?

A $\frac{3}{4}$ B $\frac{9}{12}$ C $\frac{10}{15}$ D $\frac{16}{18}$

3 ___ C

4 Marlene and Jason each took an online test. Marlene answered $\frac{3}{5}$ of the questions correctly. Jason answered a greater fraction of the questions correctly. Which of the following fractions could represent the fraction Jason answered correctly?

F $\frac{2}{3}$ G $\frac{6}{10}$ H $\frac{1}{2}$ J $\frac{3}{8}$

4 ___ F

---

5 The model below shows $\frac{28}{100}$ shaded. Which of the following decimals is equivalent to $\frac{28}{100}$?

A 2.8   B 2.08   C 0.28   D 0.028

5 ___ C

6 Candace is knitting a scarf. The scarf is 4.6 feet long. If she knits another 1.75 feet, how long will the scarf be?

F 6.35 feet   G 5.81 feet   H 5.35 feet   J 2.85 feet

6 ___ F

7 The art teacher has 46 boxes of crayons. Each box has 8 crayons. How many crayons are there altogether?

A 248   B 288   C 328   D 368

7 ___ D

8 Ms. Ayala had 152 pencils. She divided the number of pencils equally among 13 students. She kept the leftover pencils in her desk. What is the greatest number of pencils Ms. Ayala could have given each student?

F 9   G 10   H 11   J 12

8 ___ F

9 Josie draws a rectangle. She colors $\frac{3}{8}$ of the rectangle red and $\frac{1}{4}$ of the rectangle blue. How much of the whole rectangle does she color?

A $\frac{1}{8}$ B $\frac{1}{2}$ C $\frac{5}{8}$ D $\frac{3}{4}$

9 ___ C

10 Tia, Veronica, Pam, and Lily are sisters. Tia is 8 years old and she is 2 years older than Pam. Pam is 5 years younger than Veronica and Veronica is 4 years younger than Lily. Which list has the sisters in order from youngest to oldest?

F Tia, Veronica, Pam, Lily

G Lily, Veronica, Tia, Pam

H Tia, Pam, Veronica, Lily

J Pam, Tia, Veronica, Lily

10 ___ G

Answers (Grade 6)

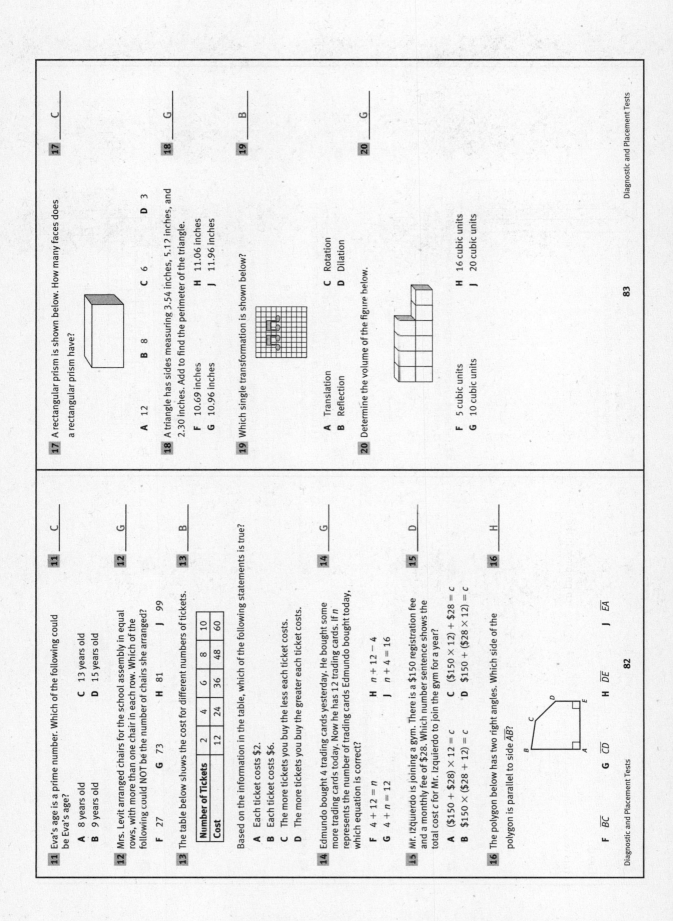

11 Eva's age is a prime number. Which of the following could be Eva's age?

A 8 years old   C 13 years old
B 9 years old   D 15 years old

11   C

12 Mrs. Levit arranged chairs for the school assembly in equal rows, with more than one chair in each row. Which of the following could NOT be the number of chairs she arranged?

F 27   G 73   H 81   J 99

12   G

13 The table below shows the cost for different numbers of tickets.

Number of Tickets	2	4	6	8	10
Cost	12	24	36	48	60

Based on the information in the table, which of the following statements is true?

A Each ticket costs $2.
B Each ticket costs $6.
C The more tickets you buy the less each ticket costs.
D The more tickets you buy the greater each ticket costs.

13   B

14 Edmundo bought 4 trading cards yesterday. He bought some more trading cards today. Now he has 12 trading cards. If n represents the number of trading cards Edmundo bought today, which equation is correct?

F $4 + 12 = n$ H $n + 12 - 4$
G $4 + n = 12$ J $n + 4 = 16$

14   G

15 Mr. Izquierdo is joining a gym. There is a $150 registration fee and a monthly fee of $28. Which number sentence shows the total cost c for Mr. Izquierdo to join the gym for a year?

A $(\$150 + \$28) \times 12 = c$ C $(\$150 \times 12) + \$28 = c$
B $\$150 \times (\$28 + 12) = c$ D $\$150 + (\$28 \times 12) = c$

15   D

16 The polygon below has two right angles. Which side of the polygon is parallel to side $\overline{AB}$?

F $\overline{BC}$ G $\overline{CD}$ H $\overline{DE}$ J $\overline{EA}$

16   H

17 A rectangular prism is shown below. How many faces does a rectangular prism have?

A 12   B 8   C 6   D 3

17   C

18 A triangle has sides measuring 3.54 inches, 5.17 inches, and 2.30 inches. Add to find the perimeter of the triangle.

F 10.69 inches   H 11.06 inches
G 10.96 inches   J 11.96 inches

18   G

19 Which single transformation is shown below?

A Translation   C Rotation
B Reflection   D Dilation

19   B

20 Determine the volume of the figure below.

F 5 cubic units   H 16 cubic units
G 10 cubic units   J 20 cubic units

20   G

Answers (Grade 6)

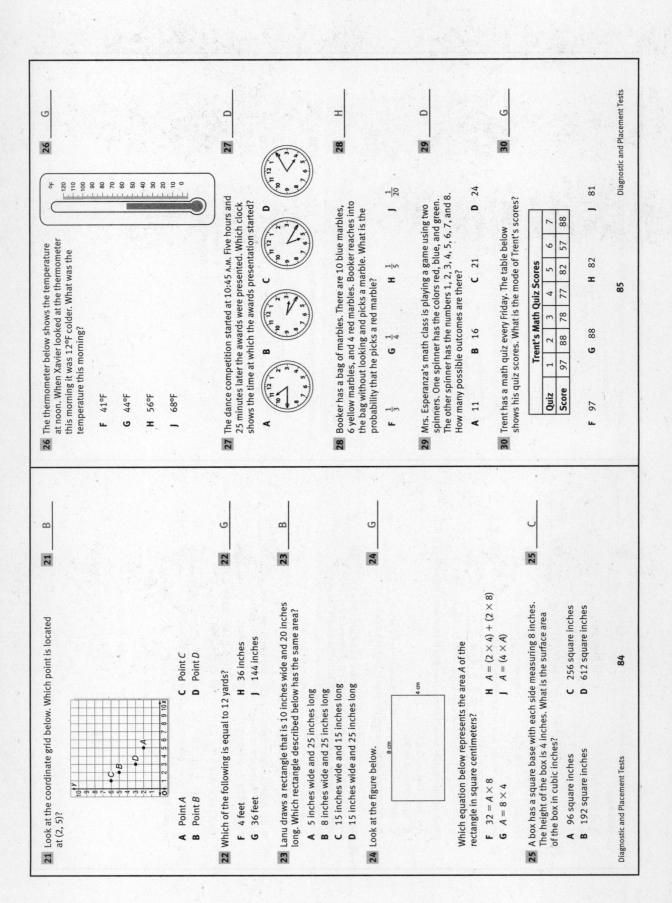

21 Look at the coordinate grid below. Which point is located at (2, 5)?

A Point A   C Point C
B Point B   D Point D

21 B

22 Which of the following is equal to 12 yards?

F 4 feet   H 36 inches
G 36 feet   J 144 inches

22 G

23 Lanu draws a rectangle that is 10 inches wide and 20 inches long. Which rectangle described below has the same area?

A 5 inches wide and 25 inches long
B 8 inches wide and 25 inches long
C 15 inches wide and 15 inches long
D 15 inches wide and 25 inches long

23 B

24 Look at the figure below.

24 G

Which equation below represents the area A of the rectangle in square centimeters?

F $32 = A \times 8$ H $A = (2 \times 4) + (2 \times 8)$
G $A = 8 \times 4$ J $A = (4 \times A)$

25 A box has a square base with each side measuring 8 inches. The height of the box is 4 inches. What is the surface area of the box in cubic inches?

A 96 square inches   C 256 square inches
B 192 square inches   D 612 square inches

25 C

26 The thermometer below shows the temperature at noon. When Xavier looked at the thermometer this morning it was 12°F colder. What was the temperature this morning?

F 41°F
G 44°F
H 56°F
J 68°F

26 G

27 The dance competition started at 10:45 A.M. Five hours and 25 minutes later the awards were presented. Which clock shows the time at which the awards presentation started?

A   B   C   D

27 D

28 Booker has a bag of marbles. There are 10 blue marbles, 6 yellow marbles, and 4 red marbles. Booker reaches into the bag without looking and picks a marble. What is the probability that he picks a red marble?

F $\frac{1}{3}$ G $\frac{1}{4}$ H $\frac{1}{5}$ J $\frac{1}{20}$

28 H

29 Mrs. Esperanza's math class is playing a game using two spinners. One spinner has the colors red, blue, and green. The other spinner has the numbers 1, 2, 3, 4, 5, 6, 7, and 8. How many possible outcomes are there?

A 11   B 16   C 21   D 24

29 D

30 Trent has a math quiz every Friday. The table below shows his quiz scores. What is the mode of Trent's scores?

Trent's Math Quiz Scores

Quiz	1	2	3	4	5	6	7
Score	97	88	78	77	82	57	88

F 97   G 88   H 82   J 81

30 G

Answers (Grade 7)

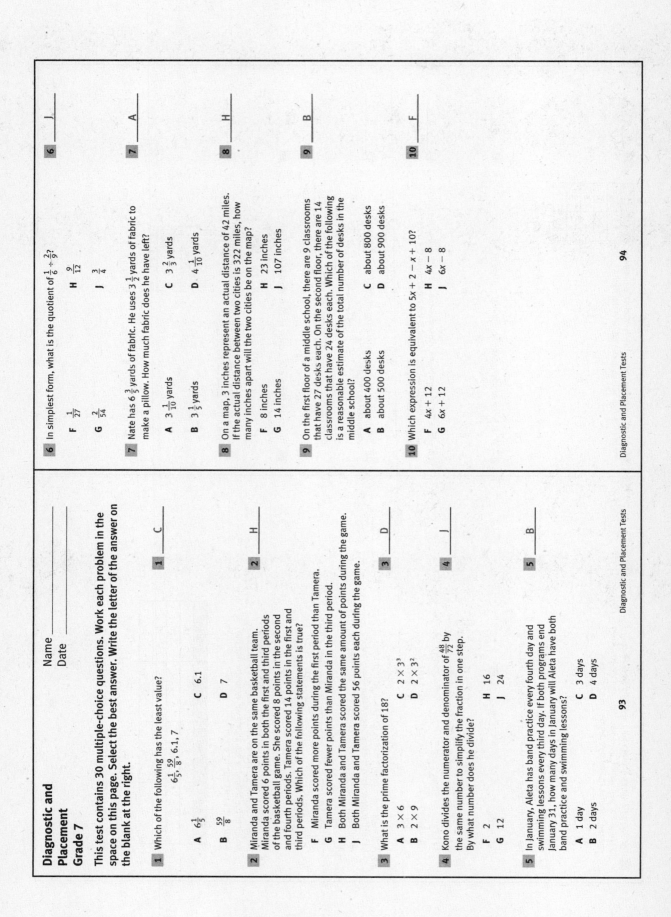

Diagnostic and Placement
Grade 7

Name _____
Date _____

This test contains 30 multiple-choice questions. Work each problem in the space on this page. Select the best answer. Write the letter of the answer on the blank at the right.

1 Which of the following has the least value?

$$6\frac{1}{5}, \frac{59}{8}, 6.1, 7$$

  A $6\frac{1}{5}$ C 6.1

  B $\frac{59}{8}$ D 7

1   C

2 Miranda and Tamera are on the same basketball team. Miranda scored 6 points in both the first and third periods of the basketball game. She scored 8 points in the second and fourth periods. Tamera scored 14 points in the first and third periods. Which of the following statements is true?

  F Miranda scored more points during the first period than Tamera.

  G Tamera scored fewer points than Miranda in the third period.

  H Both Miranda and Tamera scored the same amount of points during the game.

  J Both Miranda and Tamera scored 56 points each during the game.

2   H

3 What is the prime factorization of 18?

  A 3×6 C 2×3^3

  B 2×9 D 2×3^2

3   D

4 Kono divides the numerator and denominator of $\frac{48}{72}$ by the same number to simplify the fraction in one step. By what number does he divide?

  F 2   H 16

  G 12   J 24

4   J

5 In January, Aleta has band practice every fourth day and swimming lessons every third day. If both programs end January 31, how many days in January will Aleta have both band practice and swimming lessons?

  A 1 day   C 3 days

  B 2 days   D 4 days

5   B

93   Diagnostic and Placement Tests

---

6 In simplest form, what is the quotient of $\frac{1}{6} \div \frac{2}{9}$?

  F $\frac{1}{27}$ H $\frac{9}{12}$

  G $\frac{2}{54}$ J $\frac{3}{4}$

6   J

7 Nate has $6\frac{3}{5}$ yards of fabric. He uses $3\frac{1}{2}$ yards of fabric to make a pillow. How much fabric does he have left?

  A $3\frac{1}{10}$ yards   C $3\frac{2}{3}$ yards

  B $3\frac{1}{5}$ yards   D $4\frac{1}{10}$ yards

7   A

8 On a map, 3 inches represent an actual distance of 42 miles. If the actual distance between two cities is 322 miles, how many inches apart will the two cities be on the map?

  F 8 inches   H 23 inches

  G 14 inches   J 107 inches

8   H

9 On the first floor of a middle school, there are 9 classrooms that have 27 desks each. On the second floor, there are 14 classrooms that have 24 desks each. Which of the following is a reasonable estimate of the total number of desks in the middle school?

  A about 400 desks   C about 800 desks

  B about 500 desks   D about 900 desks

9   B

10 Which expression is equivalent to $5x + 2 - x + 10$?

  F $4x + 12$ H $4x - 8$

  G $6x + 12$ J $6x - 8$

10   F

94   Diagnostic and Placement Tests

Answers (Grade 7)

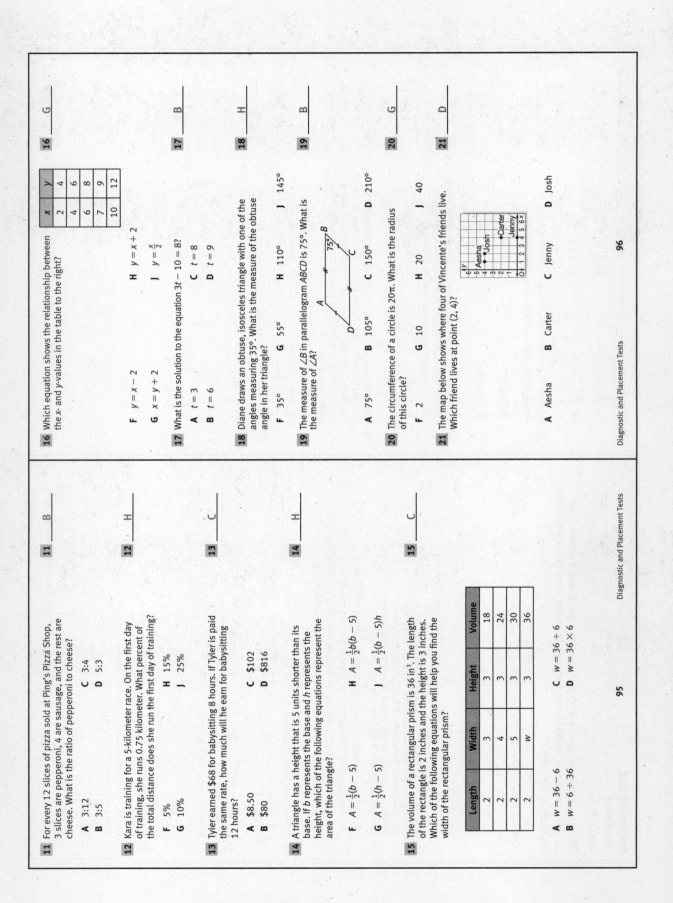

16 G   **17** B   **18** H   **19** B   **20** G   **21** D

16 Which equation shows the relationship between the x- and y-values in the table to the right?

x	y
2	4
4	6
6	8
7	9
10	12

F $\ y = x - 2$

G $\ x = y + 2$

H $\ y = x + 2$

J $\ y = \frac{x}{2}$

17 What is the solution to the equation $3t - 10 = 8$?

A $\ t = 3$

B $\ t = 6$

C $\ t = 8$

D $\ t = 9$

18 Diane draws an obtuse, isosceles triangle with one of the angles measuring 35°. What is the measure of the obtuse angle in her triangle?

F 35°   G 55°   H 110°   J 145°

19 The measure of $\angle B$ in parallelogram $ABCD$ is 75°. What is the measure of $\angle A$?

A 75°   B 105°   C 150°   D 210°

20 The circumference of a circle is 20π. What is the radius of this circle?

F 2   G 10   H 20   J 40

21 The map below shows where four of Vincente's friends live. Which friend lives at point (2, 4)?

A Aesha   B Carter   C Jenny   D Josh

---

11 B   **12** H   **13** C   **14** H   **15** C

11 For every 12 slices of pizza sold at Ping's Pizza Shop, 3 slices are pepperoni, 4 are sausage, and the rest are cheese. What is the ratio of pepperoni to cheese?

A 3:12   C 3:4

B 3:5   D 5:3

12 Kara is training for a 5-kilometer race. On the first day of training, she runs 0.75 kilometer. What percent of the total distance does she run the first day of training?

F 5%   H 15%

G 10%   J 25%

13 Tyler earned $68 for babysitting 8 hours. If Tyler is paid the same rate, how much will he earn for babysitting 12 hours?

A $8.50   C $102

B $80   D $816

14 A triangle has a height that is 5 units shorter than its base. If b represents the base and h represents the height, which of the following equations represent the area of the triangle?

F $\ A = \frac{1}{2}(b - 5)$

G $\ A = \frac{1}{2}(h - 5)$

H $\ A = \frac{1}{2}b(b - 5)$

J $\ A = \frac{1}{2}(b - 5)h$

15 The volume of a rectangular prism is 36 in³. The length of the rectangle is 2 inches and the height is 3 inches. Which of the following equations will help you find the width of the rectangular prism?

Length	Width	Height	Volume
2	3	3	18
2	4	3	24
2	5	3	30
2	w	3	36

A $\ w = 36 - 6$ C $\ w = 36 \div 6$

B $\ w = 6 \div 36$ D $\ w = 36 \times 6$

Answers (Grade 7)

28 ___F___

28 Kahlid spins a spinner 10 times. The results are shown in the tally chart below. Which of the following graphs show these results?

Spin Results	
White	⫽
Red	⫽
Blue	

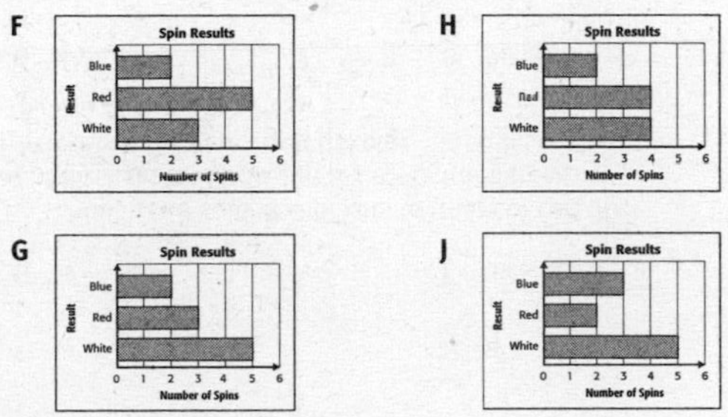

F

Spin Results

G

Spin Results

H

Spin Results

J

Spin Results

29 ___C___

29 What is the median of these data?

67, 98, 78, 75, 83, 44, 98

A 44   **B** 75   **C** 78   **D** 98

30 ___F___

30 After every run, Gabe's track coach records how many minutes it took Gabe to run a mile. The graph below shows Gabe's times. How many times did Gabe run before he was able to complete a mile in less than 10 minutes?

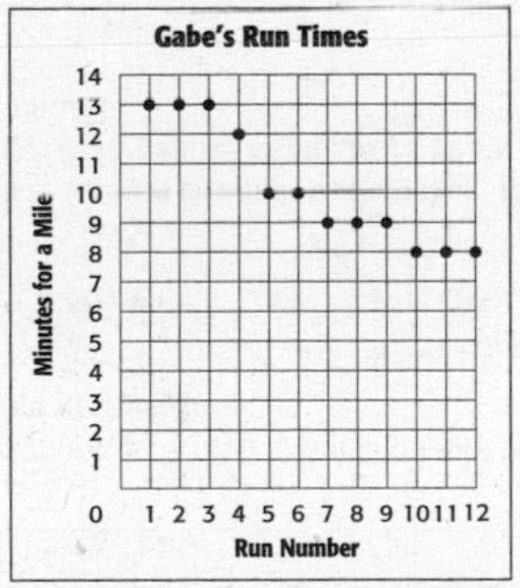

Gabe's Run Times

F 6 runs   **G** 7 runs   **H** 9 runs   **J** 10 runs

---

22 ___F___

22 Lucas attends 8 classes each day. If each class is about 45 minutes long, about how long will Lucas have been in school when he starts his fourth class of the day?

F about 2 hours   **H** about 4 hours
G about 3 hours   **J** about 5 hours

23 ___D___

23 A rectangular sandbox has a length of 60 inches, a width of 40 inches, and a depth of 6 inches. What is the volume?

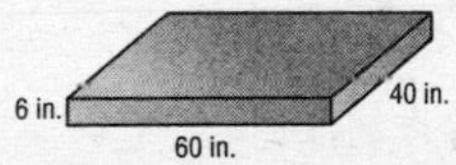

6 in.
60 in.
40 in.

A 240 cubic inches   **C** 2,400 cubic inches
B 1,440 cubic inches   **D** 14,400 cubic inches

24 ___H___

24 Which of the following is closest to the measure of the angle shown below?

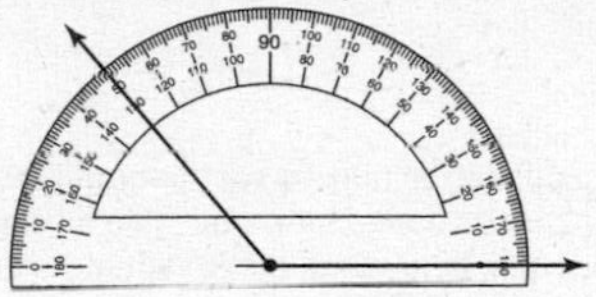

F 50°   **G** 80°   **H** 130°   **J** 180°

25 ___D___

25 A package weighs $2\frac{3}{4}$ pounds. What is the weight of the package in ounces?

A 35 ounces   **C** 43.7 ounces
B 36.8 ounces   **D** 44 ounces

26 ___J___

26 To win a prize, a player picks a door and then a box behind the door. There are 3 doors and 4 boxes behind each door. How many prizes can be won if each box has a different prize?

F 3   **G** 4   **H** 7   **J** 12

27 ___D___

27 There are 10 marbles in a bag: 1 blue, 4 yellow, 3 red, and 2 white. If you choose a marble at random, which is the probability that you will NOT choose white?

A 20%   **B** 25%   **C** 75%   **D** 80%

Answers (Grade 8)

Diagnostic and Placement

Name _____

Date _____

Grade 8

This test contains 30 multiple-choice questions. Work each problem in the space on this page. Select the best answer. Write the letter of the answer on the blank at the right.

1 Which set of numbers is in order from greatest to least?

A $4, \frac{1}{4}, \frac{2}{3}, 0.04, 40$ C $40, 4, \frac{2}{3}, \frac{1}{4}, 0.04$

B $0.04, \frac{1}{4}, \frac{2}{3}, 4, 40$ D $\frac{1}{4}, \frac{2}{3}, 0.04, 4, 40$

1 _C_

2 Charlene bought her friends lunch. The bill came to $52.80 before Charlene added an 18% service tip. How much did she add for the service tip?

F $4.75   H $9.50

G $5.70   J $10.20

2 _H_

3 Randy is playing a number game. Beginning with the number 8, he adds 4, multiples by 5, and then divides by −10. He then subtracts 2. What number does he find at the end of the game?

A −8   B −6   C 6   D 8

3 _A_

4 Which multiplication is shown by the picture below?

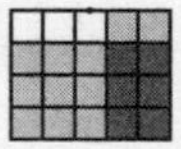

F $\frac{1}{5} \times \frac{1}{4}$ H $\frac{2}{20} \times \frac{3}{20}$

G $\frac{2}{5} \times \frac{3}{5}$ J $\frac{2}{5} \times \frac{3}{4}$

4 _J_

5 Olivia orders 4 ham sandwiches at the deli. The total amount was $30.52. How much did each sandwich cost?

A $7.63   B $7.83   C $12.63   D $122.08

5 _A_

---

6 The table below shows the charges for a taxi ride in a city.

Charges for Each Taxi Ride	
Charges	**Rate**
Mileage Charge	$0.75 Each Mile
City Gas Tax	$0.10 Each Mile
Tourist Charge	$2.50

If a taxi ride is m miles, which expression can be used to find the total charge of the ride?

F $2.50m + 0.75$ H $0.10m + 3.25$

G $0.75m + 2.50$ J $0.85m + 2.50$

6 _J_

7 Michael's age is 5 years younger than Jordan. Jordan is 4 years younger than Keanu. Keanu is 17 years old. How old is Michael?

A Michael is 12 years old, because he is 5 years younger than Keanu.

B Michael is 22 years old, because he is 5 years older than Keanu.

C Michael is 8 years old, because he is 5 years younger than Jordan, and Jordan is 13 years old.

D Michael is 18 years old, because he is 5 years older than Jordan, and Jordan is 13 years old.

7 _C_

8 Jeb's weight w is $\frac{1}{3}$ of Iago's weight a. Which equation could be used to find Jeb's weight?

F $w = a - \frac{1}{3}$ H $w = \frac{1}{3} + a$

G $w = \frac{1}{3}a$ J $w = a \div \frac{1}{3}$

8 _G_

9 The school band sold 200 tickets to their concert. If 90 of the tickets were adult tickets, what percent of the tickets sold were adult tickets?

A 18%   C 55%

B 45%   D 90%

9 _B_

10 A car travels 528 miles on 16 gallons of gas. At the same rate, how many gallons of gas are needed to travel 165 miles?

F 4   G 5   H 6   J 7

10 _G_

Answers (Grade 8)

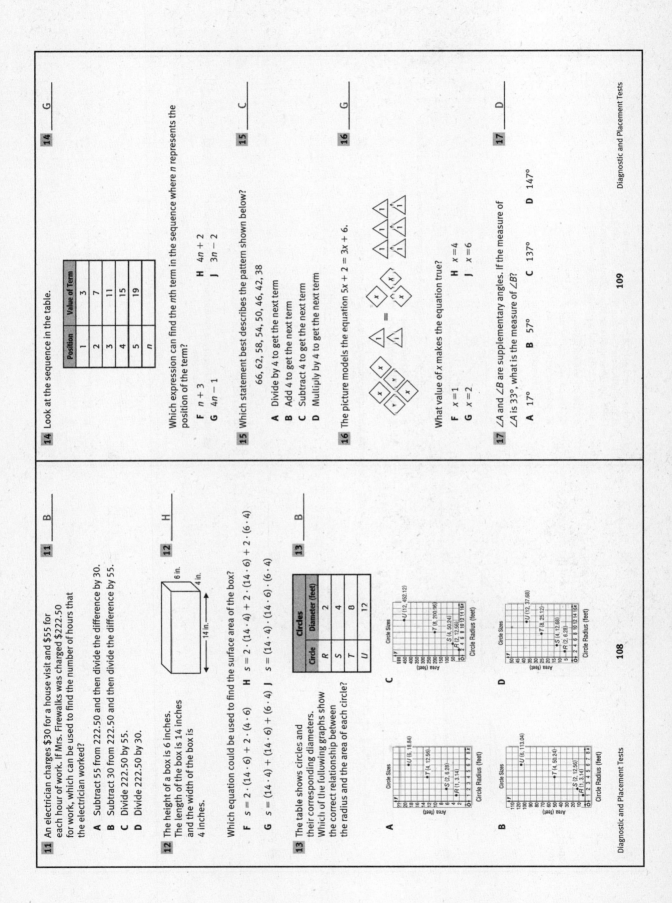

11 ____ B

An electrician charges $30 for a house visit and $55 for each hour of work. If Mrs. Firewalks was charged $222.50 for work, which can be used to find the number of hours that the electrician worked?

A Subtract 55 from 222.50 and then divide the difference by 30.
B Subtract 30 from 222.50 and then divide the difference by 55.
C Divide 222.50 by 55.
D Divide 222.50 by 30.

12 ____ H

The height of a box is 6 inches. The length of the box is 14 inches and the width of the box is 4 inches.

6 in.
14 in.
4 in.

Which equation could be used to find the surface area of the box?

F $s = 2 \cdot (14 \cdot 6) + 2 \cdot (4 \cdot 6)$
G $s = (14 \cdot 4) + (14 \cdot 6) + (6 \cdot 4)$
H $s = 2 \cdot (14 \cdot 4) + 2 \cdot (14 \cdot 6) + 2 \cdot (6 \cdot 4)$
J $s = (14 \cdot 4) \cdot (14 \cdot 6) \cdot (6 \cdot 4)$

13 ____ B

The table shows circles and their corresponding diameters. Which of the following graphs show the correct relationship between the radius and the area of each circle?

Circles	
Circle	Diameter (feet)
R	2
S	4
T	8
U	12

14 ____ G

Look at the sequence in the table.

Position	Value of Term
1	3
2	7
3	11
4	15
5	19
n	

Which expression can find the nth term in the sequence where n represents the position of the term?

F $n + 3$ H $4n + 2$
G $4n - 1$ J $3n - 2$

15 ____ C

Which statement best describes the pattern shown below?

66, 62, 58, 54, 50, 46, 42, 38

A Divide by 4 to get the next term
B Add 4 to get the next term
C Subtract 4 to get the next term
D Multiply by 4 to get the next term

16 ____ G

The picture models the equation $5x + 2 = 3x + 6$.

What value of x makes the equation true?

F $x = 1$ H $x = 4$
G $x = 2$ J $x = 6$

17 ____ D

$\angle A$ and $\angle B$ are supplementary angles. If the measure of $\angle A$ is 33°, what is the measure of $\angle B$?

A 17°   B 57°   C 137°   D 147°

Answers (Grade 8)

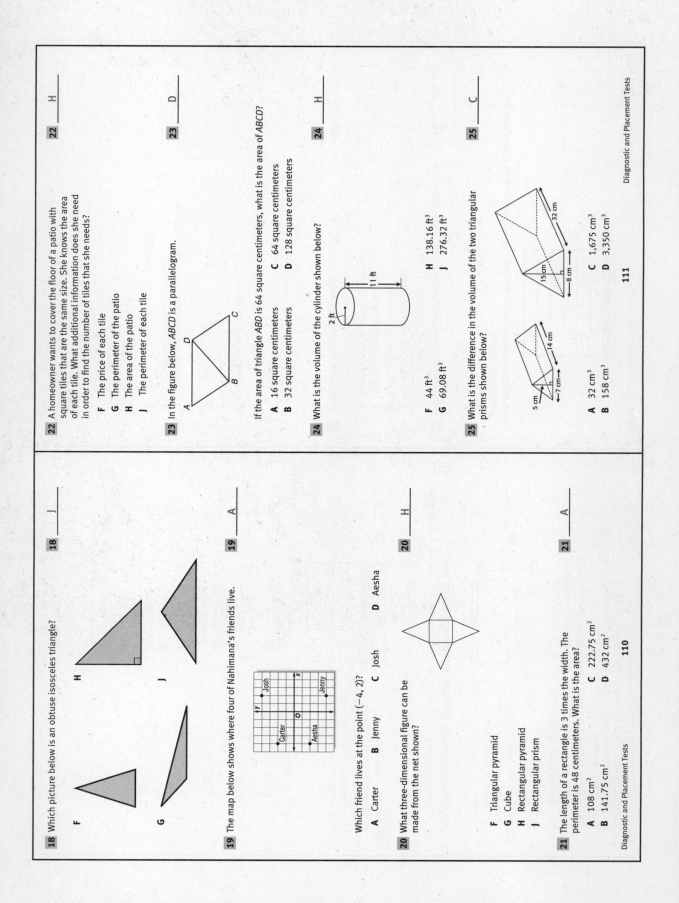

18 Which picture below is an obtuse isosceles triangle?

F

H

G

J

18 ___ J

19 The map below shows where four of Nahimana's friends live.

Which friend lives at the point (−4, 2)?

A Carter   B Jenny   C Josh   D Aesha

19 ___ A

20 What three-dimensional figure can be made from the net shown?

F Triangular pyramid
G Cube
H Rectangular pyramid
J Rectangular prism

20 ___ H

21 The length of a rectangle is 3 times the width. The perimeter is 48 centimeters. What is the area?

A 108 cm²
B 141.75 cm²
C 222.75 cm²
D 432 cm²

21 ___ A

22 A homeowner wants to cover the floor of a patio with square tiles that are the same size. She knows the area of each tile. What additional information does she need in order to find the number of tiles that she needs?

F The price of each tile
G The perimeter of the patio
H The area of the patio
J The perimeter of each tile

22 ___ H

23 In the figure below, *ABCD* is a parallelogram.

If the area of triangle *ABD* is 64 square centimeters, what is the area of *ABCD*?

A 16 square centimeters
B 32 square centimeters
C 64 square centimeters
D 128 square centimeters

23 ___ D

24 What is the volume of the cylinder shown below?

F 44 ft³
G 69.08 ft³
H 138.16 ft³
J 276.32 ft³

24 ___ H

25 What is the difference in the volume of the two triangular prisms shown below?

A 32 cm³
B 158 cm³
C 1,675 cm³
D 3,350 cm³

25 ___ C

Answers (Grade 8)

26 Juan needs to choose an outfit from his closet. He can choose from a red, green, or blue T-shirt and he can choose from a pair of blue, tan, or black pants. Which table shows all possible outfits if Juan picked one shirt and one pair of pants at random?

F

Outfits	
Shirts	**Pants**
red	blue
green	black
blue	tan

G

Outfits	
Shirts	**Pants**
red	blue
green	blue
blue	blue
red	black
green	black
blue	black
red	tan
green	tan
blue	tan

H

Outfits	
Shirts	**Pants**
red	blue
green	blue
blue	blue
red	black
green	black
blue	black
red	blue
green	black
blue	tan

J

Outfits	
Shirts	**Pants**
red	blue
green	black
blue	tan
red	blue
green	black
blue	tan

<u>G</u>

27 A jar contains 4 green marbles, 2 pink marbles, and 3 striped marbles. One marble is picked at random and then replaced. Then another marble is drawn at random again. What is the probability that both marbles are striped?

A $\frac{1}{81}$ **B** $\frac{1}{9}$ **C** $\frac{1}{3}$ **D** $\frac{1}{2}$

<u>B</u>

28 All the members of a garden club vote for a new president. The bar graph below shows the results of the election.

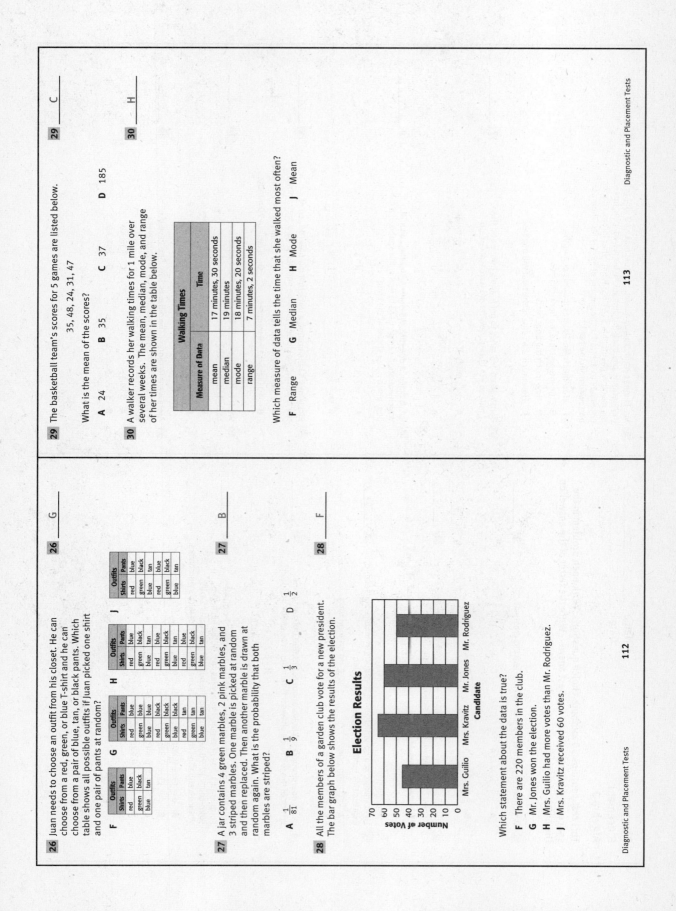

Election Results

Which statement about the data is true?

F There are 220 members in the club.
G Mr. Jones won the election.
H Mrs. Guilio had more votes than Mr. Rodriguez.
J Mrs. Kravitz received 60 votes.

<u>F</u>

29 The basketball team's scores for 5 games are listed below.

35, 48, 24, 31, 47

What is the mean of the scores?

A 24 **B** 35 **C** 37 **D** 185

<u>C</u>

30 A walker records her walking times for 1 mile over several weeks. The mean, median, mode, and range of her times are shown in the table below.

Walking Times	
Measure of Data	**Time**
mean	17 minutes, 30 seconds
median	19 minutes
mode	18 minutes, 20 seconds
range	7 minutes, 2 seconds

Which measure of data tells the time that she walked most often?

F Range **G** Median **H** Mode **J** Mean

<u>H</u>

Answers (Algebra 1)

Name _____
Date _____

This test contains 30 multiple-choice questions. Work each problem in the space on this page. Select the best answer. Write the letter of the answer on the blank at the right.

1 Which set of numbers is ordered from least to greatest?

A $\frac{3}{8}; \frac{1}{2}; 1; \sqrt{2}; 4$ C $4; \sqrt{2}; 1; \frac{1}{2}; \frac{3}{8}$

B $\frac{3}{8}; \frac{1}{2}; \sqrt{2}; 1, 4$ D $\frac{1}{2}; \frac{3}{8}; 1; 4; \sqrt{2}$

1 ___A___

2 The area of a square is 8 square meters. Which of these is closest to the length of one side of the square?

F 2 square meters   H 3.5 square meters

G 2.8 square meters   J 4 square meters

2 ___G___

3 Light travels at a speed of about 2.998×10^8 meters per second. Express this number in standard notation.

A 299,800,000   C 0.0000002998

B 0.00002998   D 29,980,000

3 ___A___

4 A thunderstorm cloud holds about 6,200,000,000 raindrops. Which of the following shows this number in scientific notation?

F 0.62×10^{10} H 6.2×10^8

G 6.2×10^9 J 62.0×10^8

4 ___G___

5 Jake goes to the grocery store and buys 3 apples, 2 cans of soup, and 1 box of cereal. The apples cost $0.89 each; the soup costs $2.98 per can; and the box of cereal costs $4.99. Write an equation that represents the total cost c of Jake's purchases.

A $c = (3 + 0.89) + (2 + 2.98) + 4.99$

B $c = (3 + 0.89) \times (3 + 2.98) + 4.99$

C $c = (3 \times 0.89) + (2 \times 2.98) + 4.99$

D $c = (3 \times 0.89) \times (2 \times 2.98) \times 4.99$

5 ___C___

6 Mr. Thomas wants to buy a boat. He must make 48 monthly payments to pay back the amount he borrowed, plus interest. His monthly payment is $161.85. What other information is necessary to determine the amount of money Mr. Thomas borrowed from the bank?

F How much Mr. Thomas makes per month

G The interest rate the bank charges

H How much the boat costs

J How much the value of the boat will increase

6 ___G___

7 Barb walked 1.3 miles to her friend's house and then $\frac{3}{4}$ mile to the library. How far did Barb walk in all?

A $1\frac{9}{40}$ miles   C $2\frac{1}{20}$ miles

B $1\frac{3}{7}$ miles   D $2\frac{1}{10}$ miles

7 ___C___

8 On average, a dog runs 5.5 times faster than a child. Which equation can be used to find s, the speed of a dog, given r, the speed of the child?

F $s = 5.5r$ H $s = r + 5.5$

G $s = \frac{5.5}{r}$ J $s = \frac{r}{5.5}$

8 ___F___

9 Ricky jogs 5 laps around a track in 8 minutes. Which of the following would be the same number of laps per minute?

A 7 laps in 9.6 minutes   C 12 laps in 19.2 minutes

B 10 laps in 15.6 minutes   D 8 laps in 20 minutes

9 ___C___

10 What is the slope and y-intercept of the equation $6x - 1 = 3y - 10$?

F $m = 2, b = 3$ H $m = 3, b = 4$

G $m = 2, b = -3$ J $m = 6, b = 9$

10 ___F___

11 Aleta went to dinner. The bill was $36. She gave the waiter a 15% tip. What was the total amount Aleta spent on the food and the tip?

A $36.15   C $38.40

B $37.50   D $41.40

11 ___D___

Answers (Algebra 1)

16 ___ J

16 A rectangle is cut along its diagonal. The measure of ∠A is 55°. What is the measure of ∠B?

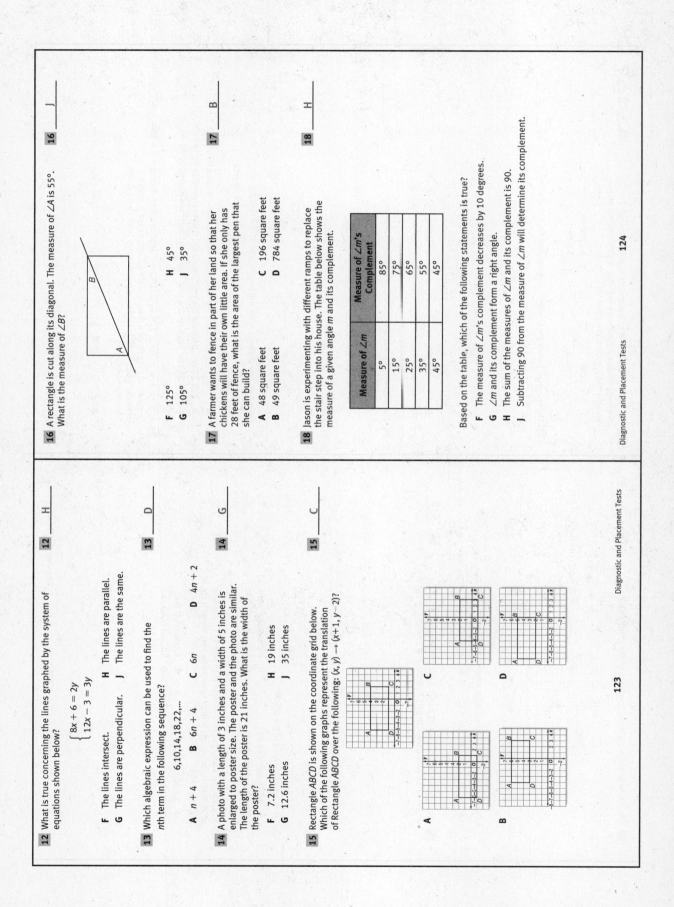

F 125°   H 45°
G 105°   J 35°

17 ___ B

17 A farmer wants to fence in part of her land so that her chickens will have their own little area. If she only has 28 feet of fence, what is the area of the largest pen that she can build?

A 48 square feet   C 196 square feet
B 49 square feet   D 784 square feet

18 ___ H

18 Jason is experimenting with different ramps to replace the stair step into his house. The table below shows the measure of a given angle m and its complement.

Measure of ∠m	Measure of ∠m's Complement
5°	85°
15°	75°
25°	65°
35°	55°
45°	45°

Based on the table, which of the following statements is true?

F   The measure of ∠m's complement decreases by 10 degrees.
G   ∠m and its complement form a right angle.
H   The sum of the measures of ∠m and its complement is 90.
J   Subtracting 90 from the measure of ∠m will determine its complement.

---

12 ___ H

12 What is true concerning the lines graphed by the system of equations shown below?

$$\begin{cases} 8x + 6 = 2y \\ 12x - 3 = 3y \end{cases}$$

F   The lines intersect.   H   The lines are parallel.
G   The lines are perpendicular.   J   The lines are the same.

13 ___ D

13 Which algebraic expression can be used to find the nth term in the following sequence?

6,10,14,18,22,...

A $n + 4$ B $6n + 4$ C $6n$ D $4n + 2$

14 ___ G

14 A photo with a length of 3 inches and a width of 5 inches is enlarged to poster size. The poster and the photo are similar. The length of the poster is 21 inches. What is the width of the poster?

F   7.2 inches   H   19 inches
G   12.6 inches   J   35 inches

15 ___ C

15 Rectangle *ABCD* is shown on the coordinate grid below. Which of the following graphs represent the translation of Rectangle *ABCD* over the following: $(x, y) \rightarrow (x + 1, y - 2)$?

193   Texas Diagnostic and Placement Tests

Answers (Algebra 1)

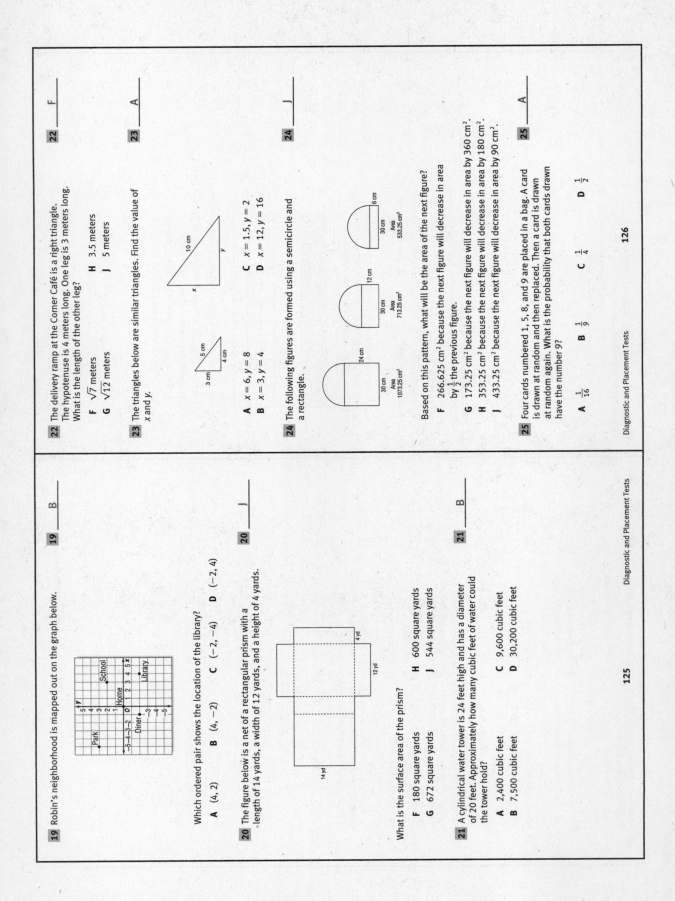

19 ___B___

Robin's neighborhood is mapped out on the graph below.

Which ordered pair shows the location of the library?

A (4, 2)   B (4, −2)   C (−2, −4)   D (−2, 4)

20 ___J___

The figure below is a net of a rectangular prism with a length of 14 yards, a width of 12 yards, and a height of 4 yards.

14 yd
12 yd
4 yd

What is the surface area of the prism?

F 180 square yards   H 600 square yards
G 672 square yards   J 544 square yards

21 ___B___

A cylindrical water tower is 24 feet high and has a diameter of 20 feet. Approximately how many cubic feet of water could the tower hold?

A 2,400 cubic feet   C 9,600 cubic feet
B 7,500 cubic feet   D 30,200 cubic feet

22 ___F___

The delivery ramp at the Corner Café is a right triangle. The hypotenuse is 4 meters long. One leg is 3 meters long. What is the length of the other leg?

F $\sqrt{7}$ meters   H 3.5 meters
G $\sqrt{12}$ meters   J 5 meters

23 ___A___

The triangles below are similar triangles. Find the value of x and y.

3 cm
5 cm
4 cm

10 cm
x
y

A $x = 6, y = 8$ C $x = 1.5, y = 2$
B $x = 3, y = 4$ D $x = 12, y = 16$

24 ___J___

The following figures are formed using a semicircle and a rectangle.

24 cm
30 cm
Area
1073.25 cm²

12 cm
30 cm
Area
713.25 cm²

6 cm
30 cm
Area
533.25 cm²

Based on this pattern, what will be the area of the next figure?

F 266.625 cm² because the next figure will decrease in area by ½ the previous figure.
G 173.25 cm² because the next figure will decrease in area by 360 cm².
H 353.25 cm² because the next figure will decrease in area by 180 cm².
J 433.25 cm² because the next figure will decrease in area by 90 cm².

25 ___A___

Four cards numbered 1, 5, 8, and 9 are placed in a bag. A card is drawn at random and then replaced. Then a card is drawn at random again. What is the probability that both cards drawn have the number 9?

A $\frac{1}{16}$ B $\frac{1}{9}$ C $\frac{1}{4}$ D $\frac{1}{2}$

Answers (Algebra 1)

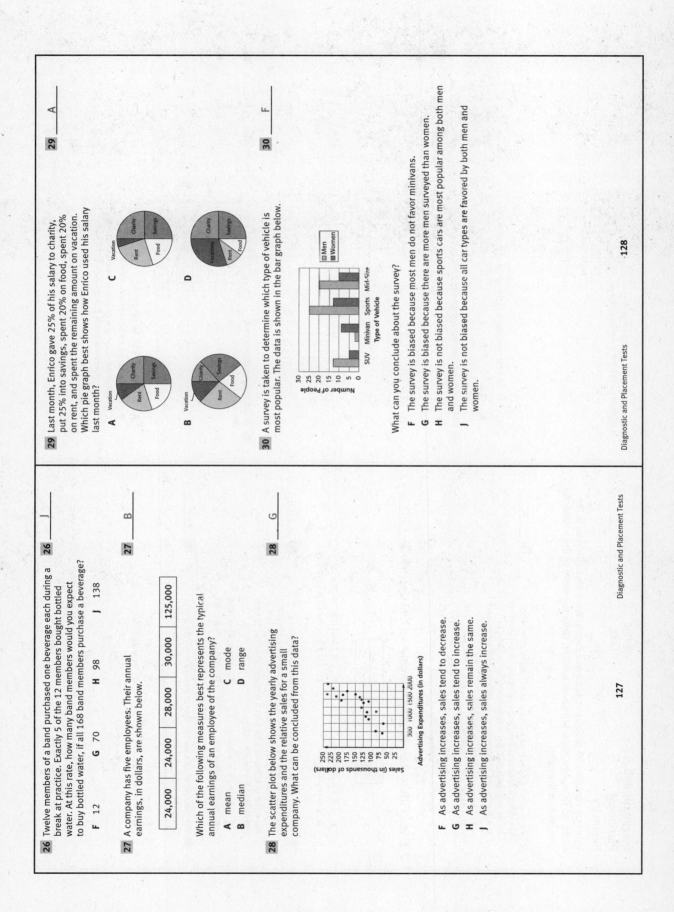

26 Twelve members of a band purchased one beverage each during a break at practice. Exactly 5 of the 12 members bought bottled water. At this rate, how many band members would you expect to buy bottled water, if all 168 band members purchase a beverage?

F 12   G 70   H 98   J 138

26 ___ J ___

27 A company has five employees. Their annual earnings, in dollars, are shown below.

| 24,000 | 24,000 | 28,000 | 30,000 | 125,000 |

Which of the following measures best represents the typical annual earnings of an employee of the company?

A mean   C mode
B median   D range

27 ___ B ___

28 The scatter plot below shows the yearly advertising expenditures and the relative sales for a small company. What can be concluded from this data?

F As advertising increases, sales tend to decrease.
G As advertising increases, sales tend to increase.
H As advertising increases, sales remain the same.
J As advertising increases, sales always increase.

28 ___ G ___

29 Last month, Enrico gave 25% of his salary to charity, put 25% into savings, spent 20% on food, spent 20% on rent, and spent the remaining amount on vacation. Which pie graph best shows how Enrico used his salary last month?

29 ___ A ___

30 A survey is taken to determine which type of vehicle is most popular. The data is shown in the bar graph below.

What can you conclude about the survey?

F The survey is biased because most men do not favor minivans.
G The survey is biased because there are more men surveyed than women.
H The survey is not biased because sports cars are most popular among both men and women.
J The survey is not biased because all car types are favored by both men and women.

30 ___ F ___

Answers (Geometry)

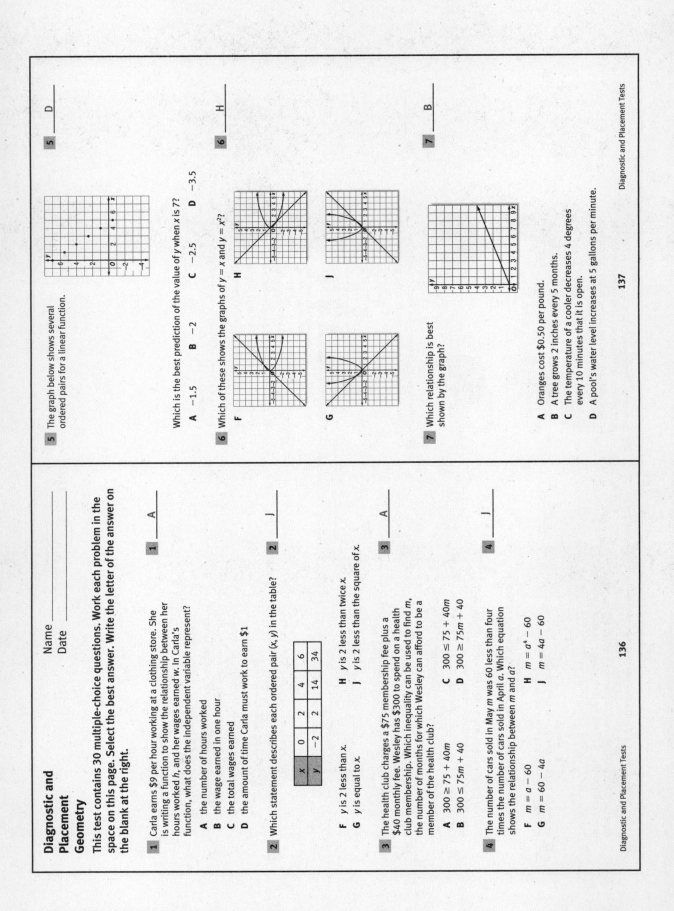

Diagnostic and Placement

Geometry

Name _____

Date _____

This test contains 30 multiple-choice questions. Work each problem in the space on this page. Select the best answer. Write the letter of the answer on the blank at the right.

1 Carla earns $9 per hour working at a clothing store. She is writing a function to show the relationship between her hours worked h, and her wages earned w. In Carla's function, what does the independent variable represent?

  A the number of hours worked

  B the wage earned in one hour

  C the total wages earned

  D the amount of time Carla must work to earn $1

1   A

2 Which statement describes each ordered pair (x, y) in the table?

x	0	2	4	6
y	−2	2	14	34

  F y is 2 less than x.

  G y is equal to x.

  H y is 2 less than twice x.

  J y is 2 less than the square of x.

2   J

3 The health club charges a $75 membership fee plus a $40 monthly fee. Wesley has $300 to spend on a health club membership. Which inequality can be used to find m, the number of months for which Wesley can afford to be a member of the health club?

  A $300 \geq 75 + 40m$

  B $300 \leq 75m + 40$

  C $300 \leq 75 + 40m$

  D $300 \geq 75m + 40$

3   A

4 The number of cars sold in May m was 60 less than four times the number of cars sold in April a. Which equation shows the relationship between m and a?

  F $m = a − 60$

  G $m = 60 − 4a$

  H $m = a^4 − 60$

  J $m = 4a − 60$

4   J

5 The graph below shows several ordered pairs for a linear function.

5   D

6 Which is the best prediction of the value of y when x is 7?

  A −1.5   **B** −2   **C** −2.5   **D** −3.5

6 Which of these shows the graphs of $y = x$ and $y = x^2$?

  F

  G

  H

  J

6   H

7 Which relationship is best shown by the graph?

  A Oranges cost $0.50 per pound.

  B A tree grows 2 inches every 5 months.

  C The temperature of a cooler decreases 4 degrees every 10 minutes that it is open.

  D A pool's water level increases at 5 gallons per minute.

7   B

Answers (Geometry)

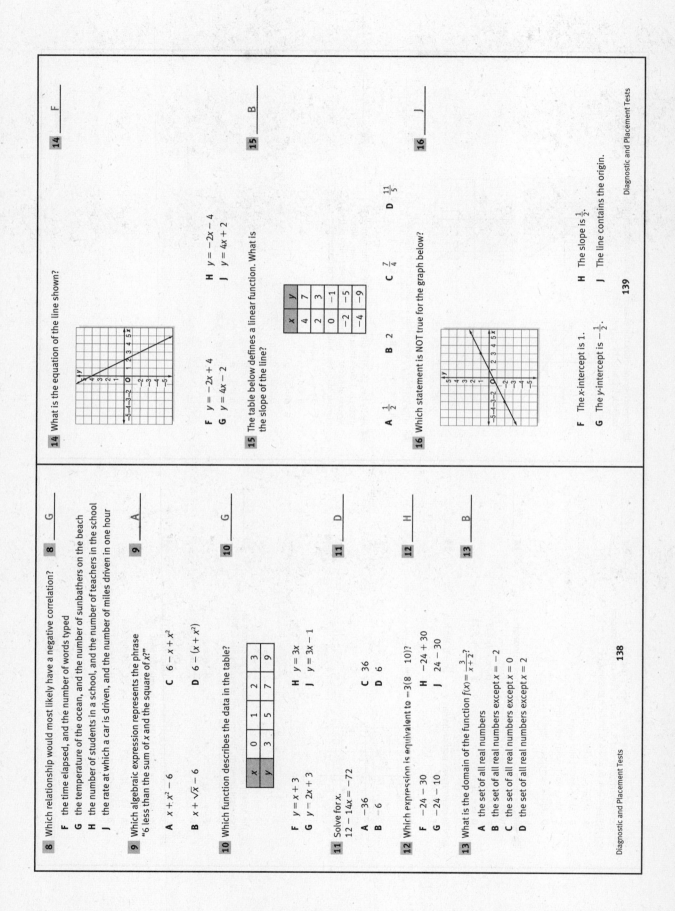

8 Which relationship would most likely have a negative correlation?

F the time elapsed, and the number of words typed

G the temperature of the ocean, and the number of sunbathers on the beach

H the number of students in a school, and the number of teachers in the school

J the rate at which a car is driven, and the number of miles driven in one hour

8 _____ **G**

9 Which algebraic expression represents the phrase "6 less than the sum of x and the square of x"?

A $x + x^2 - 6$ **C** $6 - x + x^2$

B $x + \sqrt{x} - 6$ **D** $6 - (x + x^2)$

9 _____ **A**

10 Which function describes the data in the table?

x	0	1	2	3
y	3	5	7	9

F $y = x + 3$ **H** $y = 3x$

G $y = 2x + 3$ **J** $y = 3x - 1$

10 _____ **G**

11 Solve for x.

$12 - 14x = -72$

A -36 **C** 36

B -6 **D** 6

11 _____ **D**

12 Which expression is equivalent to $-3(8 - 10)$?

F $-24 - 30$ **H** $-24 + 30$

G $-24 - 10$ **J** $24 - 30$

12 _____ **H**

13 What is the domain of the function $f(x) = \frac{3}{x + 2}$?

A the set of all real numbers

B the set of all real numbers except $x = -2$

C the set of all real numbers except $x = 0$

D the set of all real numbers except $x = 2$

13 _____ **B**

14 What is the equation of the line shown?

F $y = -2x + 4$ **H** $y = -2x - 4$

G $y = 4x - 2$ **J** $y = 4x + 2$

14 _____ **F**

15 The table below defines a linear function. What is the slope of the line?

x	y
4	7
2	3
0	−1
−2	−5
−4	−9

A $\frac{1}{2}$ **B** 2   **C** $\frac{7}{4}$ **D** $\frac{11}{5}$

15 _____ **B**

16 Which statement is NOT true for the graph below?

F The x-intercept is 1.   **H** The slope is $\frac{1}{2}$.

G The y-intercept is $-\frac{1}{2}$.   **J** The line contains the origin.

16 _____ **J**

Answers (Geometry)

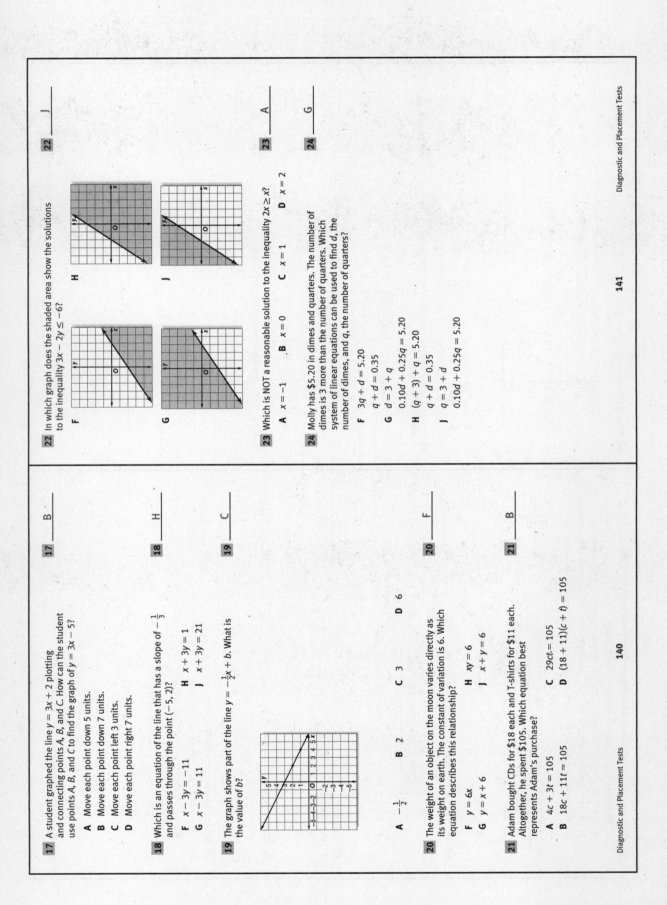

17 ___ B

A student graphed the line $y = 3x + 2$ plotting and connecting points A, B, and C. How can the student use points A, B, and C to find the graph of $y = 3x - 5$?

A Move each point down 5 units.
B Move each point down 7 units.
C Move each point left 3 units.
D Move each point right 7 units.

18 ___ H

Which is an equation of the line that has a slope of $-\frac{1}{3}$ and passes through the point $(-5, 2)$?

F $x - 3y = -11$ H $x + 3y = 1$
G $x - 3y = 11$ J $x + 3y = 21$

19 ___ C

The graph shows part of the line $y = -\frac{1}{2}x + b$. What is the value of b?

A $-\frac{1}{2}$ B 2   C 3   D 6

20 ___ F

The weight of an object on the moon varies directly as its weight on earth. The constant of variation is 6. Which equation describes this relationship?

F $y = 6x$ H $xy = 6$
G $y = x + 6$ J $x + y = 6$

21 ___ B

Adam bought CDs for $18 each and T-shirts for $11 each. Altogether, he spent $105. Which equation best represents Adam's purchase?

A $4c + 3t = 105$ C $29ct = 105$
B $18c + 11t = 105$ D $(18 + 11)(c + t) = 105$

22 ___ J

In which graph does the shaded area show the solutions to the inequality $3x - 2y \leq -6$?

F   G   H   J

23 ___ A

Which is NOT a reasonable solution to the inequality $2x \geq x$?

A $x = -1$ B $x = 0$ C $x = 1$ D $x = 2$

24 ___ G

Molly has $5.20 in dimes and quarters. The number of dimes is 3 more than the number of quarters. Which system of linear equations can be used to find d, the number of dimes, and q, the number of quarters?

F $3q + d = 5.20$
   $q + d = 0.35$

G $d = 3 + q$
   $0.10d + 0.25q = 5.20$

H $(q + 3) + q = 5.20$
   $q + d = 0.35$

J $q = 3 + d$
   $0.10d + 0.25q = 5.20$

Answers (Geometry)

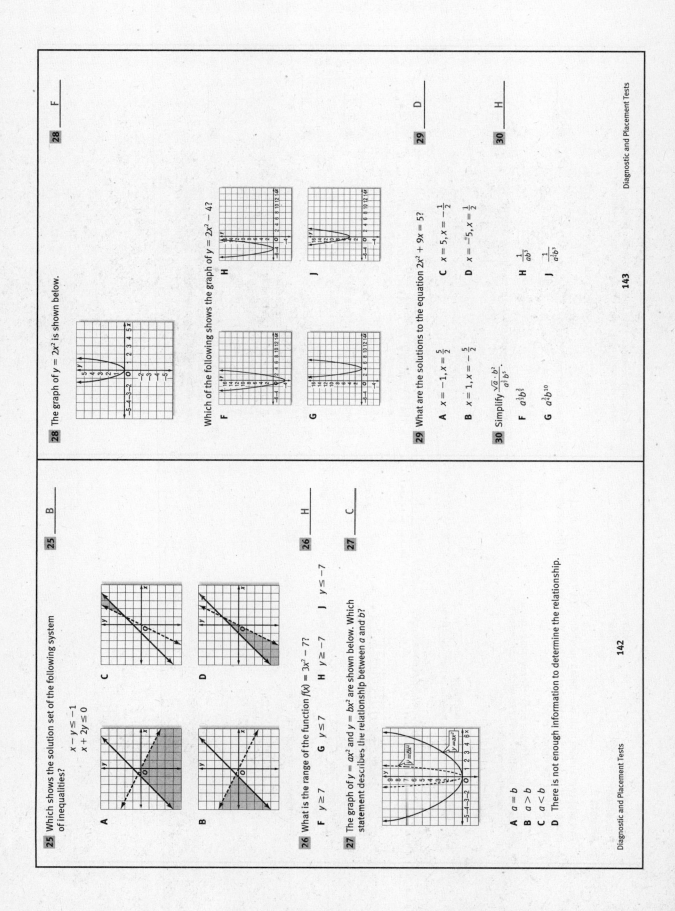

25 _____ B

Which shows the solution set of the following system of inequalities?

$$x - y \le -1$$
$$x + 2y \le 0$$

A

B

C

D

26 _____ H

What is the range of the function $f(x) = 3x^2 - 7$?

F $y \ge 7$ G $y \le 7$ H $y \ge -7$ J $y \le -7$

27 _____ C

The graph of $y = ax^2$ and $y = bx^2$ are shown below. Which statement describes the relationship between a and b?

A $a = b$
B $a > b$
C $a < b$
D There is not enough information to determine the relationship.

28 _____ F

The graph of $y = 2x^2$ is shown below.

Which of the following shows the graph of $y = 2x^2 - 4$?

F

G

H

J

29 _____ D

What are the solutions to the equation $2x^2 + 9x = 5$?

A $x = -1, x = \frac{5}{2}$
B $x = 1, x = -\frac{5}{2}$
C $x = 5, x = -\frac{1}{2}$
D $x = -5, x = \frac{1}{2}$

30 _____ H

Simplify $\frac{\sqrt{a} \cdot b^2}{a^3 b^5}$.

F $a^{\frac{1}{3}} b^{\frac{2}{3}}$
G $a^{\frac{3}{4}} b^{10}$
H $\frac{1}{ab^3}$
J $\frac{1}{a^3 b^3}$

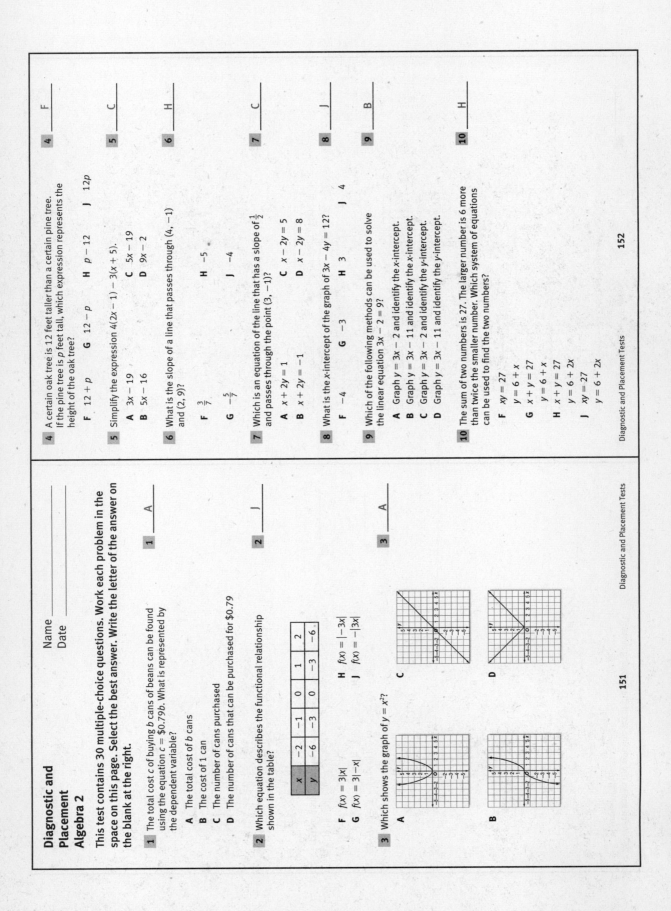

Diagnostic and Placement
Algebra 2

Name _____
Date _____

This test contains 30 multiple-choice questions. Work each problem in the space on this page. Select the best answer. Write the letter of the answer on the blank at the right.

1 The total cost c of buying b cans of beans can be found using the equation $c = \$0.79b$. What is represented by the dependent variable?

A The total cost of b cans
B The cost of 1 can
C The number of cans purchased
D The number of cans that can be purchased for $0.79

1 __ A

2 Which equation describes the functional relationship shown in the table?

x	-2	-1	0	1	2
y	-6	-3	0	-3	-6

F $f(x) = 3|x|$
G $f(x) = 3|-x|$
H $f(x) = |-3x|$
J $f(x) = -|3x|$

2 __ J

3 Which shows the graph of $y = x^2$?

A

B

C

D

3 __ A

4 A certain oak tree is 12 feet taller than a certain pine tree. If the pine tree is p feet tall, which expression represents the height of the oak tree?

F $12 + p$ G $12 - p$ H $p - 12$ J $12p$

4 __ F

5 Simplify the expression $4(2x - 1) - 3(x + 5)$.

A $3x - 19$ C $5x - 19$
B $5x - 16$ D $9x - 2$

5 __ C

6 What is the slope of a line that passes through $(4, -1)$ and $(2, 9)$?

F $\frac{3}{7}$ H -5
G $-\frac{5}{7}$ J -4

6 __ H

7 Which is an equation of the line that has a slope of $\frac{1}{2}$ and passes through the point $(3, -1)$?

A $x + 2y = 1$ C $x - 2y = 5$
B $x + 2y = -1$ D $x - 2y = 8$

7 __ C

8 What is the x-intercept of the graph of $3x - 4y = 12$?

F -4 G -3 H 3 J 4

8 __ J

9 Which of the following methods can be used to solve the linear equation $3x - 2 = 9$?

A Graph $y = 3x - 2$ and identify the x-intercept.
B Graph $y = 3x - 11$ and identify the x-intercept.
C Graph $y = 3x - 2$ and identify the y-intercept.
D Graph $y = 3x - 11$ and identify the y-intercept.

9 __ B

10 The sum of two numbers is 27. The larger number is 6 more than twice the smaller number. Which system of equations can be used to find the two numbers?

F $xy = 27$
  $y = 6 + x$

G $x + y = 27$
  $y = 6 + x$

H $x + y = 27$
  $y = 6 + 2x$

J $xy = 27$
  $y = 6 + 2x$

10 __ H

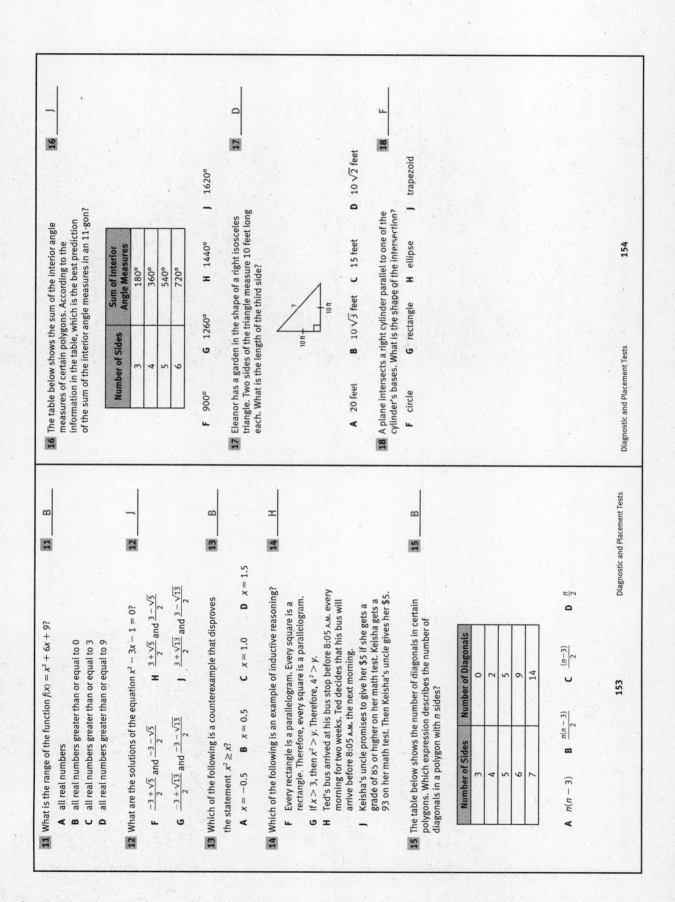

11 What is the range of the function $f(x) = x^2 + 6x + 9$?

A all real numbers

B all real numbers greater than or equal to 0

C all real numbers greater than or equal to 3

D all real numbers greater than or equal to 9

11 ___ **B**

12 What are the solutions of the equation $x^2 - 3x - 1 = 0$?

F $\dfrac{-3+\sqrt{5}}{2}$ and $\dfrac{-3-\sqrt{5}}{2}$ H $\dfrac{3+\sqrt{5}}{2}$ and $\dfrac{3-\sqrt{5}}{2}$

G $\dfrac{-3+\sqrt{13}}{2}$ and $\dfrac{-3-\sqrt{13}}{2}$ J $\dfrac{3+\sqrt{13}}{2}$ and $\dfrac{3-\sqrt{13}}{2}$

12 ___ **J**

13 Which of the following is a counterexample that disproves the statement $x^2 \geq x$?

A $x = -0.5$ B $x = 0.5$ C $x = 1.0$ D $x = 1.5$

13 ___ **B**

14 Which of the following is an example of inductive reasoning?

F Every rectangle is a parallelogram. Every square is a rectangle. Therefore, every square is a parallelogram.

G If $x > 3$, then $x^2 > y$. Therefore, $4^2 > y$.

H Ted's bus arrived at his bus stop before 8:05 A.M. every morning for two weeks. Ted decides that his bus will arrive before 8:05 A.M. the next morning.

J Keisha's uncle promises to give her $5 if she gets a grade of 85 or higher on her math test. Keisha gets a 93 on her math test. Then Keisha's uncle gives her $5.

14 ___ **H**

15 The table below shows the number of diagonals in certain polygons. Which expression describes the number of diagonals in a polygon with n sides?

Number of Sides	Number of Diagonals
3	0
4	2
5	5
6	9
7	14

A $n(n-3)$ B $\dfrac{n(n-3)}{2}$ C $\dfrac{(n-3)}{2}$ D $\dfrac{n}{2}$

15 ___ **B**

16 The table below shows the sum of the interior angle measures of certain polygons. According to the information in the table, which is the best prediction of the sum of the interior angle measures in an 11-gon?

Number of Sides	Sum of Interior Angle Measures
3	180°
4	360°
5	540°
6	720°

F 900°   G 1260°   H 1440°   J 1620°

16 ___ **J**

17 Eleanor has a garden in the shape of a right isosceles triangle. Two sides of the triangle measure 10 feet long each. What is the length of the third side?

A 20 feet   B $10\sqrt{3}$ feet   C 15 feet   D $10\sqrt{2}$ feet

17 ___ **D**

18 A plane intersects a right cylinder parallel to one of the cylinder's bases. What is the shape of the intersection?

F circle   G rectangle   H ellipse   J trapezoid

18 ___ **F**

Answers (Algebra 2)

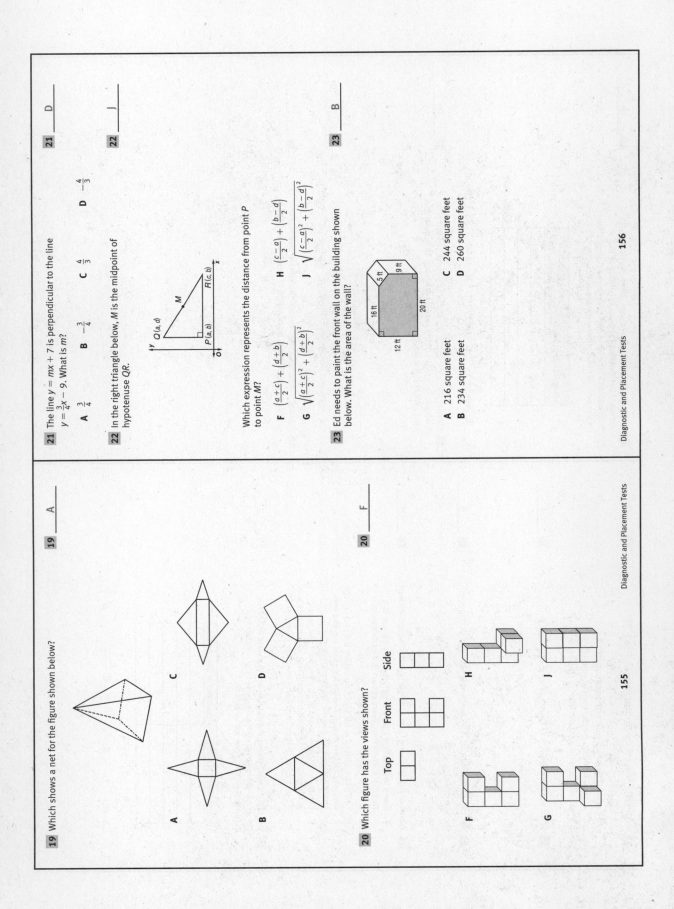

19 Which shows a net for the figure shown below?

A

B

C

D

19 _____ A

20 Which figure has the views shown?

Top   Front   Side

F

G

H

J

20 _____ F

---

21 The line $y = mx + 7$ is perpendicular to the line $y = \frac{3}{4}x - 9$. What is m?

A $\frac{3}{4}$ B $-\frac{3}{4}$ C $\frac{4}{3}$ D $-\frac{4}{3}$

21 _____ D

22 In the right triangle below, M is the midpoint of hypotenuse QR.

Which expression represents the distance from point P to point M?

F $\left(\frac{a+c}{2}\right) + \left(\frac{d+b}{2}\right)$ H $\left(\frac{c-a}{2}\right) + \left(\frac{b-d}{2}\right)$

G $\sqrt{\left(\frac{a+c}{2}\right)^2 + \left(\frac{d+b}{2}\right)^2}$ J $\sqrt{\left(\frac{c-a}{2}\right)^2 + \left(\frac{b-d}{2}\right)^2}$

22 _____ J

23 Ed needs to paint the front wall on the building shown below. What is the area of the wall?

A 216 square feet   C 244 square feet
B 234 square feet   D 260 square feet

23 _____ B

Answers (Algebra 2)

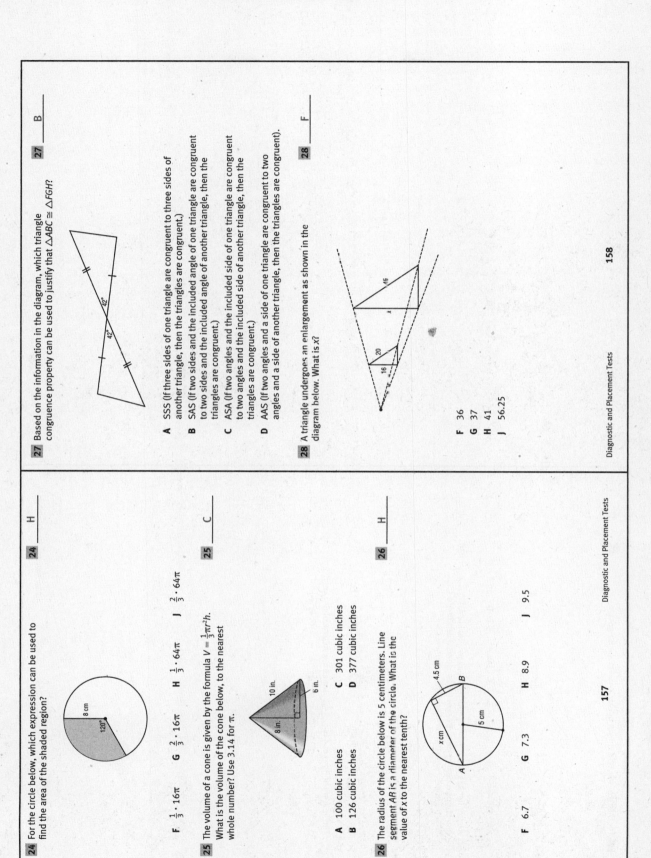

24 For the circle below, which expression can be used to find the area of the shaded region?

8 cm
120°

F $\frac{1}{3} \cdot 16\pi$ **G** $\frac{2}{3} \cdot 16\pi$ **H** $\frac{1}{3} \cdot 64\pi$ **J** $\frac{2}{3} \cdot 64\pi$

24 ___H___

25 The volume of a cone is given by the formula $V = \frac{1}{3}\pi r^2 h$. What is the volume of the cone below, to the nearest whole number? Use 3.14 for π.

10 in.
8 in.
6 in.

A 100 cubic inches   **C** 301 cubic inches
B 126 cubic inches   **D** 377 cubic inches

25 ___C___

26 The radius of the circle below is 5 centimeters. Line segment AB is a diameter of the circle. What is the value of x to the nearest tenth?

4.5 cm
B
x cm
5 cm
A

F 6.7   **G** 7.3   **H** 8.9   **J** 9.5

26 ___H___

27 Based on the information in the diagram, which triangle congruence property can be used to justify that $\triangle ABC \cong \triangle FGH$?

42°
42°

A SSS (If three sides of one triangle are congruent to three sides of another triangle, then the triangles are congruent.)

B SAS (If two sides and the included angle of one triangle are congruent to two sides and the included angle of another triangle, then the triangles are congruent.)

C ASA (If two angles and the included side of one triangle are congruent to two angles and the included side of another triangle, then the triangles are congruent.)

D AAS (If two angles and a side of one triangle are congruent to two angles and a side of another triangle, then the triangles are congruent).

27 ___B___

28 A triangle undergoes an enlargement as shown in the diagram below. What is x?

20
16
16
x

F 36
G 37
H 41
J 56.25

28 ___F___

Answers (Algebra 2)

29 _____ D

30 _____ J

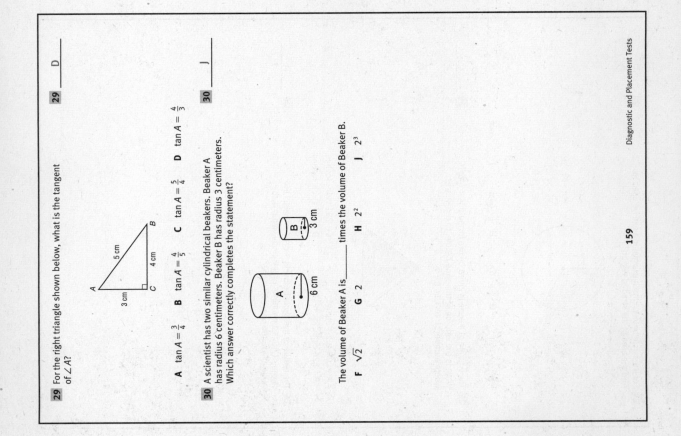

29 For the right triangle shown below, what is the tangent of ∠A?

3 cm, 5 cm, 4 cm — triangle with vertices A, C, B

A $\tan A = \frac{3}{4}$ **B** $\tan A = \frac{4}{5}$ **C** $\tan A = \frac{5}{4}$ **D** $\tan A = \frac{4}{3}$

30 A scientist has two similar cylindrical beakers. Beaker A has radius 6 centimeters. Beaker B has radius 3 centimeters. Which answer correctly completes the statement?

A — 6 cm
B — 3 cm

The volume of Beaker A is _____ times the volume of Beaker B.

F $\sqrt{2}$ **G** 2 **H** 2^2 **J** 2^3